MANAGING AGGRESSIVE BEHAVIOUR
IN CARE SETTINGS

MANAGING AGGRESSIVE BEHAVIOUR IN CARE SETTINGS
Understanding and applying low arousal approaches

Andrew A. McDonnell, BSc, MSc PhD

*Clinical Psychologist and Director of
Studio3 Training Systems, Honorary Research Fellow,
Department of Nursing and Midwifery,
University of Stirling*

WILEY-BLACKWELL

A John Wiley & Sons, Ltd., Publication

This edition first published 2010
© 2010 John Wiley & Sons Ltd.

Wiley-Blackwell is an imprint of John Wiley & Sons, formed by the merger of Wiley's global Scientific, Technical, and Medical business with Blackwell Publishing.

Registered Office
John Wiley & Sons Ltd, The Atrium, Southern Gate, Chichester, West Sussex, PO19 8SQ, UK

Editorial Offices
The Atrium, Southern Gate, Chichester, West Sussex, PO19 8SQ, UK
9600 Garsington Road, Oxford, OX4 2DQ, UK
350 Main Street, Malden, MA 02148-5020, USA

For details of our global editorial offices, for customer services, and for information about how to apply for permission to reuse the copyright material in this book please see our website at www.wiley.com/wiley-blackwell.

Library of Congress Cataloging-in-Publication Data

McDonnell, Andrew A.
  Managing aggressive behaviour in care settings : understanding and applying low arousal approaches / Andrew A. McDonnell.
    p. cm.
  Includes bibliographical references and index.
  ISBN 978-0-470-51232-6 (cloth) 978-0-470-51231-9 (pbk.)
  1. Aggressiveness–Treatment. 2. Violence–Treatment. 3. Psychiatric hospital patients.
I. Title.
  [DNLM: 1. Aggression. 2. Arousal. 3. Evidence-Based Medicine. 4. Social Behavior
Disorders–therapy. 5. Violence. WM 600 M478m 2010]
  RC569.5.A34M43 2010
  616.85′82–dc22
                                                                        2009043679

A catalogue record for this book is available from the British Library.

Typeset in 10/12pt Minion by Aptara Inc., New Delhi, India.
Printed in Singapore by Markono Print Media Pte Ltd.

1 2010

To Denise, Liam, Keiran, Callum and Matthew

Contents

Preface

Being confronted by an angry individual can be a powerful and emotional experience. Exposure to aggressive behaviour in care environments presents major challenges for organizations that attempt to balance their responsibilities to their employees and service consumers. Responses to these behaviours need to be both effective and socially acceptable. This book is based on more than 20 years of experience of the author as a practising clinical psychologist in a variety of care environments. The development of humane responses to manage aggressive behaviours has been the central focus of the author's career. In the early 1980s the author experienced a variety of training courses in managing aggression. In many cases staff were taught predominantly physical responses to aggressive behaviours, which often used techniques developed for self-defence. An examination of the research at this time revealed only limited evidence for the effectiveness of such training. The response was to create a series of training programmes from an evidence-based perspective. It was decided at an early stage to develop a non-violent response that encompassed de-escalation strategies and physical management within a clear person-centred philosophy. This philosophy has come to be described as a 'low arousal approach'. The approach eventually led to the creation of an independent training organization called Studio3 Training Systems. This organization now develops training programmes across Europe, Africa and the Middle East.

This book aims to present evidence for low arousal approaches. In Chapter 1 there is an attempt to place the approaches described in this book within a theoretical framework. Chapters 2 and 3 describe the development of low arousal approaches and a core three-day training course to help carers to manage challenging behaviours. The next five chapters outline the application of this training to a variety of different care environments (such as intellectual disabilities, autism, mental health services for children and adults and services for older adults). Each of these chapters attempts to provide background information on managing aggressive behaviours that is relevant to its distinctive area. Each chapter also presents real-life case examples. Chapter 9 reviews the research evidence for the effectiveness of staff training in physical interventions. Suggestions for future research using a range of methodologies are furthermore discussed. Chapter 10 presents an overview of many of the key issues raised in the book.

Acknowledgements

There are a vast number of people who need to be mentioned. First, the author greatly appreciates the efforts of the staff at Studio3 Training Systems, who have been great champions of low arousal approaches. I am not going to list names, but I rather thank you for your dedication and passion. I am especially indebted to Professor Peter Sturmey for his practical advice and unflinching academic support. Regine Anker has provided an organized and structured approach to the completion of this book. Rather like a marathon the last part has been the most painful and difficult. There are also numerous services which have helped to pioneer these approaches, and to name them all would require much space. But to my colleagues in Birmingham in the United Kingdom and the National Autistic Society I am very much indebted. In Ireland special mention must be given to my colleagues at Gheel Autism Services in Dublin, who have both questioned and supported me. I am quite aware of the many people who have been involved with the ideas and views described in this book. Many service users have actively been involved throughout this process, and I have to acknowledge how much of the information in this book has involved listening to our customers and learning from them.

1

Understanding Violence and Aggression in Care Settings

Mankind must evolve for all human conflict a method which rejects revenge, aggression, and retaliation. The foundation of such a method is love.
—Attributed to Dr Martin Luther King

Aggressive and violent behaviours present significant challenges to individuals and the society as a whole. Social scientists tend to view the capacity to commit interpersonal violence as a universal capability (McCall & Shields, 2008). The financial costs of interpersonal violence to employers can be extremely high, especially when the indirect costs are calculated along with the direct costs (Di Martino, 2005). Evidence has been found from archaeological examination of early Neanderthal skeletons about the occurrence of violence-related trauma, although the frequency of the deaths caused by it is still a moot point (Berger & Trinkhaus, 1995). Aggressive behaviours have remained a major topic of concern for many years in human services. Physical aggression can generate fear among care staff who are often expected to manage such behaviours in their day-to-day work (Singh, Lloyd & Kendall, 1990), and it can also generate strong emotional reactions in them (Bromley & Emerson, 1995).

The management of aggressive and violent behaviour in care settings is an important topic. This chapter will examine definitions of violence and aggression and will provide some basic knowledge of the theoretical approaches to the subject. Responses to violence and aggression will be discussed at both an individual and an organizational level. Finally, the training response to violence and aggression management will be examined.

Managing Aggressive Behaviour in Care Settings: Understanding and applying low arousal approaches
By Andrew A. McDonnell © 2010 John Wiley & Sons, Ltd

Definitions of Aggression and Violence

Definitions of constructs such as violence and aggression are important for researchers, as they often determine the responses of individuals. The terms violence and aggression are often used interchangeably. An understanding of these definitions can be important for both practitioners and researchers.

There are many definitional problems in defining violence and aggression. Anderson and Bushman (2002) regard the difference between aggression and violence to be a matter of degree. According to their definition aggression is the behaviour intended to produce deliberate harm to another, and violence is the behaviour that has extreme harm (such as murder) as its intent.

There are dangers to viewing aggressive behaviours as a homogeneous 'lump'. Specific definitions can help to provide clearer interpretations of data. To illustrate this point a distinction between verbal and physical aggression can be useful. Verbal aggression is reported as being far more common than physical aggression in hospital settings (Hahn et al., 2008). Understanding these differences can have positive implications for human service providers. At a macroscopic level staff responses to verbal and physical aggression may create different training needs.

Intentionality is a construct that has implications for both researchers and practitioners. Bandura (1973) distinguished between angry and instrumental aggression. Angry aggression is associated with highly charged emotional sequelae, and instrumental aggression is the term used to describe aggression that has a clear purpose. This is useful in distinguishing between explosive aggressive acts and those which have a planned component.

According to the UK law, in the case of aggressive behaviour there is a distinction made between the act (known in Latin as *actus reus*) and the intent (known in law as *mens rea* or a 'guilty mind'). Consider the example of a street thief who uses intimidation and openly aggressive behaviour to obtain money. This aggression is clearly instrumental in its presentation, as it is designed to obtain the primary goal of hard cash. This should be distinguished from an aggressive situation in which an individual may be overtly angry in order to achieve a goal but remains reasonably in control of their behaviour. In contrast an individual may experience an elevated arousal level and may actually lose control of their responses. In the latter circumstance the aggression and the violence may be less premeditated and more driven by emotional arousal. (In Chapter 2 this distinction will be used to formulate staff and service responses to aggression).

Aggressive behaviour can also vary in terms of its everyday presentation. Gomes (2007) distinguished between overt and covert aspects of aggression. Overt aggression includes, but is not limited to, hitting, shoving and pushing, whereas covert aggression includes actions such as rumour spreading, gossiping and social isolation, which are not readily observable to others not enmeshed in the experience of the aggression. Bullying would fit into either the overt or the covert category, although most forms of bullying tend to be covert in nature.

Definitions also need to account for violence and aggression not just at an individual level but also at organizational and societal levels. Tiered definitions of violence can help to clarify key issues for researchers and practitioners. Bowie (2002) distinguished four categories of violence in the workplace: first, intrusive violence, which includes planned acts especially those involved in committing a crime; second, consumer-related violence, which includes violence committed by both service consumers and staff; third, relationship violence, which includes bullying and harassment in the workplace; and finally, organizational violence, which is caused by organizational structures and systems.

Formulating violence and aggression in such a 'systemic' manner would appear to enhance the explanatory power of such models. However, there is the real danger of such definitions leading to the mantra that it is the systems which need to be changed rather than the individuals. In reality violence and aggression can be conceptualized at a variety of explanatory levels.

Theoretical Approaches to Aggression and Violence

Drive and instinct theories

Psychodynamic approaches stress the importance of early life experiences in determining aggressive behaviour (Freud, 1930). Theories of aggression in the early decades of the twentieth century tended to focus on aggressive behaviour as being predominantly instinctive in nature. Models that combined both instinctual and environmental elements emerged after the Second World War. MacDougall (1947) proposed a hydraulic model of the behaviour in which emotions build up to a point at which they need to be released. Dollard, Doob, Miller, Mowrer and Seers (1939) maintained that the environment was more critical in the maintenance of aggression. They viewed behaviour as goal directed and held the view that the blocking of goals consequently leads to frustration and ultimately aggression.

These early models tended to focus on highly simplistic explanations of human aggression. A good example of this involves the concept of catharsis. Cathartic theories of aggression tended to stress the positive benefits of the release of anger or hostility. The concept of catharsis has been associated with purging and cleansing. The idea that violence and aggression can be released in some manner would appear to have high face validity. In reality such constructs are difficult to quantify. Consider the following two examples: In the first, a young man may be encouraged in therapy to strike or hit objects to reduce his aggressive tendencies. In the second, after returning from war soldiers were observed to display lower levels of violent and aggressive behaviours. In both these examples a release or purging of aggression is assumed. The construct of catharsis is used in a contextually different manner – one reflects an individual perspective, whereas the other stresses a societal effect.

Evolutionary models

Ethologist Konrad Lorenz (1966) described violence and aggression in terms of societies and larger groups. He proposed that humans were naturally aggressive and that they consequently release aggression through activities such as sports and military conflict. He furthermore argued that animals, especially the males, were biologically programmed to fight over resources. This behaviour should be considered part of the Darwinian process of natural selection, as aggression leading to death or serious injury may eventually lead to extinction of animals unless it has such a role. According to his approach aggressive behaviour could be adaptive in nature.

The evolutionary perspective on violence appears to have some attraction for researchers. These approaches tend to stress the adaptive nature of violence and aggression. There are, however, problems with this perspective. It could be argued that aggression and violence should be less prominent in developed Western societies, where presumably there are fewer individuals who need to compete for resources. The evidence for this assumption is limited. The murder rates among the Ju'hoansi of the Kalahari are similar to (or higher than) those of modern North American cities (Lee, 1979). In contrast, many stratified forager societies, such as those of the American Northwest, not only have historically had very high rates of violence but also have had culturally sanctioned, institutionalized violence as legitimate social activity.

Animal studies made famous by Calhoun (1962) show that crowding in the animal world results in what he calls the behavioural sink. In his now-classic study Calhoun provided a cage of rats with food and water that was replenished to support any increase in population, in a small quarter-acre plot in Maryland, USA. What Calhoun built was a quarter-acre pen, calling it a 'rat city', which he seeded with five pregnant females. Calhoun calculated that the habitat was sufficient to accommodate as many as 5000 rats. Instead, the population levelled off at 150 and throughout the two years that Calhoun kept watch never exceeded 200.

Calhoun claimed that the level of overpopulation produced clear behavioural effects. He reported that normal behaviour and reproductive habits in the rats began to fail. Aggressive behaviour increased when the animals competed for scarce resources. This work has been subjected to great scrutiny and has received considerable criticism (Ramsden & Adams, in press). These animal models may appear quite attractive, but the explanation of this behaviour by crowding alone might not neatly apply to models of human aggression and violence.

This view of the role of evolutionary factors in violence and aggressive behaviours is not necessarily pessimistic. An acknowledgement of the human capacity for violence does not necessarily mean that the person cannot control their behaviour. This does not mean that societies cannot alter their patterns of violence and aggression, as there are clearly huge situational components to this behaviour.

Operant models

Operant approaches have stressed the importance of the environment in causing and maintaining aggressive behaviours (Skinner, 1953, 1957). Reinforcement of behaviour, both positive and negative, has a causal effect on antecedent stimuli and behaviour. Early behavioural research tended to focus on the study of animals and aggressive behaviours. Skinner (1959) reported that he could induce aggressive behaviour among pigeons by rewarding a hungry pigeon if it attacked another bird. Azrin, Hutchinson and Hake (1966) reported aggression in pigeons when reinforcement was withdrawn leading to extinction.

Applying work conducted on animals to non-laboratory settings has been a major focus of applied behaviour analysts. Behaviourists often stress the role of directly observable behaviours and the reinforcement contingencies that maintain behaviours. Early studies attempted to apply behavioural methods to real-world settings. For example Fuller (1949) applied a shaping procedure to assist a person with intellectual disability to move their arm.

There is little doubt that the application of scientific approaches to behaviour analysis has led to significant positive developments in care settings. Early approaches tended to focus on the manipulation of consequences to behaviours. The use of token economy systems to control and manage behaviours can provide some insight into the change and adaptation of behavioural technologies. Token economies tended to be used in larger institutional systems in the past (Ayllon & Azrin, 1968). The advent of behavioural approaches which concentrate more on the antecedents of the behaviour (Goldiamond, 1974) has made these approaches less popular. However token systems are still in use in some institutional settings (Moore, Tingstrom, Doggett & Carlyon, 2001) and in some services for people with intellectual disabilities and autism (Kahng, Boscoe & Byrne, 2003).

The primary goal of a token economy is to increase desirable behaviour and decrease undesirable behaviour (Kazdin, 1982). Tokens are used to shape positive behaviours. In some cases individuals can lose tokens for bad behaviours. The decline in the applications of these systems may be more moral in nature than scientific. The use of response cost and fines can be perceived by practitioners in a negative manner and may be extremely controlling (Corrigan, 1995). Despite these reservations some researchers still believe in the positive aspect of these methods (Matson & Boisjoli, 2009).

The operant models began to focus more on the antecedents of behaviours rather than on the consequences; this was called the 'constructional approach' (Goldiamond, 1974). Further development of the behavioural model has included the introduction of distant antecedent events which may also influence behaviour. Wahler and Fox (1981) used the term 'setting events' for them, which was later superseded by the term 'establishing operations' (Michael, 1993). Deprivation and satiation are commonly used constructs in behaviour analysis (Murphy, McSweeney, Smith & McComas, 2003). That is to say the level of reinforcement can greatly influence behaviour. As a rule reinforcers are more powerful if the individual has been deprived of them.

Over the last decade there has been a substantial move away from interventions based on consequential punishment to those based on reinforcement contingencies (Donnellan et al., 1988; LaVigna & Donnellan, 1986; Lerman & Vorndran, 2002). Positive behaviour support is a development of applied behaviour analytic interventions in which 'to remediate problem behaviour, it is necessary first to remediate problem contexts. There are two kinds of deficiencies: those that relating to environmental conditions and those relating to behaviour repertoires' (Carr ct al., 1999, p. 4).

Despite the optimism there have been criticisms levelled at these approaches. First, the implementation of these interventions can be time consuming (Donnellan et al., 1988). Second, staff turnover can affect the consistency of the programmes (Reid & Parsons, 2002). Third, many behavioural interventions are conducted on an informal basis, that is to say without professional guidance or in written form. A recent survey of behavioural programme implementation in Canada reported that 54% of behavioural interventions were conducted on an informal basis (Feldman, Atkinson, Foti-Gervais & Condillac, 2004).

Cognitive models

Behavioural models are sometimes referred to as 'black box' approaches, as internal events are not viewed as causal in them. Cognitive theories stress the role of internal events in the maintenance of behaviours (Salkovskis & Rachman, 1997). Cognitive constructs have extended and enriched the early behavioural approaches. Bandura (1973) described a social learning model of aggressive behaviour in which learning could take place both directly and indirectly. The later development of the self-efficacy theory (Bandura, 1977, 1985, 1995, 1997) introduced cognitive constructs which included the beliefs and expectations of the individuals.

Cognitive models of aggressive behaviours have tended to focus primarily on the responses of individuals. Novaco (1975, 1978) introduced a cognitive behavioural formulation of aggressive behaviour in which an individual's appraisal of events was critical in the maintenance of aggression. In essence a person may encounter aggressive behaviour, and their appraisal of the situation determines their emotional and behavioural responses. Novaco and Welsh (1989) argued that people who engage in aggressive behaviours often interpret everyday social interactions as threatening, which leads to the experience of anger and the open expression of an aggressive response.

Weiner's attributional model of helping behaviour has also been proposed as an explanatory model for staff behaviour. In this model staff attributions and emotional responses determine their helping behaviour (Allen, 1999a; Dagnan, Trower & Smith, 1998; Wanlesss & Jahoda, 2002). In sum, if an individual's behaviour is perceived as not necessarily within their control, then the behavioural responses to them should be more positive. Cognitive behavioural approaches would appear to provide a useful explanatory framework for aggressive behaviours. Cognitive behavioural approaches such as the attributional model of Weiner (1986) may offer a pragmatic explanatory framework to staff responses to aggressive behaviour in learning disabilities settings (Allen, 1999a; Dagnan et al., 1998). There is little doubt that the influence and application of behavioural and cognitive behavioural approaches in care environments are substantial (Turnbull, 1999).

Transactional models of aggression

Models of aggression and violence need to account for the wide differences in the manifestations of these behaviours. In psychology the importance of personality and situational characteristics has been heatedly debated. Mischel (1968) argued cogently that situational characteristics influence behaviour and that personality traits have little influence. Mischel (2004) later presented a model which reflected the complex interaction of these variables.

The power of situational factors and how they can interact with individual characteristics can be best illustrated by violence at football matches. Early sociological studies stressed the rule-governed nature of football fans who committed acts of premeditated violence (Marsh, Rosser & Harre, 1978). It would be easy to stereotype these individuals as generally being predisposed to aggressive behaviours, but in fact the data do not tend to support this view. Stott and Adang (2004) examined statistics from the English National Criminal Intelligence Service and found that the majority of the individuals who were arrested during the 2004 European Football Championships had no prior involvement with football-related violence. An understanding of group processes and categorization (see Tajfel & Turner, 1979) and crowd behaviour may account for some of this behaviour. Intuitively, there will be some individuals who have the capacity to be violent and aggressive in a variety of situations. In addition the vast majority of football fans never commit acts of aggression and violence.

The example of aggression and violence at football matches illustrates the complex interaction of variables that relate to aggression and violence. It could be argued that the study of situations in which individuals manage to control their aggressive behaviours may be as useful for researchers as those in which they do not.

The general aggression model

In the field of aggression, Anderson and Bushman (2002) proposed a detailed model of aggression and violence which included elements of both the situation and the person. In their theory a person's internal state is the sum of the interactions between cognitions, affect and arousal. These are described as the 'routes' to aggressive behaviours. Cognitions include hostile thoughts and aggressive scripts and may come to be highly salient or accessible to an individual. Affect includes negative or hostile feelings and anger. Arousal involves the person's physiological state that may be the result of factors unrelated to anger, such as exercise or the use of drugs. These three routes are highly interconnected.

Anderson and Bushman (2002) distinguished between behavioural outcomes that can be relatively automatic (immediate appraisal) or controlled (reappraisal). The inferences a person makes about the situation are related to their internal state and social learning history. An important part of the appraisal process is the person's resources to reflect upon the situation. Resources include the available time and the person's cognitive capacities to analyse the circumstances. When an outcome or course of action is important to the person, and the immediate action is unsatisfying, reappraisal is more likely to take place.

In this model there is a complex interaction between both internal and external stimuli and how individuals process information. The idea that information processing is a key component of aggressive and violent behaviours has been proposed by other researchers (i.e. Huesmann, 1988). More recently Metcalfe and Mischel (1999) proposed the existence of two interrelated memory systems, namely the hot and cool systems, involved in the execution of aggressive behaviour. The information stored in the cool system is narrative and episodic (e.g. autobiographical events) and is associated with a neutral mood. The cool system is responsible for novelty monitoring, semantic priming, problem solving, metacognition, control processes, planning and comprehension and is important for non-impulsive and self-controlled behaviours. The hot system stores the emotionally salient aspects of events and less elaborated memories. The hot system is important for rapid automatic responses that are more inflexible, stereotyped and affectively primary. Both systems do not always directly lead to actions or responses.

A recent analysis of information processing approaches to understanding aggressive behaviours has highlighted that aggressive behaviour should not be viewed as fully automatic and as a consequence out of the individual's control and that hot and cool processes may sometimes interact in a complex manner; it is possible for both components to operate during an aggressive or violent episode (Richetin & Richardson, 2008). The distinction between hot and cool processes as an explanatory construct for aggressive and violent behaviour would appear to have considerable face validity. Variables which may mediate these processes could include alcohol (MacDonald, Zanna & Holmes, 2000) and stress (Hennessy & Wiensenthal, 1999), both of which have been associated with aggressive behaviours. These factors may reduce an individual's capacity to process information.

Anderson and Bushman (2002) described another aspect of their theory, which is called 'scripts'. Scripts are collections of primarily well-rehearsed, exceptionally related concepts in memory, often involving contributory links, aims and action strategies. This theory proposes that when children watch violence in the mass media, they gain knowledge of aggressive scripts. Repeated practice of these scripts can generate associations to other notions in memory and amplify the strengths of these links. This idea of scripts illustrates how everyday behaviour may eventually produce aggressive behaviours in some individuals and not in others. This is because these scripts will vary dramatically among individuals.

The present author has used the general aggression model to demonstrate the complex interactions that can result in aggressive behaviours. The complexity of this model has great usefulness, as it would appear to have face validity and explanatory power (it appears to provide explanations to many complex observations). Theories also need to be high in predictive power. That is to say clear testable predictions should be generated (Hyland, 1981). Complexity in this case can rather be a 'double-edged sword'.

Theoretical debates about the comparative efficacy of specific models of aggression will undoubtedly continue in the future. In conclusion aggression is regarded as a phenomenon determined by multiple factors (Patterson & Leadbetter, 1999). This complex transaction between the environment, affect and cognition has to be formulated within a cognitive-behavioural multidimensional model. In sum,

> [v]iolence is the result of interaction between a few important biological inputs and many strong situational inputs and environmental influences. (McCall & Shields, 2008)

Applying this theoretical knowledge about the causes and maintenance of aggressive behaviours to non-laboratory settings is a major challenge for researchers. This book aims to have a pragmatic approach to the application of current scientific information to help to produce more effective management of these behaviours. The next section will describe some of the issues relating to violence in care environments.

Violence and Aggression in Care Settings

Workplace violence and aggression is acknowledged to be a serious problem. A recent European survey of workplace violence and aggression estimated that 1 in 20 workers experiences violence in the workplace with the highest rates being reported in the Netherlands, France, the United Kingdom and Ireland (Parent-Thirion, Macías, Hurley & Vermeylen, 2007). Aggressive behaviour in health care settings is a serious problem for service providers (Beech & Leather, 2006). This problem is not a new phenomenon. An advisory committee of the UK health services showed that violence was commonplace in health care, and specific areas such as accident and emergency, psychiatry and community care carried the highest risk (Health & Safety Advisory Committee, 1987). More recent official figures from the Security Management Service of the National Health Service (NHS) in the United Kingdom recorded 43,301 incidents of physical assault against NHS staff working in mental health and learning disability settings in 2004–2005 across England. This includes one assault for every five staff in mental health and learning disability settings.

In residential services violence and aggression can have a significant impact. Zuidema, Derksen, Verhey and Koopmans (2007) in a survey of Dutch nursing homes for older adults reported that more than 80% of these individuals presented with agitation/aggression, apathy and irritability. There are a number of studies which report associations between organic brain damage and aggressive behaviour in older adults (Pulsford & Duxbury, 2006).

There has also been considerable research investigating rates of aggression and violence in services for people with intellectual disabilities. Allen (2000a) in a recent review of the literature on aggression has reported that weapons may be used by between 17% and 29% of individuals with intellectual disabilities who present with aggressive behaviours. Physically aggressive symptoms such as hitting, kicking and biting occurred less often (in less than 13% of the sample). In services for people with intellectual disabilities, studies have reported data on complete populations through state registers. Jacobson (1982a, 1982b) reported data from the New York state register, which contained records on over 30,000 individuals living with their own families, in community residences or in hospitals. The register included data on both children and adults. The overall prevalence of relevant behaviours included 10.9% for physical assault, 4.3% for property destruction, 1.4% for coercive sexual behaviour, 8.1% for actively resisted supervision and 5.9% for verbally abusing others (Jacobson, 1982a).

A recent meta-analytic review of 86 studies on challenging behaviours identified risk markers of challenging behaviours in people with intellectual disabilities and autism (McClintock, Hall & Oliver, 2003). Risk markers were identified for a number of presenting problems. In the case of aggression these included a higher prevalence of males with a diagnosis of autism and deficits in expressive communication.

Hahn and colleagues (2008) reviewed the published literature of aggression and violence in hospital settings. They identified 31 studies rated as being of good or moderate research quality. Several themes emerged from this review. First, staff experienced more verbal than physical aggression. Second, health care professionals working in general hospitals were at high risk for experiencing various forms of violence at some point during their career and also during the time frame of one year. Third, they found that threats and verbal violence were more common among patients than visitors. In addition, hospital patients tend to be more violent than visitors. The authors identified a number of important situational factors that were associated with aggression. Organizational factors, such as prolonged waiting times and difficult interactions between professionals and service consumer, were associated with aggressive behaviour. Frustrating experiences also contribute to aggression in general hospitals, especially in relation to medical procedures that induced pain and/or anxiety and procedures that encouraged the patients to feel as though they were not being taken or treated seriously (Winstanley, 2005). These findings do appear to increase the risk of aggression and violence against nurses.

Although surveys appear to present a negative picture the representation of the complex nature of these behaviours may be affected by recording difficulties. Surveys vary in their use of definitions and may not represent true levels of violence and aggression. Violence and aggression may in some cases be under-reported (Lion, Snyder & Merrill, 1981). In contrast surveys and increased public awareness may over-emphasize the level and impact of verbal aggression. Distinguishing between verbal and physical aggression in surveys is important. A good example of this is found in surveys which report high levels of verbal aggression. Nijman, Bowers, Oud and Jansen (2005) reported that 80–90% of mental health nurses had experienced verbal aggression in the previous year. Logically a great deal of verbal behaviour does not escalate into full-blown violent acts. Verbal aggression nearly always precedes physical aggression, but the inverse is not necessarily a correct assumption. It could be argued that verbal aggression in many cases may potentially predict lower levels of physical aggression.

The nature of aggressive behaviours

Emerson and colleagues (2001) in a study of the total population reported a number of forms of aggression, which included the following: hitting others with hands (75%), hitting others with objects (41%), scratching others (27%), pulling others' hair (23%) and pinching (20%) and biting (16%) others. The use of objects requires more detailed investigation. Similarly, the categories do not specify the body location that was hit and whether people were hit with a clenched fist or open hand(s). The type of objects used was also unspecified. There is limited data about the physical manifestations of aggression and violence.

Institutional/organizational aggression and violence

Violence and aggression should not just be viewed from the individual perspective; the system can potentially cause and maintain such behaviours. Bowie (2002) described the relationship between organizational structures and management and their susceptibility to violence. Similarly, Braverman (2002) identified that organizational systems can be 'crisis prone' or that alternatively they can have a positive culture of crisis preparedness.

There are numerous documented cases of institutional structures condoning and in some cases colluding with aggression and violence. Institutional structures can lead to acts of abuse, especially where negative subcultures are allowed to develop. Martin (1984) reviewed inquiries in UK hospitals over a 15-year period. His analysis identified that isolated staff groups committed acts which to some extent became normalized. In a number of inquiries new staff tended to act as 'whistle-blowers' who often challenged cultures in which violent and other abusive acts became normalized.

There are ample numbers of social psychological studies which have tended to demonstrate that the so-called ordinary people can commit extreme acts of violence. In some cases people can be made to deliver electric shocks to individuals in contrived laboratory situations (Milgram, 1974). In the classic Stanford prison experiment students were asked to role-play as both guards and prisoners in a mock-up prison in the basement of the Stanford University psychology department. In a matter of days guards started to display controlling and abusive behaviours that led to the termination of the experiment (Haney, Banks & Zimbardo, 1971). One of the themes of these studies is to show the ability of individuals to normalize and justify their behaviour especially in group contexts.

Byrne and Stowell (2007) cogently described the negative ethos of some prisons: 'The image of prisons as institutions of reform has been supplanted by the reality of the prison system whose stated purpose is undermined by a culture of fear, violence, and control' (p. 554). These few examples serve to illustrate the role of organizational cultures in maintaining aggressive behaviours. A useful area of research is to reframe the power of institutions. If we accept that these settings and cultures can maintain aggression and violence, then it must be possible to create organizations and structures with a violence- and aggression-free positive ethos (Braverman, 2002).

Responses to the Prevention of Aggression and Violence

The views of cultures about the management of these behaviours can vary dramatically. A natural extension of organizational approaches to preventing violence and aggression is the societal approach. In the last decade there has been the trend to move away from single-factor solutions to violence to complex strategies which involve interventions at a variety of levels. This approach has been called the public health model of violence prevention.

The recent World Health Organization document (Butchart, Phinney, Check & Villaveces, 2004) described four steps in the public health model: 'The first step is to define the problem using the systematic collection of information. The second step is to identify and research the risk and protective factors that increase or decrease the likelihood of violence, including those that can be modified through interventions. The third step is to determine what works in preventing violence by developing and evaluating interventions tailored to the demographic and socioeconomic characteristics of the groups in which they are to be implemented. The fourth step is to implement effective and promising interventions in a wide range of settings and, through ongoing monitoring of their effects on the risk factors and the target problem, to evaluate their impact and cost-effectiveness'.

Primary prevention seeks to prevent the onset of violence. The goal is to alter some factor in the environment, to bring about a change in the status of the host or to change the behaviour so that violence is prevented from developing. An example of this would be the application of positive parenting programmes. Secondary prevention aims to halt the progression of violence once it is established. This is achieved by early detection or early diagnosis followed by prompt, effective treatment. An example of secondary prevention is conflict resolution within schools. Tertiary prevention is concerned with rehabilitation of people with an established violent behaviour, which would encompass behavioural change programmes within a prison setting.

There is a conflict between public health and judicial approaches to violence and aggression management. Consequence-based methods to managing aggressive behaviours are reflected in many penal systems. The strategy of prevention of violence and aggression may prove to be cost-effective when compared with consequence-based methods. A Rand Corporation study compared the following four types of interventions to reduce crime among youth (including violent crime) in the United States: providing high-school students with incentives to graduate; parent training; delinquent supervision programmes; and home visits and day care. All interventions except home visits were found to be more cost-effective than the 'three strikes and you're out' law of the state of California that incarcerates individuals for 25 years to life if convicted of three serious crimes (King, 2004). The public health and criminal justice systems do have some fundamental differences in approaches; these include proactive versus reactive strategies and preventive versus punitive responses to violence (Sade, 2004).

There are difficulties with the public health approach to violence prevention. Most notable is that multi-layered interventions may not always produce short-term outcomes. The systematic evaluation of the model requires comparisons across service settings and cultures. Despite these reservations the systematic approach to violence prevention using such a model would appear to be a positive and constructional approach. In many ways it is also an optimistic strategy.

> Violence leaves no continent, no country and few communities untouched.
>
> Although it appears everywhere, violence is not an inevitable part of the human condition, nor is it an intractable problem of 'modern life' that cannot be overcome by human determination and ingenuity. (Butchart, Phinney, Check & Villaveces, 2004, p. 77)

Although the prevention of violence and aggression is a laudable aim, it is unlikely that all of these behaviours could be eradicated in care settings. These approaches also require significant financial investment and may take years or even decades to have an impact. For both practitioners and researchers it would appear logical to develop prevention and management approaches in tandem. The development of effective behaviour management approaches represents a logical step.

Managing Violence and Aggression in Care Settings

As discussed earlier, Bowie (2002) distinguished four typologies of violence: intrusive violence, consumer-related violence, relationship violence and organizational violence. Both consumer-related violence and organizational violence would primarily encompass violence in care environments. Global interventions such as the public health model may have an effect on both organizational and consumer-related violence.

The development of crisis responses in care settings needs to take account of factors that may immediately reduce the risk of harm. Crisis interventions should be distinguished from longer-term interventions. McDonnell and Anker (2009) distinguished between behaviour change and behaviour management strategies. According to their definition behaviour change 'involves changes in intensity, frequency or episodic severity that maintain across situations and time', and behaviour management involves 'strategies which contain a behaviour and reduce the risk of harm to service users and staff without attempting to alter the behaviour per se'. In this model, reductions in intensity, frequency or episodic severity of aggressive behaviours may occur, but the primary goal is one of safety and containment. Managing these behaviours effectively and safely in care contexts would appear to have potential benefits to both staff and service users. At an organizational level these could include reduction of restrictive practices such as physical interventions, seclusion and mechanical restraint. In addition the reduction of injuries to both carers and service users could also be an achievable goal (Deveau & McDonnell, in press). Intuitively, training staff in crisis responses may also have an effect on the reduction of violence and aggression.

The training response to aggression and violence in care settings

This chapter has highlighted the complex interaction of variables which can lead to violence. In care settings the behaviour of staff can be a significant factor. Morrison (1990) proposed a model of aggression and violence in psychiatry, which emphasized that people are more aggressive and violent when they are being 'controlled' by care staff. The behaviour of staff and other carers may inadvertently trigger aggressive behaviours in services for people with intellectual disabilities (Hastings & Remington, 1994)

The nature of interactions between staff and service users can also influence aggressive behaviour. Whittington and Wykes (1994) interviewed psychiatric nurses within 72 hours of an assault: 86% of assaults appeared to have been preceded by aversive stimulation from nursing staff, 60% of incidents were preceded by staff approaching the person or initiating physical contact, 51% involved frustrating a person in their goals or refusing a request, and 38% included requests or activity demands to the person.

Staff and service users are also at risk of injury when managing aggressive behaviours. Staff training is one approach to managing this difficulty. The need for advice and training on how to manage these behaviours and for carers to defend themselves non-violently, while also ensuring client safety, has been acknowledged by researchers (Allen, MacDonald, Dunn & Doyle, 1997; Rusch et al., 1986).

This book will focus on the training response to the management of aggressive behaviour in care settings. Training staff to de-escalate violent and aggressive situations and to safely manage physical violence is an important goal. Although, staff training would appear to be an obvious approach, the effectiveness of training in aggression management, which includes physical interventions, is based on limited outcome data (Allen, 2000b; McDonnell et al., 2009). A theme of this literature is the poor quality of the research (Stubbs et al., 2009; Beech & Leather, 2006).

The content of training is important, but another element of importance is the values base. Paterson and Leadbetter (2002) argued, 'Training involves more than the acquisition of skills and knowledge; it involves either explicitly or implicitly the transmission of a culture and a value base' (p. 141).

Many behaviour management training approaches are available (Beech & Leather, 2006). The current situation would indicate that in the area of behaviour management anecdotal evidence for these systems still predominates. The development of behaviour management within a person-centred and evidence-based model would potentially have significant benefits. The remainder of this book will describe the development and evaluation of a training course to support staff to manage violence and aggression in care settings. The training system has the title of the 'Studio3 approach'. It was developed and evolved over a 20-year period. The next two chapters will describe the development of the training, and the subsequent five chapters will describe the application of the approach in a variety of care contexts. The final two chapters will review the current evidence for the training system and suggest future areas of research for both academics and clinical practitioners.

2

The Development of a Low Arousal Approach

Background

Managing aggressive behaviour involves prevention, de-escalation and in extreme cases physical management. This chapter will describe the development and evolution of a de-escalation model which is now routinely called a 'low arousal approach' (McDonnell, Waters & Jones, 2002) – this approach is a central tenet of this book.

Managing verbal and physical aggression is an important day to day skill required of workers in care environments. Verbal aggression appears to be more common than physical aggression in care environments (Kiely & Pankhurst, 1998). De-escalating or defusing verbal aggression has received relatively little empirical evaluation (McDonnell & Sturmey, 1993a), and currently, there are no standard evidence-based models of de-escalation (Patterson & Leadbetter, 1999).

The most commonly used model to help staff understand and defuse aggressive behaviours is the assault cycle (Kaplan & Wheeler, 1983). Kaplan and Wheeler proposed a five-stage assault cycle which contains a triggering phase, an escalation phase and a crisis phase followed by a recovery phase and a depression phase. This model is extensively cited in the literature (Breakwell, 1997; Patterson & Leadbetter, 1999) and would appear to have high face validity, but with regard to the scientific basis of this cycle there is little objective experimental evidence.

Understanding the assault experience should in theory at least lead to the development of de-escalation strategies. In conclusion aggressive behaviour is

Managing Aggressive Behaviour in Care Settings: Understanding and applying low arousal approaches
By Andrew A. McDonnell   © 2010 John Wiley & Sons, Ltd

a multi-faceted phenomenon unlikely to be explained by one single model. To develop any de-escalation approach in care environments a number of key issues require careful examination. In the next section the role of trauma experiences will be examined.

Trauma-Informed Behaviour Management Approaches

In Chapter 1 it was noted that aggression can occur in a variety of settings (Anderson & Bushman, 2002). People in care environments may have either experienced or been exposed to trauma. Early childhood trauma has been linked to the development of a number of mental health difficulties including schizophrenia (Read, Perry, Moskowitz & Connolly, 2001). There is now a considerable body of knowledge which links trauma with significant groups of people in care environments (Jennings, 2004). 'Trauma-informed' services are not specifically designed to treat symptoms or syndromes related to sexual or physical abuse or other trauma, but they are informed about, and are sensitive to, trauma-related issues which are present in survivors (Harris & Fallot, 2001). There also remains the intriguing speculation that early trauma may cause damage to the arousal mechanisms in the brain.

In sum, models and approaches to behaviour management skills need to account for the traumatized nature of the populations in their care. A good example of this has been the development of more humanistic approaches such as the Tidal Model to managing severe mental illness (Buchanan-Barker & Barker, 2008). This model stresses the complex interaction of the individuals and their carers and the distress that the carers experience. This model has gained significant influence in psychiatric nursing (Barker, 2005; Brookes, 2006). A major part of this approach is to encourage nurses to work with individuals in distress in order to assist them with their recovery.

An implicit assumption about models of care which attempt to be less judgmental or interventionist and more person centred is that they tend to avoid the use of punitive approaches. In the intellectual disabilities field the avoidance of punitive consequences has been one of the guiding principles for non-aversive approaches, most exemplified in the so-called positive behavioural supports (Carr et al., 1999). In intellectual disability services trauma has been acknowledged as an important factor in the presentation of aggressive and violent behaviours. Person-centred approaches that acknowledge this factor tend to avoid the use of punitive consequences or sanctions. In essence an individual in distress could potentially be re-traumatized by the application of such methods. This would explain the rationale of giving choices rather than boundaries to people who present with aggressive behaviours (Pitonyak, 2004).

The Role of Staff Expectations and Beliefs in the Maintenance of Aggression

Attempts have been made to explain staff behaviour in care environments from a cognitive behavioural perspective (Dagnan, Trower & Smith, 1998). Attribution models stress that staff perceptions of a situation mediate their behavioural responses. Staff may have negative thoughts about working with a particular individual in a service setting – 'Oh, God! I'm not working with him again.' – which directly affect their deeper-held beliefs reflected in thoughts such as 'I can't cope with stress'. Altering these thought processes can help staff in their interactions with service users. It is not unusual for staff to catastrophize events; often this is typified by predictions about negative future outcomes – 'It is only a matter of time before I really get badly hurt', or 'He is a ticking bomb'. In addition if the person is perceived as in control of their behaviour the use of punitive consequences may seem attractive to staff.

There is a growing body of knowledge which suggests that staff factors may contribute to aggressive behaviours (Whittington & Wykes, 1994). Staff who work with aggressive service users face a challenging and sometimes a dangerous task. All of them come with their own learning history of managing aggressive behaviour and conflict resolution. Psychologist Albert Bandura has stated, '[P]eoples' levels of motivation, affective states and actions are based on what they believe, than in what is objectively true' (Bandura, 1997, p. 21). This view of human behaviour has changed the focus from simple environmental contingencies to a closer examination of the thoughts and beliefs of individuals and how these mediate their behaviour.

In terms of aggressive behaviour we can view aggression and violence as a complex interaction between the person and their environment. Staff's thinking style and perception of situations may influence how they behave when service users are aggressive and whether they follow written plans and the way they instruct other staff to manage the service user's behaviour. Staff may instruct new staff implicitly or explicitly about certain rules to be followed. For example, in a particular situation, an experienced staff or supervisor might say to a new staff, 'Leave George alone. If you mess with him too much you'll get hurt like the last staff who got injured.' These interactions with peers can develop into rules and 'scripts' (Anderson & Bushman, 2002), such as 'If you interact with George, then you will get hurt.' Such rules appear to be confirmed when the staff member does avoid interacting with George and does not get hurt. Thus, learning such rules prevents the staff member from working with George.

Sometimes the personal experiences that the staff bring to care situations may in turn lead to negative scripts (see Anderson & Bushman, 2002). These core beliefs (Beck, 1975) can be quite rigid and difficult to change and may be learnt since childhood. For example a staff member may hold the belief that people who misbehave should be punished. This belief may lead to negative interactions with service users that may further lead to, for example, excessive demands being placed on these individuals. The author has even encountered care environments in which service users are compelled to write letters of apology after incidents. In these circumstances staff are attempting to assert control in a rather subtle manner and moreover are assuming that the individual was in control of their behaviour at the time of the violent act.

A more contemporary view is that some aggressive behaviour can be viewed as automatic. In these circumstances (especially where heightened arousal is concerned) an individual may at times not be in control of their behaviour (Richetin & Richardson, 2008).

The Role of Staff Reflective Practices

If the behaviour of staff inadvertently triggers aggressive behaviours, then altering these behaviours may have an impact on the management of aggressive behaviours. The construct of reflective practice in which an individual evaluates their performance in situations and learns from both positive and negative experiences (Schon, 1987) is useful to apply to staff who may experience violence and aggression in care settings. It is possible that aggressive behaviours are triggered by staff, although in many cases they may be unaware of their influence. In these circumstances it may be difficult to expect staff to examine their own contribution to these situations.

The reflective process requires colleagues to provide both positive and negative feedback. Challenging thoughts and altering beliefs is an integral part of cognitive behaviour therapy (see Beck, 1974). Understanding the attribution process can assist in this process. A staff member may experience the same event but may view the person as less directly in control of their behaviour (an external attribution) – 'Oh, he does not like loud noises', or 'Maybe I approached him too fast and scared him' (that is to say attributing blame and cause to themselves). These types of thoughts may lead staff to perceive the person as less in control of their behaviour and view themselves as active contributors to the situation. In these circumstances staff may think of solutions that focus on their own behaviour rather than manipulating the service user's behaviour per se.

Research has identified that staff's perception of the service user's control of their behaviour may have an impact on their helping behaviour towards those individuals (Dagnan et al., 1998; Weiner, 1986). In essence the more positively a staff member or carer feels towards a service user, the more likely they are to help that individual. It is the author's experience that in crisis situations staff sometimes become fearful and fail to see the person and focus too much on their fear. This can lead to what social psychologists have described as 'deindividuation' (Zimbardo, 1969). A number of studies have demonstrated that the more detached the people are from those who they are supposed to be supporting, the more likely they are to engage in punitive approaches. Social psychological experiments have demonstrated with reasonable consistency that individuals can conduct punitive approaches, especially if the people towards whom these approaches are directed are in some way viewed as different (Milgram, 1974).

Behaviour management strategies need to develop a questioning approach to managing behaviours, which should include an honest and critical appraisal of the staff member's contribution to violence and aggression. In order to achieve this, encouraging an open dialogue in human services about the role of staff beliefs and expectations in the maintenance of aggressive behaviours is crucial.

History and Evolution of the Low Arousal Approach

The term 'low arousal approach' was first used in 1994 (McDonnell, McEvoy & Dearden, 1994). The approach was then reformulated within a cognitive behavioural framework (McDonnell, Waters & Jones, 2002). The original ideas of the author were developed in the late 1980s and early 1990s whilst working in three distinctive areas. The first was a specialist high-staff-ratio support service for adults with intellectual disabilities and autism. The second area was a community service for people with intellectual disabilities. The third area was a hospital for people with intellectual disabilities and most notably a secure area for people with severe challenging behaviours. All three of these work areas involved working with people who presented with aggressive behaviours with varying levels of resources. It was very noticeable that there was a great need to manage behaviours in a dignified and socially acceptable manner. The behaviour management approach was developed as a response to the observational data that staff and carers often adopted punitive consequences to behaviours. It was also clear that the behaviour of staff appeared to directly trigger challenging behaviours in some cases. Furthermore, the use of physical interventions appeared to be used in an unplanned and unsafe manner.

The development of a coherent model of defusion and de-escalation required a rationale. The obvious area of investigation was the link between physiological arousal and behaviour.

The Link between Arousal and Behaviour

Arousal is a construct, which has proved difficult to define. For more than 100 years researchers appeared to be unable to agree if it was a unitary or a multifaceted construct (Pfaff, 2005). Recent research in neurobiology has indicated that there is a generalized arousal mechanism in the brain that feeds cortical functions (Pfaff, 2005): 'Generalized arousal is higher in an animal or human being who is (S) more alert to sensory stimuli of all sorts, and (M) more motorically active, and (E) more reactive emotionally' (Pfaff, 2005, p. 5). This relatively simple definition relates arousal to information processing. Novel, unpredictable stimuli will lead to an increased arousal response. The link between arousal and information processing was originally described by Yerkes and Dodson (1908) and came to be known as the Yerkes–Dodson law. This law maintains that performance and arousal are linked in a classic inverted-U shape and proposes that high levels of arousal lead to decrease in human performance. The original study examined the performance of mice in a learning task, in which electric shocks were delivered for incorrect responses. This has been used as an analogy to show that arousal reducing information processing has an optimum level (Easterbrook, 1959).

Critics of the Yerkes–Dodson law argue that high levels of arousal have survival value (Zajonc, 1980) and in some circumstances may increase performance in specific situations (Hanoch & Vitouch, 2004). Despite these criticisms the construct of arousal is considered useful in understanding the regulation of emotion (Pfaff, 2005), and arousal and stress are considered to be important in the moderation of emotions (Reich & Zautra, 2002).

The mediating effects of arousal are a major focus in aggression management. Linsley (2006) identified this role thus:

> [W]hile arousal is not necessarily associated with violence in itself, there is a strong association between arousal, violence and aggression. (p. 45)

An understanding of the mediating role of arousal can lead to such responses from carers that may reduce and manage extremely aggressive situations. In sum, heightened states of arousal do not always lead to physically aggressive responses, but it is comparatively rare to come across aggressive incidents which do not contain this factor. Similarly, verbal aggression does not always lead to physical aggression, although physical aggression is quite often preceded by verbal aggression.

A model of arousal which mediates certain forms of aggressive behaviours could provide a useful explanatory framework. A central premise is that an individual's internal physiological state of arousal influences cognitive processing of environmental sensory stimuli. Extending this view we would contend that the regulation of arousal mediates behavioural responses to environmental stressors. Individuals seek a state of *arousal equilibrium*, that is to say the optimum arousal level required for an individual to function in an environment; this is similar to the bodily state of homeostasis. The author proposes that arousal be thought of in three distinct areas of a Gaussian curve (see Figure 2.1). The

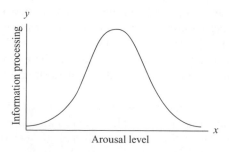

Figure 2.1. The Gaussian curve.

majority of individuals spend their time in a state of arousal equilibrium. In the case of people who present with aggressive behaviours two distinct arousal groupings will have an effect on behaviour; both appear at the tail end of the arousal curve. Individuals will be *hyper-aroused* and highly reactive to environmental sensory stimuli; in these circumstances 'hot' processes (Anderson & Bushman, 2002) have a powerful influence. In other situations people will be *hypo-aroused* and exhibit low responses to sensory stimuli.

The inverted-U shape described in Figure 2.1 has strong links to the constructs of stress and anxiety. Stress and anxiety have been proposed as factors in aggressive behaviours of people with autism spectrum disorder (ASD; Groden, Cautela, Prince & Berryman, 1994; Howlin, 1998) and in everyday work situations (Chen & Spector, 1992). An understanding of the stress response may be useful in the development of effective behaviour management strategies.

Lazarus and Folkman (1984) described a transactional model of stress, emphasizing the interaction between an individual and his/her environment. Stress is experienced when the demands of the stressors outweigh the coping responses and there is a clear interaction between environmental and physiological events. Implicit in this model is the cognitive appraisal of threat. To help account for challenging behaviours such as aggression and self-injurious behaviours we propose that physiological arousal may mediate stress.

This model suggests that there is a transaction between the person's internal state of arousal and the interaction with environmental stressors. The reduction of environmental arousal should decrease stress and anxiety and should therefore reduce the frequency and intensity of challenging behaviours.

Extreme levels of hyper-arousal may lead to a person becoming less responsive to environmental stimuli and appearing to 'shut down'. Goodwin and colleagues (2006) reported lower sensitivity to environmental stimulation in five individuals with ASD compared with the non-ASD controls; these individuals also had higher baseline heart rates than the controls. It is possible that higher levels of internal arousal may make some individuals less responsive to environmental stimuli. In this instance the internal arousal state became more dominant. This may well provide an explanatory framework of some forms of catatonic-type behaviours observed in some individuals with autism and certain forms of schizophrenia (Rogers, 1992).

There are several testable hypotheses that can be extrapolated from this model. First, basal physiological arousal measures should be able to identify groups of individuals with high and low responsivity on parameters such as heart rate and skin conductance (see Goodwin et al., 2006; Hirstein, et al., 2001). Second, reducing generalized physiological arousal should reduce challenging behaviours. Third, the more unpredictable the sensory stimuli are, the greater the levels of arousal experienced, leading to increases in challenging behaviours. Fourth, extreme forms of hyper-arousal may lead to reduced attention to external stimuli. To summarize, there would appear to be a consensus that high states of unregulated arousal can have a negative effect on human performance. The remainder of this chapter will present a model which focuses on the reduction of arousal in aggressive situations.

A Low Arousal Model of Behaviour Management

A low arousal approach is predominantly a staff-based intervention which focuses on reducing arousal in crisis situations. Organizationally there is an emphasis on strategies which aim to reduce confrontation through primarily staff-based reduction of arousal. Immediate staff-based strategies focus on the reduction of requests and demands and on the non-verbal cues and triggers employed by staff in conflict situations. The general reduction of rules and boundaries which may also create a culture of control are an implicit aspect of the approach. Encouraging staff on training courses to examine their own negative thinking styles and beliefs about individuals with challenging behaviours is a major element of the methods. Finally, designing physical interventions which minimize arousal and avoid punitive or painful approaches is a critical element.

A more recent reformulation of the approach acknowledges the potential role of cognitive behavioural frameworks in shaping staff behaviour (McDonnell, Waters & Jones, 2002). There are four key components considered that are central to low arousal approaches, which include both cognitive and behavioural elements:

(1)   decreasing staff demands and requests to reduce potential points of conflict around an individual;

(2)   avoidance of potentially arousing triggers, e.g. direct eye contact, touch, and removal of spectators to the incident;

(3)   avoidance of non-verbal behaviours that may lead to conflict, e.g. aggressive postures and stances; and

(4)   challenging staff beliefs about the short-term management of challenging behaviours.

Key Elements of the Low Arousal Approach

Pre-crisis intervention

There are opportunities in which the service user's arousal level increases, making it necessary for staff to intervene to avoid escalation in behaviours. Typically an individual will start to show signs of panic or distress (increased vocalization, threatening behaviours, excessive behaviours). In behavioural terms this involves the altering of antecedent events in an attempt to avoid both verbal and physical aggression. There are six key strategies that could be used at this point, namely diversion strategies, managing aversive stimuli, managing staff demands, managing response chains, managing requests and demand reduction in crises.

Diversion strategies

Obsessive behaviours such as a person repeating a verbal request to staff could be addressed by staff through, for example, changing the topic of conversation to a highly preferred subject. The use of tangible rewards such as a drink to interrupt the behavioural sequence is also possible. Often a simple strategy to manage aggressive behaviour and the other behaviours that reliably precede it is to divert the person's attention towards some other activity. In line with a low arousal approach these activities and the method used to redirect the person should not be arousing or provoke aggressive behaviour themselves. For example, a staff member might ask a service user to move away from a provocative situation and engage in another activity. If a service user is irritated by a noisy peer in their workshop a staff member might ask them to go help another staff member elsewhere in the workshop for a while with the staff praising them for co-operative behaviour. Alternatively, a staff member might ask a service user to engage in some other behaviour. For example, if a service user is aggressive whilst waiting for their bus home a staff member might ask them to help put the magazines away and then spend time reading their favourite magazine with them.

These diversionary strategies have a good scientific basis in applied behaviour analysis. Instructions and reinforcement to engage in some other and perhaps incompatible behaviour have an extensive research base to support that they reduce aggressive behaviour. The mere presence of reinforcing and engaging materials may reduce aggressive behaviour in some service users. For others materials must be present, and staff must additionally provide prompts and reinforcement for engaging in these activities.

Managing aversive stimuli

We have all learned to avoid the place that is too crowded, too noisy, too hot or too cold or smells bad. We may simply avoid entering such settings or escape them once we enter them. As well as our motor behaviour our verbal behaviour is often effective at managing aversive stimuli. We may say to another person, 'I am not going in there', and thereby avoid an aversive stimulus. We may say, 'Get me out of here,' or some equivalent to escape some aversive stimulus. We may do so with a certain degree of sophistication, such as when we say, 'Let's go get a breath of fresh air!' We may also manage aversive stimuli by simply removing them in various ways. We may close the door, put the lid of the toilet down or spray air freshener to mask an unpleasant odour. Some of our interpersonal interactions also serve similar functions. 'Let's not talk about that any more' and 'I'm just not going to talk to Susan if she behaves in that way' are great ways to terminate aversive social stimuli of one kind or another.

Aggressive behaviour may also be reinforced by removal of aversive stimuli in the physical or social environment. Escape from noise, crowds and excessive stimuli may all be important factors in maintaining aggressive behaviour. People with ASDs may be especially sensitive to excessive stimulation and may have idiosyncratic sensitivities to certain kinds of sensory stimuli (for a fuller explanation, see Chapter 5). Further, some care environments may inadvertently be highly aversive. For example, crowded buses, noisy congregate rooms with TVs and radios playing and staff and peers trying to talk above the dim are all too common. Likewise many people may experience aversive social situations, such as staff members who present too many requests, nag or frequently reprimand or roommates who are noisy or irritating.

Managing staff demands

One area of staff demand that can lead to service user aggression is staff presentation of requests to engage in difficult tasks. These tasks may include requests to engage in educational tasks, work tasks, self-help tasks, household chores and social interaction. Research over 30 years has robustly demonstrated these effects with a wide range of population, and they can be observed routinely in many types of population and settings. Applied behaviour analytic research has construed these naturally occurring sequences of interactions as follows: A staff member makes a request. This request is an antecedent stimulus, that is to say a triggering or activating event which occurs before the behaviour. This is then followed by gradual escalation in the intensity and frequency of the behaviour, including aggression. The staff member may repeat the request or intensify it in some way, for example by asking repeatedly, talking more loudly or offering physical guidance. At this point the staff member may personally experience mild or sometimes highly intensive aversive stimuli. For example, one may observe a staff member becoming tense or exhibiting facial expressions, such as tensing the forehead or scowling. As the service user engages in aggressive behaviour the staff then terminates the request, talks more quietly, walks away from the service user or removes the service user from the physical location at which the requests were made. This has two effects. First, the service user's aggressive behaviour is negatively reinforced by the removal of the aversive task demand. Sometimes it may also be positively reinforced if a staff member presents interesting or pleasant tasks. Second, the staff member's removal of the request is negatively reinforced by the removal of the service user's aversive behaviour. Over time this pattern of interaction may result in the mutual shaping of both staff behaviour and the service user's behaviour. For example, a service user may learn that less intense behaviours, such as turning away, whining or threatening, become effective in terminating staff requests. Likewise, staff may learn to present only the most essential requests such as bathing, eating and necessary medical and related activities to the service user. This pattern of learning may sometimes result in very low rates of aggression, as staff learn to present requests infrequently and to engage in other acceptable forms of staff behaviour, such as documenting that opportunities, choices and training was offered but that the service user chose to not participate.

Novaco and Welsh (1989) argued that people who engage in aggressive behaviours often interpret everyday social interactions as threatening, which leads to experience anger and the open expression of aggressive response. A simple request from a member of staff to a person who is hyper-aroused may be sufficient to trigger an episode of severe aggression.

Managing response chains

The term assault cycle (Kaplan & Wheeler, 1983) has been used to describe interactions between individuals in which verbal behaviours between people interact and escalate, which can then lead to a conflict phase followed eventually by conflict resolution. Staff readily see aggressive behaviour and some of the more dramatic behaviour, such as threatening others or destruction of property, that sometimes precede aggression. However, other subtler behaviour may also reliably precede this more dramatic behaviour. For example, a person may tense their forehead, make a fist, pace more rapidly or talk more loudly before engaging in more dramatic behaviour that leads to aggression. Such sequences of behaviour are known as response chains.

A response chain is a predictable sequence behaviour that leads to a behaviour that is followed by a reinforcer. For example, a service user might first approach a housemate, threaten them, push them and finally go to the office for counselling. If the counselling acts as a reinforcer, then several things take place. The most obvious one is that the counselling reinforces pushing their peer. However, other learning also takes place. First, engaging in aggression and the stimuli it produces are paired with counselling. The stimuli that the aggression produced may be both external and observable such as the housemate saying, 'She's going to get me!' and internal to the person, such as muscle tension, heart racing and other internal changes that occur at the same time as the aggressive act. Thus, aggressive behaviour and the stimuli it produces are reliably paired with counselling in the office. In this way they may function as discriminative stimuli for the reliable availability of future reinforcing stimuli and may themselves become secondary reinforcers. This analysis may be applied to all members of the response chain.

This analysis of response chains that end with aggressive behaviour or that have aggressive behaviour as a component has important implications for low arousal approaches to interventions for aggression and for staff training. The first implication is that if the first part of the response chain is reinforced the service user may well not show aggressive behaviour. Thus, if the service user approaches a peer, a staff member might take the person to the office to talk to them. Over time, if this is implemented reliably, it might be possible to modify the procedure to talking to the service user outside the office or eventually in the room in which the aggressive act might typically take place. A second implication is that if the service user has some alternate, acceptable way of talking to a member of staff in the office, then that behaviour should be made as likely as possible. For example, staff might give the person appointment cards that they can hand over to request a counselling session or work with the service user to make a schedule for a counselling session. In this way strengthening a competing acceptable communication behaviour may weaken aggressive behaviour that is maintained by access to a counselling session.

Managing requests

The behaviour of staff can inadvertently reinforce aggressive behaviour. One mechanism for this involves high levels of demands and requests, leading to challenging behaviours. Since staff requests are one variable that may provoke aggression, modifying staff requests, such as eliminating or otherwise changing the frequency or other aspects of requests, may reduce aggressive behaviour. Managing staff requests is one key element of a low arousal model. However, removing all requests has significant limitations. First, completely removing all requests may be impossible. For example, service users must comply with health-related and life-saving procedures, such as taking medication, complying with medical procedures, keeping out of danger and refraining from engaging in dangerous behaviour like eating rubbish. Service users must also engage in activities that result in socially acceptable appearance, such as bathing and dressing, and must refrain from socially unacceptable behaviour, such as approaching strangers. Removing all requests also results in social isolation, unavailability of the opportunity to learn appropriate behaviour and a failure to learn other, new reinforcing activities. This sometimes results in service users' lives being so restrictive that they spend much of their day in the corner of a room or otherwise isolated, not engaging in any meaningful or enjoyable activity. Thus, removal of all staff requests is neither possible nor desirable.

Demand reduction in crises

This is a critical element of the approach. One strategy to managing demand-related aggression is to temporarily reduce or remove all requests from a person. Such an intervention may be appropriate during a crisis when there is considerable danger to the service user and staff or as an initial starting point in an intervention. The author has had considerable success in adopting this approach with individuals who have assaulted staff. The most common strategy is to suggest, 'What you are currently doing is not working. So stop the normal routine, back off, and let the individual and yourself have a cooling off period'. In these circumstances staff often feel that the service user is too much in control. McDonnell and colleagues (1998) described an intervention that employed a low arousal approach with an adult with a borderline learning difficulty, who lived in a locked hospital ward. Although at follow up after 18 months there was a significant reduction in aggressive episodes, one staff member who did accept the positive improvements reported that staff were 'giving in' far too much.

This element of a reduction in staff power and control is a critical element of the approach. In cases in which staff's fear of physical aggression is very apparent it is sometimes understandable why more rules are often imposed on individuals in their care.

Managing the critical incident

There are situations in which staff and carers are confronted by a verbally aggressive individual, which in some situations can lead to physical aggression. In these circumstances the arousal level of the service user may be extremely high, leading to reduction in the ability to process information. Staff avoidance of arousing stimuli in these situations is a critical element of the approach. Managing staff responses is important for both moral and pragmatic reasons. Essential to the approach is the view that violent responses elicit violent responses, thus creating behavioural response chains that increase the likelihood of violence.

Verbal de-escalation

A critical element of verbal de-escalation is a reduction of verbal interaction. There is some evidence that high speech volumes are physiologically arousing

(Argyle, 1986). Raised voices should be avoided, and a gentle tone should be adopted by staff. The avoidance of requests in these circumstances is very important. Individuals experiencing high states of arousal will process information more slowly (Huesmann, 1998). Therefore, reducing decision-making in times of crisis is likely to reduce physiological arousal.

Awareness of non-verbal behaviours as a trigger for aggression

There is a substantial amount of literature which looks at the role of non-verbal behaviours (see Argyle, 1986). Low arousal approaches by definition attempt to avoid non-verbal physiological arousing behaviours.

- Stay calm, or more correctly give the appearance of being calm. Staff members need to control their breathing and avoid sudden movements and increases in the pitch of their voice. Like the commonly used phrase states, 'Do not pour fuel on an open fire', it is advisable that in a conflict situation a staff member should appear calm and not increase arousal, especially when the service user they are managing is hyper-aroused (McDonnell, Dearden & Richens, 1991).
- Direct eye contact has been seen to increase physiological arousal in laboratory studies (Mehrabian, 1972). Avoiding eye contact in situations in which a person may already be in a state of hyper-arousal would appear to be logical. Physical touch also has an arousing element (Argyle, 1986). Avoiding touch would again represent a sensible low arousal strategy. It is the author's experience that carers often seek to comfort individuals by touching them. In normal day-to-day interaction touch may have a positive effect for some individuals. In cases of aggressive behaviours touch may increase arousal and panic responses. For some populations such as people with autism touch may have a negative effect even in everyday situations (O'Neill & Jones, 1997).
- Interpersonal space is also a key element of the approach. Research has also demonstrated that individuals are often wary of people invading their personal space (Hayduk, 1983). Invading a person's space can lead to increased physiological arousal and in some circumstances even assault (Kinzel, 1970). A low arousal approach would suggest that when a person is upset we should avoid invading their space.

Post-incident recovery

The aftermath of a behavioural incident can be potentially traumatizing to both carers and service users. There are a number of strategies which may be helpful in these circumstances. These include 'critical-incident' debriefing for staff, maintaining a positive relationship with the distressed individual, developing longer-term therapeutic interventions, developing organizational responses and designing environments from a low arousal perspective.

Critical-incident debriefing

Staff in care environments can often experience high levels of stress and in some cases 'burnout' (Braverman, 2002). Supporting staff after exposure to incidents of aggression is an important aspect of the approach. Linsley (2006) has described debriefing as follows: 'The debriefing process involves groups of people witnessing an incident recounting their impressions and understanding of the event in a systematic and structured form. It is designed to enable the person to re-experience the incident in a controlled and safe environment in order to make sense of and become reconciled with the traumatic event' (p. 81).[1]

First-line or immediate debriefing can be distinguished from more in-depth psychological or trauma counselling (Tehrani, 2002). Despite the apparent popularity of debriefing, there remains very little effective outcome data in the empirical literature. There are several methodological issues surrounding this literature, which include the lack of randomization of study samples and the problem that debriefing is often a component of a service response and therefore difficult to evaluate as an intervention per se (Rick, Perryman, Young, Guppy & Hillage, 1998). The best evaluated critical-incident debriefing system in care environments for staff experiences of aggression is the Assaulted Staff Action Program (Flannery, 1998), with claims that this approach consistently reduces workplace trauma (Flannery, 2002; Flannery, Penk & Corrigan, 1999).

The low arousal approaches described in this chapter involve taking 'a step backwards' by staff when confronted with high-risk situations. This may mean exposure to verbal and in some cases physical aggression for prolonged periods of time. Immediate debriefing may help staff to cope with the emotional aftermath of such episodes. In addition their thoughts and underlying belief structures may be altered as a consequence of their experiences. Therefore, an understanding of staff perceptions and attributions is a critical element.

Maintaining a positive relationship with the distressed individual

Maintaining relationships with distressed individuals is a complex task. In modern psychiatric nursing the predominant model of care examines the nature of the relationship between the nurse and the patient (Peplau, 1952). The Tidal Model (Barker, 2005) uses the relationship between the nurse and the consumer in a positive manner, focusing on the individual's attempts to make sense of

---

[1] © Linsley, Paul, *Violence and Aggression in the Workplace: A Practical Guide for All Healthcare Staff*. Oxford: Radcliffe Publishing; 2006. Reproduced with the permission of the copyright holder.

the world. In this approach a distressed individual is encouraged to 'tell their own story'. Buchanan-Barker and Barker (2008) further argued, 'Many of the significant descriptions of recovery were developed by people who had been (or still were) psychiatric "patients" and who professed a more optimistic, empowering approach to identifying the help people might need to deal with problems of human living' (p. 94).

These types of person-centred approaches are a component of approaches to working with people with dementia (see Kitwood, 1997, Chapter 8) and people with intellectual disability and/or autism (Pitonyak, 2004). Maintaining a positive relationship with individuals who present with severe episodes of aggression may be problematic for carers. There are implications for service providers in altering staff's negative attributional styles; especially, as in Weiner's attributional model, these negative thinking styles may make staff less inclined to help and work with service users in a positive manner (Dagnan et al., 1998). The concept of malignant alienation (Watts & Morgan, 1994) has been used to describe the difficulties that therapists face when working with individuals whom they do not like. It is difficult to sometimes 'see the person' especially if they have the potential for severe aggression. In their description of nurses working with people who have psychopathy in secure forensic environments in the United Kingdom, Moran and Mason (1996) described a process of alienation: 'Few psychiatric nurses prefer to care for this patient group and tend to dislike this population' (p. 189). A low arousal approach adopts a person-centred approach to crisis management. In care environments when a carer is confronted by aggression or even a victim of a serious assault, this approach would suggest that the person may be expected to show a high degree of tolerance in these circumstances. In the author's experience it is impractical to assume that all staff can work in this way. However, in most situations it is possible to find individuals who do think positively about the person.

Developing longer-term therapeutic interventions

The crisis intervention described above should only be the beginning and definitely not the end of an intervention. Leaving an individual in a low-demand environment for prolonged periods of time can eventually lead to an increase in challenging behaviours, as the person will become bored and inactive. Increasing demands after a cooling-off period is often the next stage. One approach is to fade in requests very gradually. This may be done in three possible ways. First, staff may gradually increase the frequency of requests. Second, they may intersperse difficult requests with easy requests. Third, they may gradually fade in difficult requests by fading in easy, then slightly difficult and finally the most difficult requests.

The low arousal approach described in this chapter stresses the importance of the role of psychological trauma which may lead to panic anxiety in individuals in care environments. There are several evidence-based therapeutic interventions for these problems. Cognitive behavioural therapy has been recommended as the intervention of choice for these disorders in the United Kingdom (NICE, 2007). There is also some evidence for specific trauma interventions such as eye movement desensitization and reprogramming (Foa, Keane & Friedman, 2000).

Developing organizational responses

Managing crisis in a more acceptable manner does not in itself change the behaviour. Creating organizations which support staff to adopt low arousal strategies is an area which has received less emphasis. The interaction between the person, the situation and the organization can produce situations in which aggressive behaviours are maintained rather than reduced.

People who develop challenging reputations can evoke powerful fearful responses in staff (Singh, Lloyd & Kendall, 1990). The author has found during many years of working with staff in these situations that these service users attract large number of 'rules and boundaries'. Rules may be defined as guidance or instructions which restrict an individual's freedom of choice on a day-to-day basis. Boundaries often refer to limit-setting strategies that are placed on people. In lay terms an overuse of rules and boundaries can actually increase the likelihood of conflict rather than reduce it. Often staff and carers may be unaware that they are exacerbating a situation. Good examples of verbal rules can be 'Stop repeating things to me' or 'You can ask that once'. Larger boundaries can involve the three-strike rule. That is to say if a person is aggressive in a situation three times, then a punitive consequence is placed on the individual – 'That's it. You are not going to the cinema today, as your behaviour is unacceptable'.

Community houses can often environmentally appear to be positive places to live at a superficial level. On closer examination these houses may contain a surfeit of rules and boundaries. The restriction of access to kitchens, inflexible routines and locked internal doors can create an inadvertent culture of coercion. Low arousal strategies sometimes involve the reduction of general rules and boundaries in a service rather than just focusing on the behaviour of the individual and the critical incident per se. In these circumstances it is often more effective to reduce unnecessary rules and restrictions. Although such approaches can be challenging for staff and carers, empowering individuals with intellectual disabilities to make choices can lead to reductions in challenging behaviours (Pitonyak, 2004). The role of empowerment would appear to transcend this area.

Designing environments from a low arousal perspective

The design of care environments may assist in the effectiveness of low arousal approaches. Crowded environments can lead to aggressive behaviours (see Calhoun, 1962, in Chapter 1 of this book). Large institutional environments have been historically associated with abusive practices (Martin, 1984).

Intuitively, environmental factors such as heating, light and noise may play a strong mediating role. In the author's experience people who show signs of hyper-arousal are often managed effectively in individualized environments in which the potential for interpersonal violence and aggression can be avoided. In psychiatric services, practices such as seclusion or quiet rooms are often used to remove an individual from communal areas. Logically, smaller environments that could be made secure could potentially reduce the need for such practices.

Conclusions

This chapter has described the low arousal approach, which is a model of managing aggressive behaviours in care settings. The model involves the reduction of demands in crisis situations and a focus on avoiding non-verbal and verbal cues and triggers to aggression. Furthermore, carers are encouraged to reflect on their own contribution to aggressive behaviours.

3

Developing a Core Training Course

This chapter describes the rationale, development, structure and dissemination of a training course to manage aggressive behaviour in people with intellectual disability and its subsequent application to other populations and settings. This work began in the late 1980s when the resettlement of adults with intellectual disability was in full swing in the United Kingdom, and agencies were setting up many new community services. Thus, many new agencies were establishing group homes, day services and crisis support services for people with intellectual disability in community settings. Many of these services involved hiring and training new staff in community settings or retraining staff from institutional settings. Unfortunately, many of these services did not have community-based services to support the people with intellectual disability and aggressive behaviour effectively. This forms the background in which this course was developed. Subsequently, the course has been widely implemented and used for other populations. The last part of this chapter briefly describes those developments.

Rationale for the Training Course

Service need

The policy of deinstitutionalization in the United Kingdom and the United States in the last two decades has led to an increase in the number of people being supported in community-based settings. This has created a challenge

Managing Aggressive Behaviour in Care Settings: Understanding and applying low arousal approaches
By Andrew A. McDonnell © 2010 John Wiley & Sons, Ltd

to service providers to maintain the placements of individuals who present with violence and aggression. Aggressive behaviours have been implicated in the breakdown of family placements (Rousey, Blacher & Hauneman, 1990), placement in more restrictive settings such as institutions (Hill & Bruininks, 1984), breakdown of community placements and subsequent readmission to hospital services (Allen, 1999; Lakin, Hill, Hauber, Bruininks & Heal, 1983). Aggressive and violent behaviours give rise to injury to carers and peers (Hill & Spreat, 1987) and may in some circumstances be associated with high staff turnover and lower job satisfaction (George & Baumeister, 1981; Razza, 1993).

Despite a need for staff to be able to manage these behaviours, comparatively little emphasis has been placed on training to staff to manage high-risk situations and protect both themselves and service users from harm. The development of more effective behaviour management technologies would have positive benefit for both researchers and practitioners (Allen, 2002) and enable more effective support of individuals in community settings (Hanson & Weiseler, 2002; Lakin & Larson, 2002).

Limitations to current practices

A second motivation for developing a new course was the limitations in current practices. These limitations included training that used painful locking of joints and restrictive physical holds, training that took too long for many community staff to attend and the widespread use of training that had not been scientifically evaluated. For example, in the United Kingdom a commonly used course was 'control and restraint' (Gilbert, 1988; Tarbuck, 1992). As part of an information-gathering exercise the author attended four control and restraint training courses between 1987 and 1992. The training varied between two and eight days in length. The vast majority of the training courses involved the practice of physical intervention skills rather than preventative, diffusion and redirection strategies. For example, the eight-day training course contained approximately 40 physical techniques, including the so-called breakaway skills. These are physical disengagement skills mostly developed from a variety of martial arts, which assist staff to break free from low-intensity assaults such as the grabbing of hair or clothing.

Two of the four training courses contained little or no information about diffusion skills, and some failed to present a rationale for the use of diffusion and other preventative skills. Further, the evidence base for teaching these techniques appeared to be primarily anecdotal in nature (McDonnell & Gallon, 2006). Third, the physical breakaway skills included hyperflexion of joints, which inflicted considerable pain on the author and other training course participants. Fourth, approximately five distinctive physical restraint holds were demonstrated to the author. All of these courses employed prone (face-down) holds. In one case a four-person hold was taught to course participants. Fifth, the majority of the physical skills training took place in gymnasiums on matted areas, creating a quasi-military, authoritarian atmosphere rather than a respectful approach to service users who show aggressive behaviour. Finally, the author witnessed a number of course participants receiving minor injuries on training courses which were mostly bruising and complaints of painful joints from a minority of course participants. These injuries did not appear to be perceived as a problem by the course trainers. Indeed, one trainer, when challenged about the injuries, argued that they were only minor in nature.

Some of these concerns were also reflected in an anonymous national survey of U.K. psychiatric nursing training in the management of aggression. Of those staff who attended the training, 29.9% reported receiving an injury while attending training courses in control and restraint. The content of training also appeared to be quite variable. This survey reported that over 21% of staff received no training in defusion skills on a variety of in-service training courses; 67% of training courses routinely taught prone (face-down) restraint holds (Wright et al., 2002). Prone restraint holds have been associated with restraint-related fatalities (McDonnell, 2007; Nunno, Holden & Tollar, 2006). Despite the widespread training of staff in physical interventions, little outcome data have been provided to support the rationale for this type of training (McDonnell & Gallon, 2006).

Personal interest

The author has a long history of training as an instructor in the Japanese martial art of jiu jitsu. Hence he had extensive practical knowledge of physical intervention methods of managing aggressive behaviour. This gave him an insight into the difficulties of both the safety and the application of these methods. He has also had considerable practical experience of working directly with people with intellectual disabilities and challenging behaviours. Additionally, the author had just taken up a job as a clinical psychologist in a large geographical area with responsibility for delivering services to approximately 400 people with intellectual disability and 300 community staff working in group homes, a 130-bed hospital for people with intellectual disabilities and five-day service settings. Working as a practitioner in these services he has been able to directly identify the training needs of the front-line staff. Staff in these services received a wide variety of control and restraint training courses. Despite their apparent popularity with some of the front-line staff many staff did raise concerns to the author that the training appeared to focus too much on physical interventions.

Development of a Three-Day Course

In response to these unmet service needs, the limitations of current practices and personal interest in training staff to manage aggressive behaviour more effectively, the author developed a three-day course through a series of overlapping activities over a period of four years between 1988 and 1992. These activities included identifying intervention strategies that could effectively address aggression using low arousal strategies and developing a model of low arousal approaches to intervene with aggressive behaviour (see Chapter 2). Second, current practices in physical restraint were identified and evaluated through the use of an expert panel. Third, in the light of this information, effective, but non-painful, methods of physical management and restraint that appeared to be safe to staff and service users alike were then identified. Fourth, a three-day course was developed that involved both didactic and role-play methods that one instructor could deliver. Finally, this course was implemented and evaluated over a number of pilot courses and modified to result in the initial standard three-day course. The next section describes this development process.

Current physical management practices and their limitations

Even in the best services, physical management strategies may have to be used from time to time to deal with emergencies in order to protect staff and service users from injury. Staff may have to use restraint for some newly admitted service users, while professionals develop intervention plans.

In order to design a new training course, the author reviewed current courses including many unpublished training manuals. After reviewing their syllabi and training materials some common limitations were found, which included confidential information obtained on a variety of U.S. and U.K. training systems. Because of the secrecy surrounding these training materials, publicly reporting them was not possible. For the purposes of this chapter there were a number of consistent themes which emerged from this review:

- Some courses placed little emphasis on or only paid lip service to the prevention of aggressive behaviour.
- Some courses presented intervention methods without any rationale as to why these intervention methods might be required.
- Some courses had been designed for other populations and thus appeared not to address the needs of staff working with intellectual disability, addressed irrelevant situations or taught irrelevant skills.

- Some courses did not operationally define their intervention methods. This made it difficult to divine exactly what the procedures were. It also made it impossible to train staff in these methods.
- Some courses attempted to teach staff too many holds. One course which was five days long taught at least nine distinctive holds including their variations. It seemed very unlikely that staff would even properly acquire and moreover retain the large number of physical intervention skills that some courses attempted to teach. This could easily result in staff using intervention methods inaccurately.
- The use of pain compliance methods such as the locking of wrists and main joints to the extent that extreme pain could be experienced by service users appeared to be relatively commonplace.
- Teaching methods varied widely on training courses, ranging from demonstrative teaching that involved few practice trials of physical methods to intensive repetition of methods. The use of role-play methods, a practice in which staff were placed in stressful situations, was also variably applied across courses.
- The majority of restraint holds tended to focus on the restriction of movement.
- The implementation of some over long training courses on a large scale in services that served hundreds of people with intellectual disability in community settings seemed unlikely.

Identification of potentially effective, safe, non-painful, acceptable forms of restraints

Staff training in the management of aggressive behaviours often involves the teaching of physical interventions (Allen, 2001; Leadbetter, 2002; McDonnell et al., 2009). Selecting physical skills that are appropriate to people with intellectual disabilities is a complicated area of research, since the criteria for selecting physical skills are not always made explicit. Effectiveness is one important dimension. The restraint method must be effective in preventing aggressive behaviour from occurring and also in preventing injuries that result from aggressive behaviour to the service user, other service users and staff.

A second consideration is the safety of the restraint method. Whereas prevention of aggressive behaviour may avoid injuries, the restraint method itself may result in injuries and in a few cases even death. For example reddening of the skin, bruising and other injuries can occur during the application of both personal and mechanical restraints. Pro re nata medication may render the service user drowsy, and they may fall. Of great concern is the problem of restraint-related death. This has been reported in both institutional and community service settings in the United States (Morrison, Duryea, Moore & Nathanson-Shinn, 2002; Weiss, 1998) as well as the United Kingdom (Paterson et al., 2003). In the United Kingdom the enquiry into the death of a psychiatric patient (Rocky Bennett) who was restrained in a face-down position for over 20 minutes in 2003 and the restraint holds televised by the BBC in the documentary *McIntyre Undercover* in 1999 have heightened the interest in this area. In the United Kingdom this has led to the development of a national accreditation scheme for physical interventions (British Institute of Learning Disabilities [BILD], 2001) that involves the author along with a number of concerned individuals and training organizations.

Improper application of methods is also thought to have an influence on restraint-related deaths (Nunno et al., 2006). The death of a 16-year-old boy named Gareth Myatt in a secure facility for young people in the United Kingdom illustrates this example. Initial reports appeared to indicate that the young man was held in a seated position on a bed using what is described colloquially as a double-embrace hold. Further investigation has revealed that a third member of staff had pushed the young man's head between his knees, compromising his breathing and leading to his death.

Prone (face-down) restraint holds have been associated with sudden deaths during restraint (Morrison et al., 2002). The debate about position is still contested, with some authors arguing that it is a less important factor in restraint-related deaths (Paterson, 2007) and others calling for a ban of these methods in the United Kingdom and the rest of Europe (McDonnell, 2007).

There is now a small empirical literature about the safety of specific restraint methods. This literature reliably finds that emergency restraint is less safe than planned restraint. This supports the importance of training staff to use restraint in order to reduce service user injuries. Safety is only one index; specific methods need to be evaluated in terms of safety, effectiveness and social validity (McDonnell & Jones, 1999).

Finally, restraint methods must also be acceptable to staff, family members and service users (McDonnell, 1998). Some methods of restraint appear to be humiliating and degrading along with being unnecessarily painful; they may cause distress and trauma to both the service user and staff and may perhaps be sexualized in some circumstances. Two studies by McDonnell and colleagues (1993, 2000) and another one which involved the views of service users (Cunningham, McDonnell, Sturmey & Easton, 2002) have found that staff, professionals, members of the public and service users rate prone and supine physical restraints as more unacceptable than restraint in a seated position (these studies are discussed in Chapter 8 in more detail).

Empirical studies of current practices

In order to evaluate current practices in restraint the author set up two panels: a panel of reviewers and a panel of martial arts experts. The reviewer panel read the research literature in this area to identify currently recommended restraints. It then taught these restraint methods to the martial artists. The martial artists then practised these holds and evaluated which ones were dangerous and/or painful. The details of the evaluation process are given next.

The first panel included a school teacher, a children's care manager and a clinical psychologist (the author), all with national coaching qualifications in jiu jitsu. This panel reviewed six training studies which were current at that time (Fein, Gareri & Hansen, 1981; Gertz, 1980; Infantino & Musingo, 1985; Lehmann, Padilla, Clark & Loukes, 1983; Patterson, Turnbull & Aitken, 1992; St Thomas's Psychiatric Hospital, 1976). The panel found that three studies provided sufficient topographical information about the physical interventions taught (Fein et al., 1981; Infantino & Musingo, 1985; St Thomas's Psychiatric Hospital, 1976). The panel then identified a pool of approximately 40 physical interventions including breakaway and physical restraint techniques from the remaining papers.

Eight people who had black belts in the martial art of jiu jitsu with at least 800 hours of experience in physical intervention training volunteered to participate in the martial arts panel. The author selected these people to participate because of their high degree of technical knowledge and skill, which might reduce the potential risk of injury when using restraint. The assessments of physical techniques took place at the University of Birmingham in June 1994.

The members of the reviewer panel taught a sample of 20 techniques to the eight subjects. Groups of volunteers were trained by the author for approximately 20 minutes per method. Each physical technique was then judged by the expert panel as achieving a reasonable level of competency in a non-resisting passive situation. A role-play test was then used. The martial arts experts agreed to struggle and attempt to break away from the person applying the hold. It was also decided that this test should take place in an ordinary room without the use of mats or other safety aids to assess the ecological validity of the methods. In the case of physical restraint procedures the individuals were instructed to actively resist being restrained or held. The physical restraint procedures examined included the prone and supine holds reported in the social validity studies (Lefensky, De Palma & Lociercero, 1978; Harvey & Schepers, 1977) and variations of one-person basket holds; a number of unpublished methods in the United Kingdom were also investigated. The panel members taught these procedures to the volunteers until they collectively agreed that they had reached a safe standard to carry out the method in more realistic circumstances. This process took place over two days. Table 3.1 lists 11 of the categories of major restraint holds and physical disengagement that were judged to be unsafe and not suitable for inclusion in the Studio3 syllabus.

Five categories of restraint hold were examined: two variations of a one-person basket hold (standing and seated); a supine hold that Harvey & Schepers (1977) had recommended for use with people with intellectual disabilities; a prone face-down hold used in psychiatric services for adults in the United States

Table 3.1. Physical methods rejected after panel assessment and role-play demonstration

Method title	Method description	Type of injury caused	Number of test trials	Decision	General comments
Single-person standing basket hold	Staff member stands behind the service user with their bodies touching. The service user's arms are crossed. Staff member holds the service user's wrists, pulling them towards the service user's sides.	None	3	Rejected	Restriction of breathing around abdomen when hold applied with force.
Single-person seated basket hold	Staff member sits with the service user between their legs with the bodies touching. The service user's arms are crossed. The staff member holds the service user's wrists, pulling them towards the service user's sides.	None	3	Rejected	As above. Also, application of method mediated by size of participant.
Gooseneck wrist lock	The staff member places their hand (same side) over the service user's hand. Pressure is applied to the fingers and back of the service user's hands, pushing them towards the elbow. The staff member cradles the service user's arm between their elbow and side.	None	3	Rejected	Startled responses noted when method applied. Pain in joint persisted after application even though no external signs of injury.
Variations of gooseneck wrist locks	The staff member places their hand (same side) over the service user's hand. Pressure is applied to the fingers and the back of the hands, pushing them towards the elbow. The staff member cradles the service user's arm between their elbow and side and manipulates the wrist in either the upward or the downward direction.	None	3	Rejected	Startled responses noted when method applied. Pain in joint persisted after application.

Bar armlock	The staff member holds the service user's wrist so that the palm is facing upward. The staff member places the other hand underneath the service user's elbow and applies upward pressure.	None	3	Rejected	Strong experience of pain, possibilities of serious injuries such as a broken arm if applied with force.
Prone hold (Lefensky et al., 1978)	Two staff members hold the service user in a prone (face-down) position; one staff member sits on the service user's legs, while the other staff member sits astride of the service user's abdomen, holding both the service user's arms with theirs.	Minor	3	Rejected	Take-down to floor caused injuries to knees when applied with force. One individual received a carpet burn to face. Restriction of breathing reported.
Prone hold composite (see Figure 3.1)	The service user is held in a face-down cruciform position. Two staff members immobilize the service user's arms, and another staff member lies across the service user's legs.	Minor	3	Rejected	Take-down to floor caused injuries to knees when applied with force. One individual received a carpet burn to face. Restriction of breathing reported.

(*Continued*)

Table 3.1. (*Continued*)

Method title	Method description	Type of injury caused	Number of test trials	Decision	General comments
Supine hold (Harvey & Schepers, 1977)	Two staff members stand facing the service user. They grab the service user's wrists and place the crook of their arm in the service user's elbow and their palm on the service user's shoulder. Staff members sweep the service user's leg away. One member of staff straddles the service user's body, and the other lies across the service user's legs.	Minor	3	Rejected	Take-down to floor rapidly on one occasion caused a participant to bang their head on floor.
Hair-pulling method (head press)	The service user grabs the staff member's hair so that their hand makes a fist. Staff member places both their hands (palms down) on the service user's hand and presses downwards	None	3	Rejected	Locking of wrist was difficult to avoid. The pain inflicted was deemed excessive
Biting disengagement	The service user has bitten another service user. The staff member approaches from the rear and uses the forefinger of their hand to apply upward pressure under the service user's nose. The other hand applies downward pressure to the jaw.	None	3	Rejected	Pain experienced was reported by participants as excessive
Rear choke hold	The service user has grabbed the staff member around the neck, with their long arm bone applying backward pressure to the staff member's throat. The staff member uses their elbow in a backward motion and strikes the service user's ribcage, stamping on the feet of the service user at the same time.	Minor	3	Rejected	The force of the strike required to weaken the person's grip was deemed to be excessive.

Figure 3.1. Composite prone hold.

(Lefensky et al., 1978), which had many features in common with this class of holds; and a composite prone restraint hold which had many features of these types of holds. Figure 3.1 shows a modified example of the last type of hold.

This last hold involves three members of staff, one of whom restricts leg movement, while the other two hold the arms straightened out. There are many variations of this class of holds, including bending the arms to avoid the obvious armlock or pressing them to the side of the service user's body. This class of methods was rejected for several reasons:

- Pressure on the abdomen appeared to restrict breathing, particularly in people who had excessive weight around their stomach area.
- The positions of the arms effectively locked them in an extremely painful hold.
- Injuries occurred to the knees, the shoulders and, on full application, the face when attempting to get the trial subjects to the floor.
- Holds requiring three or more staff were deemed to be impractical for many services with poor ratios of staff to service users.
- Prone and supine restraint holds were difficult to implement when practised rapidly and realistically by the volunteers. There were also minor bruises to a number of the volunteers and one carpet burn from a face-down hold.

Two methods that required bending a service user's wrist, which had been colloquially termed 'swan' or 'goose' wrist locks, were examined in detail. These were also rejected because of the abnormal rotation of the wrist joint, which inflicted a considerable degree of pain on the volunteers. Several breakaway skills were excluded because they were judged as having the potential to inflict much pain on the person who role-played a service user. The locking of elbow joints was discarded, as were methods which applied focused pressure to nerve endings. The biting assistance method which was rejected by the panel involved applying upward pressure underneath the person's nose. The deliberate use of pain was also a factor in several disengagement methods. Three two-handed strangulation methods were removed from the syllabus because of the rarity of their occurrence.

The method of Harvey and Schepers (1977) is supposed to be used when a staff member is grabbed around the neck from the rear. Harvey and Schepers described the method as follows: 'the staff member bends his or her arm slightly and with moderate force jabs his or her elbow into the solar plexus area of the resident' (p. 31). The volunteers found that when their airway was restricted there was a possibility to elbow their assailant very hard in the solar plexus such that the attacker actually collapsed to the ground. This technique was deemed highly effective but dubious, unsafe and unacceptable as a method to work with people with intellectual disability.

Some methods to deal with service users pulling the hair of staff also presented significant difficulties when practised rapidly. A number of procedures which recommended the placing of hands on top of individuals' hands to reduce movement were excluded when two martial arts volunteers accidentally inflicted severe pain on the other person's wrists when executing the procedure with speed. There were two interventions involving breakaway skills during which our experts injured another volunteer, resulting in a bleeding nose and swollen and sprained finger and thumb.

Table 3.2 shows the difference between the Studio3 physical interventions syllabus before (around 1990) and after (around 2000) this exercise. In 1990 there were 19 physical techniques that were taught over a three-day period. This was reduced to 11 methods after the expert panel evaluation, which were identified to be relatively safe and pain free. These 11 techniques were five wrist grabs, two methods to counter hair pulling from the front and the rear, a method for airway protection, one- and two-arm methods to counter biting and a method to give a member of staff assistance from biting. To illustrate these methods the five hand-grabbing holds and the teaching principles underlying them are described in detail.

In Figure 3.2 a simple wrist release procedure is shown. In all of these methods the function of this behaviour is most commonly that a person is requesting something in a nonverbal manner. Therefore, it is assumed that a staff member would try to acquiesce and address the request before attempting to break free from the hold. In the figure the staff member has been gripped by the service user with the service user's thumb on top of their hand. All wrist grabs have a weak point (the area where the service user's finger and thumb overlap). To

Table 3.2. Changes in physical intervention syllabus, 1990–2000

Methods taught around 1990	Methods taught around 2000
Six wrist releases	Five wrist releases
Hair pulling (front)	Hair pulling (front)
Hair pulling (rear)	Hair pulling (rear)
Hair pulling (staff seated)	Removed from the core training module
Airway protection (one- and two-arm)	Airway protection (one- and two-arm)
Strangulation (front)	Removed from the core training module
Strangulation (rear)	Removed from the core training module
Strangulation (staff member pushed against wall)	Removed from the core training module
Separating fights between service users	Removed from the core training module
Biting	Biting
Giving assistance to a member of staff who is being bitten	Giving assistance to a member of staff who is being bitten
Over- and under-arms rear grabs to the abdomen	Removed from the core training module
A 'walk-around' chair restraint method	First part of the procedure described as the 'walk-around' method kept in core module, chair restraint removed
TOTAL = 19	TOTAL = 11

break free the staff member rotates their wrist using their body weight (not just arm strength) and pulls their wrist free.

Figure 3.3 shows a staff member being grabbed by a service user with the user's thumb on the underside of the staff member's arm. The principle used is the same as above with the exception that the staff member applies the force in a downward motion to break free.

Figures 3.4–3.6 show a hold that is relatively common (in the author's experience). In intellectual disability settings it is often used by a service user in distress to pull a member of staff to a preferred area or object. In essence the person normally 'wants something'. In these circumstances a staff member should try and move with the service user and where possible meet the person's need. With children and adults this type of grab can be followed by the service user placing their knee in the staff member's groin area. Therefore, safely and effectively breaking this grip is a priority. In this example the staff member is grabbed very firmly by the service user with both of their hands (see Figure 3.4). To break the grip the staff member places their hands together in a prayer like pose (see Figure 3.5). The staff member then pulls their hands towards themselves and using their body weight they step away from the service user (see Figure 3.6). This technique illustrates that body weight

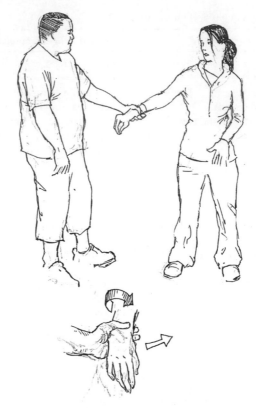

Figure 3.2. Wrist release 1.

and not physical strength is a key aspect of the Studio3 approach to physical interventions.

The chair restraint method involves two components: the first is a method employing movement to distract individuals (known as the walk-around method); the second is to use the first method to seat an individual in a chair. The chair restraint method adopted by the author involves the use of an armchair (McDonnell, Dearden & Richens, 1991c). It was also the subject of social validity research (Cunningham et al., 2002; McDonnell & Sturmey, 2000; McDonnell et al., 1993). This two-person method adopted an approach different from many restraint techniques. Emphasis was placed on allowing the service user a certain degree of movement. It was speculated that allowing movement would cause less distress to the service user and allow more physical energy to be dissipated.

First, staff were taught to introduce circular movement to the upper arms and walk the individual around a room to help distract them (see Figure 3.7).

Figure 3.3. Wrist release 2.

Figure 3.4. Two-hand release, Part A.

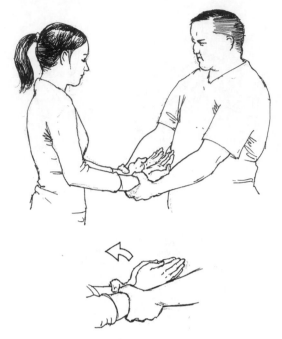

Figure 3.5. Two-hand release, Part B.

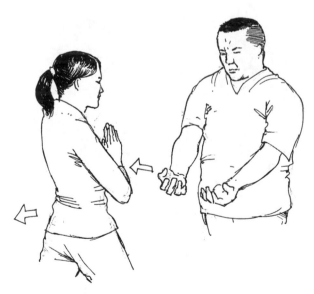

Figure 3.6. Two-hand release, Part C.

Figure 3.7. The walk-around method, Part A.

Second, emphasis was placed on keeping the individual on their feet if possible. Third, if a service user attempted to sit on the floor the staff would adopt a wide posture and lower the person to the ground (see Figure 3.8). At this point the staff would disengage from the service user (see Figure 3.9). If the service user attempted to get up and become aggressive towards the staff or other service users the walk-around method would be repeated.

If the aggression persisted staff were encouraged to move from the walking method to a chair restraint method (see Figure 3.10). This method involved the use of the body weight of staff to restrict the service user's movement.

Other considerations

In addition to issues related to content, there were a number of important decisions concerning the design of the course. One issue was the duration of training. Courses must be sufficiently long to present the information necessary and practise skills but must not be so long that organizations cannot release staff from work. The original course (McDonnell, 1988) was only two days long.

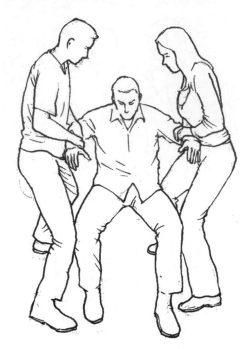

Figure 3.8. The walk-around method, Part B.

Figure 3.9. The walk-around method, Part C.

Figure 3.10. The walk-around method, Part D (using the chair).

This resulted in 75% of the time being devoted to physical interventions. This was judged to be unsatisfactory because it resulted in insufficient emphasis on preventative strategies in addition to the course being 'too pressured'. Thus, the course duration was extended to three days, which resulted in a full day each for both physical restraint and the application of breakaway skills and an entire day devoted to the non-physical components. Table 3.2 describes the formats of the two- and three-day courses.

As well as teaching preventative and physical strategies to manage aggression, other considerations were made as to the content of the class. Information about legal aspects of intervention, such as assault and the duty of care, were identified as important for staff to have some knowledge of. Additionally, some basic information on the causes of challenging behaviour, behaviour management and debriefing after episodes of aggression were identified from discussions with service providers.

Teaching methods included both group-based discussion and lecture format for informational components such as legal aspects of interventions for aggression. The instructors taught physical intervention skills using instructions, modelling, rehearsal and feedback during the role-play of physical skills. The course used repetition of physical movements using chaining methods and rehearsal, developed primarily from the author's experiences of teaching physical skills in martial arts. The use of role-play to practise physical interventions was adopted from a number of studies reported in the literature at the time (Fein et al., 1981; Patterson et al., 1992; Van Den Pol, Reed & Fuqua, 1983). The instructors also included practising skills under a high state of emotional arousal in order to aid the generalization of staff skills. Typically, a trainer would get individual course participants to experience a controlled attack that would require calling for assistance from another staff member. Very little preparation – merely that the service user was only be allowed to be controlled through use of the two-person restraint method – would be provided to staff about the nature of the situation. The trainer would raise their voice to add to the realism and increase arousal. In addition the role-play took place in front of their colleagues to further increase the arousal levels of the participants. Sometimes a video of the procedure would be reviewed for feedback purposes and to increase arousal even further. Great care was taken by the trainers to avoid stigmatizing people with intellectual disabilities. Staff were also encouraged to talk to each other about the experience after the exercise was completed.

Another consideration in designing a course to teach staff to manage aggressive behaviour in people with intellectual disability is the nature of aggressive behaviour that such people display. Many existing courses addressed situations and behaviour that did not match the author's experience of aggressive behaviour in people with intellectual disability. For example, some existing courses addressed the use of weapons and aggression that appeared to be very carefully planned. Based on anecdotal evidence and personal experience, McDonnell and colleagues (1991a) speculated that people with intellectual disability showed aggressive behaviour that was less sophisticated than that shown in other populations. Subsequently, McDonnell, Hardman, Knight, Manning and Semple (2004) reported some data which supported this idea and also reported the kinds of aggressive behaviours shown by referrals to a challenging-behaviour community service for people with intellectual disability. These data indicated that most forms of aggressive behaviour included grabbing, pushing, pulling and hitting (self-injury was also a common reason for referral). In contrast aggressive behaviours involving the use of weapons, head butting, choking and throttling occurred infrequently in the sample. The results of this anecdotal study suggested that the course should focus on the more common forms of aggressive behaviour, which seemed more reactive and largely did not involve the use of weapons in a directed and skilled manner.

The First Courses

The first pilot training course in the management of aggressive behaviour took place in Birmingham, United Kingdom, in 1987. It was a two-day workshop developed for a hospital service for people with intellectual disability. The evaluation of this course formed part of a master's thesis in clinical psychology (McDonnell, 1988). The author then expanded this training course as described earlier and delivered the core three-day training course between 1988 and

1994 to approximately 3000 care staff in services for adults and children with intellectual disabilities and services for people with ASD. This totalled 150 training courses delivered throughout the United Kingdom and Ireland.

Based on these experiences and ongoing reviews of the literature, the author published a series of three brief papers for a practitioner journal in intellectual disability (McDonnell, Dearden & Richens, 1991a, 1991b; McDonnell et al., 1991c). These three papers provided information about the development of a specific staff-training package. The first placed training within the context of organizational factors; the second provided principles for developing physical breakaway skills and a rationale for their use; and the third described a chair restraint method. Let us review these three papers in more detail.

McDonnell and colleagues (1991a) stressed the importance of organizational factors, such as policies and procedures, as the context for organizational change. Their paper emphasized developing training systems as opposed to training courses. Training courses that include physical interventions can be delivered in a non-systematic manner. Thus, they are limited because few staff may receive direct training, and there is the possibility that the effects of the training will diminish over time. In contrast, training systems include an emphasis on systematic delivery of training to targeted areas of a service. Maintenance of skills by means of follow-up training is a major component of training systems. Policies and procedures are also designed to support the delivery of the training. Hence training systems have advantages over training courses in that the delivery is systematic and they are delivered within an organizational framework. This paper was one of the first papers to address these organizational issues which were mirrored in later work (e.g. Harris, 2002).

This paper also argued that physical interventions should be specified in individual plans and that unacceptable practices should be clearly stated within these plans. Trained responses to crises should be explicit and transparent in care environments, which reduces the likelihood of abuse by carers. Restricting the number and the type of behavioural responses that are deemed to be appropriate increases the likelihood of an appropriate response being delivered by staff.

McDonnell and colleagues (1991b) described three principles involved in the training courses. They were as follows:

- First, practitioners should avoid violent situations. The best way to avoid assault is to not be in the specific place. It is the author's experience that conflict can often occur in situations that tend to be repeated. Avoiding these predictable violent situations is a more practical option than managing them.
- Second, where physical restraint is required it should not use procedures that involve painful locking of joints. The use of pain as means of coercion can damage the relationship between the carer and the service user. There

is also the possibility that a service user may consider retaliating in a similar manner.

- Third, staff should learn to use their body weight more effectively. These methods biomechanically require less physical strength but more technical skill. Physical techniques that use body weight can be applied by both male and female staff.

This paper also described a non-confrontational approach using five principles. The five principles are as follows:

1. Stay calm. Or more correctly, give the appearance of being calm. Staff members need to control their breathing and avoid sudden movements and increases in the pitch of their voice. As mentioned in Chapter 2, the commonly used phrase 'Do not pour fuel on an open fire' should be kept in mind by staff. When facing a conflict situation the staff member should appear calm and do nothing further to arouse the service user, especially if the latter is hyper-aroused.
2. Avoid physical contact. Human touch can have both calming and excitatory effects. When a service user is hyper-aroused it is possible that physical contact may increase their arousal further. Touch should be intermittent.
3. Be aware of your own bodily reactions. It is the experience of the author that staff members in these situations are not aware that their own body language is communicating fear and distress. For example, individuals may perspire or stare at the service user (which is also physiologically arousing). Aggressive postures such as folding arms should be avoided.
4. Keep your distance. Everyday social interactions tend to take place at a social distance of 3–6 feet. Research has demonstrated that close proximity to individuals who are angry or aroused may increase the likelihood of interpersonal violence.
5. Respond in a non-violent manner. This is as much a moral as a pragmatic approach. Essential to the approach is the view that violent acts elicit violent responses, thus creating behavioural response chains that increase the likelihood of violence.

This collection of strategies eventually evolved into a low arousal model (McDonnell, Waters & Jones, 2002), which is described in Chapter 2.

The third paper focused on physical restraint procedures and introduced in a limited way the notion of social validity (Wolf, 1978). For example, the author recommended that when evaluating a physical restraint procedure a person should ask themselves the question 'How would I feel being restrained in such a manner?' This paper also introduced a chair restraint method as an alternative to prone and supine holds. The paper furthermore described a physical movement in detail to illustrate how a member of staff can release themselves from a service user who has grabbed their wrists. It suggested that simple, slow movements are as effective as rapid movements.

The Core Training Course

Based on the evidence presented in this chapter a three-day training course was developed, which contained the following elements.

Day One

Introduction

The outline of the three days is presented to participants during 15 minutes. The non-confrontational philosophy and value base of the training course is briefly introduced.

Legal issues

The law and the use of physical interventions and other restrictive approaches are described. This section contains elements of the distinction between assault and battery, reasonable force, case law examples of the application of reasonable force, a decision-making process for assessing risk and the need for reactive strategies from a legal perspective. This section lasts 15 minutes.

Qualitative differences in violence

This is a group exercise using an attributional format (Weiner, 1986), the duration of which is 45 minutes. Participants are given three scenarios. Each scenario contains a situation in which physical violence occurs. The first scenario involves an older adult being assaulted outside of a post office. The second scenario involves a bar room brawl. The third involves the assault of a member of staff by a young man with autism in a residential care home. Participants are asked to rate how people think, feel and behave in these situations. Participants are then asked to describe the physical nature of the violence that each person might encounter in the three scenarios and how the persons in the scenarios might be thinking and feeling and to compare the similarities and differences in physical violence. Finally, course participants are encouraged to talk about how they would think, feel and behave if they were exposed to similar situations.

The causes of violence and aggression

This part lasts for an hour. Course participants are asked to think of the possible causes of challenging behaviour. These are then discussed in small groups ($n = 4$). The facilitator then presents a lecture which provides an explanatory framework for the causes of violence and aggression. These include environmental and biological factors and the role of communication difficulties. An emphasis is placed on the role of direct care staff in the maintenance of violence and aggression (Hastings & Remington, 1994). Staff are encouraged to think of incidents of aggression which may have been inadvertently caused by themselves.

Staff support and debriefing after incidents of aggression (duration = 1 hour)

The rationale for this element, which also lasts an hour, of the training course is to encourage course participants to discuss their cognitive and emotional responses to violent situations they may have encountered in the workplace. The facilitators are encouraged to disclose their own experiences of violence and aggression. Participants are encouraged to split into pairs and discuss their own experiences of physical aggression within a cognitive-behavioural framework (involving thoughts, feelings and behaviour). The facilitator presents information about how to debrief their colleagues and support each other in crises.

Low arousal approaches

The low arousal model is presented in a one-hour session (McDonnell et al., 1998, 2002). Staff are encouraged to think of situations in which they placed too many demands on individuals who presented with violence and aggression. Cognitive elements of the model are stressed. In particular staff are encouraged not to label diversionary strategies as 'giving in'. Group exercises are used to encourage staff on the training course to examine behaviours that are physiologically arousing (see McDonnell & Sturmey, 1993). Finally a case study illustrating the approach is presented to participants (McDonnell et al., 1998).

The distinction between managing and changing behaviours

This 30-minute long session involves presenting to participants the distinction between short-term crisis management and long-term behavioural change strategies (Gardner & Moffatt, 1990). Emphasis is placed on the use of tangible rewards and activities to distract individuals. Course participants are encouraged to think about using reinforcing behaviours in the short term to avoid physical aggression (see Donnellan et al., 1988).

Day Two

Health and safety

In this 45-minute session participants are introduced to health and safety rules for the training course. The facilitator ascertains if there is any participant who has to be excluded on medical grounds. Group trust exercises are used, and the participants are taken through a series of limb stretching movements which are based on movements from the martial art of tai chi. No hard aerobic exercises (such as press ups and squat thrusts) are employed.

Physical disengagement skills – phase 1

Four breakaway skills are taught to participants in an hour-long session. These are as follows:

Physical skill number 1. A staff member being grabbed by the wrist with the fingers and the thumb pointed upwards and the right wrist being grabbed by the other person's left hand.

Physical skill number 2. A person being grabbed by the wrist with the fingers and the thumb pointed downwards and the right wrist being grabbed by the other person's left hand.

Physical skill number 3. A person being grabbed by both the wrists from the front with their arms in parallel.

Physical skill number 4. A person grabs one wrist with both hands overlapping.

This first phase of physical interventions training involves demonstrating the physical method in entirety. The facilitator breaks all movements down into a minimum of two movements per physical technique. Participants are then encouraged to practise movements slowly for minimum of 10 trials with a partner per technique. Immediate corrective feedback is provided by the facilitators (see Van Vonderen, 2004, for a rationale).

Physical disengagement skills – phase 2

Participants are taught two techniques to counter hair pulling from the front and the rear, in a session that lasts an hour and 15 minutes. In addition, the following skills are taught:

Physical skill number 5 involves a person having their hair pulled from the front by the service user using both hands.

Physical skill number 6. This involves how to deal with a service user pulling a person's hair from behind with both hands.

Physical skill number 7 involves a technique for dealing with being bitten.

Physical skill number 8 involves dealing with being scratched on the hands and arms.

Physical skill number 9 involves breaking away from a service user who has grabbed staff's clothing.

Physical skill number 10. This involves teaching staff to protect their airway in circumstances under which a service user places their arm around the staff member's neck with their forearm pressing on the staff member's trachea.

Physical skill number 11. Finally, this skill requires staff to practise giving assistance to another member of staff who has been bitten or scratched.

These physical techniques are taught using the same format as the previous section.

Physical disengagement skills – phase 3

This session lasts an hour. All of the physical skills are practised in sequence with a minimum of 10 trials per technique. In this phase participants are encouraged by the facilitators to practise their physical skills with more force and energy. The facilitators conduct numerous short feedback sessions with the group; these aim to improve the course participants' technical ability and in addition help to prevent course participants from being over-aroused and injuring their colleagues. Course participants are requested to practise techniques selected at random with different members of their group. Finally each facilitator practises a physical skill selected at random with each course participant.

Role-play evaluation

Role-play is used in a number of training studies (Gertz, 1980; Infantino & Musingo, 1985; Patterson et al., 1992). It was decided to include role-play assessments in this training course in a session 30 minutes long. In a cognitive-behavioural framework, realistic role-play should allow participants to experience cognitive and emotional as well as behavioural responses to aggression. A minimum of six course members are selected to practise their physical disengagement skills and use of low arousal strategies with a course facilitator who role-plays a distressed service user. Each role-play lasts a maximum of three minutes. The facilitator attacks the staff member using one of the assaults mentioned in the previous modules. The course participant is given no advance warning about which type of attack is going to occur. The facilitators attempt to make the situation both realistic and stressful. This is achieved by conducting the role-plays in front of the entire group, with the facilitator making loud noises and threatening postures. Using a cognitive-behavioural framework facilitators encourage participants to discuss what they were thinking and feeling and how they were behaving during the role-plays. Positive feedback is provided to participants about their performance.

The social validity of physical restraint procedures

Three methods of physical restraint are presented to the group by means of video and physical demonstration on participants in a 45-minute-long session. The concept of social validity is explained to participants. The physical restraint methods are described in detail elsewhere (McDonnell et al., 1993; McDonnell & Sturmey, 2000; Cunningham et al., 2002). Participants are encouraged to experience the physical restraint methods themselves. The group is then encouraged to talk about their own experiences of implementing physical restraint procedures in the workplace. The chair method (McDonnell et al., 1991c) is presented as the technique of choice.

Day Three

Health and safety (duration = 30 minutes)

In a session of 30 minutes, a series of games and physical exercises are used to encourage group cohesion and establish if participants are ready to carry out physical movements.

Physical disengagement skills – phase 4

The facilitators encourage course members to demonstrate the physical skills taught to them the previous day in front of the entire group in a 45-minute session. The 11 physical skills are practised by all participants for a minimum of 10 trials per technique. The facilitators encourage participants to practise physical movements that they have difficulty in recalling.

Introduction to chair restraint – phase 1

The chair restraint method (McDonnell et al., 1991) is task analyzed into four distinct areas for an hour and 45 minutes. The first area involves practise of the initial assault, where a staff member is attacked. The second area teaches a two-person escort procedure. The third area practises the restraint of a service user in an armchair. Finally, disengaging from the service user is the fourth area. All course members are encouraged to talk about how the method makes them feel and think, in the role of both a staff member and a service user. Course participants are encouraged to practise all four stages in a slow demonstrative manner. Emphasis is placed on technical precision and learning the technique.

Chair restraint – phase 2

The chair restraint method is practised more rapidly with the course facilitators taking the role of service users for a session of one hour. In this session emphasis is placed on increasing the rapidity of the movements.

Role-play practise of chair restraint

In a session that lasts an hour, each training course participant completes a role-play test, which requires the full use of the chair restraint method. The course participant is given no advanced warning about which type of attack is going to occur. The facilitators attempt to make the situation both realistic and stressful. This is achieved by conducting the role-plays in front of the entire group and the facilitator making loud noises and assuming threatening postures. Participants are encouraged to describe their thoughts and feelings while carrying out their role-play. Positive feedback is given to course participants, and they are encouraged by the facilitators to believe that they can manage serious incidents involving aggressive behaviour. The second facilitator rates the person's ability to carry out the procedure using a role-play assessment. This rates the task analysed behavioural components of the chair restraint method.

Subsequent Applications and Developments

This course has been widely disseminated in European services for people with intellectual disability. Additionally, this course has been applied, sometimes with modifications, to children and adults with ASDs, children and adolescents, adults with mental health needs, people with acquired brain damage and older adults. Trainers have introduced the course to a variety of settings, including group homes for adults with intellectual disability, day services for adults with intellectual disability, institutional settings for adults with intellectual disability, schools for children and adolescents, residential and day service settings for people with ASDs and nursing homes. The course has been used both as part of an intervention for individual service users and as part of interventions for entire services. Thus, this course, which was originally designed, piloted and evaluated for adults with intellectual disability in residential settings, has been applied and adapted to numerous populations and settings.

This process of dissemination has resulted in two main kinds of developments. The first includes adoptions of the teaching content and methods, and the second is the training of in-service course instructors who can deliver the training courses and provide follow-up services after the initial training.

Course adaptations

Autism spectrum disorders

Autism is a pervasive developmental disorder characterized by deficits in social communication, social interaction and imagination. Adults and children with autism can present with severe violence and aggression (McClintock, Hall & Oliver, 2003). People with Asperger's syndrome can present with severe violence and aggression (Attwood, 2007).

To be applicable to this population, the core training course required few changes in the content of physical interventions. The low arousal approach was adapted to meet the needs of the population. Physiological arousal was originally proposed as an explanatory theory for ASDs (Hutt, Hutt, Lee & Ounsted, 1964). Two implications of this theory are that children and adults with ASD would be more reactive to sensory stimuli than the normal population and that they may be slower to habituate to stimuli. There is some laboratory evidence of differences in physiological responses of individuals with ASD compared with non-autistic controls (Althaus et al., 2000; Hirstein, Iversen & Ramachandran, 2001; Van Engeland, Roelofs, Verbaten & Slangen, 1991). Therefore, trainers were encouraged to emphasize sensory triggers and cue behaviours and their importance in the maintenance of challenging behaviours (see McDonnell, Mills & Jones, 2008). Intermittent holding using the walk-around method was also encouraged because of the aversion to physical contact that some individuals with ASD might have.

Children and adolescents

The core training course remained similar for this population. There was the addition of physical interventions which catered for adolescents punching staff in the face. The management of deliberate self-harm was also added to the core training course. Chair restraint is taught on an individual-needs-only basis to this population.

Adults with mental health needs

Psychiatric staff were taught some additional physical interventions – most notably three methods involving strangulation and the full chair restraint method. Emphasis was also placed by trainers on the confusion created by psychiatric illness. In addition to the core training, emergency tranquillization methods were taught, which involved restraining an individual on a bed to receive an intra-muscular injection.

Training course to manage aggression in older adults

The training course to deal with older adult was reduced to two days in length. Emphasis was placed on the person-centred method developed by the late Tom Kitwood (1997). The walk-around method was taught, as was the emphasis on wrist grabs and hair pulling. These physical behaviours were reported as the most commonly encountered by the front-line staff.

Training instructors

Throughout the 1990s the demand for the core three-day training course increased rapidly. This led to a need to train, increasing the demand for the individuals who can deliver this training. Training other trainers in the system is a necessary aspect. 'Training trainers' programmes have been relatively overlooked in discussions about training standards (Paterson & Leadbetter, 2002). There can be a conflict between training high-quality trainers in sufficient volume without sacrificing the quality of training delivery. A comparison of lead training providers in the United Kingdom led to a consistent pattern of the training rarely being assessed 'in situ'. Training trainer programmes ranged from four days to three weeks in duration. The failing of trainers also appeared to be a rarity in many of the larger training systems.

There was a clear need for a robust behaviourally based assessment system which assessed the people delivering training with clear pass and fail elements which trained high-quality trainers. The skill set of trainers had to reflect three core competencies. The ability to deliver both theoretical and physical components with an ability to conduct role-plays required a competency-based assessment model.

An interview and selection process was developed which focused on screening individuals for competencies in at least two of the areas. Potential trainers were encouraged to attend training workshops and observe trainers' skills in delivery with reference to a training manual. They were encouraged to conduct a pre-rehearsed role-play as a basic test of competency. An analysis of the candidates' strengths and weaknesses was then discussed with them, and a training plan was developed. The training course was task analyzed into six components. Each candidate was expected to deliver the training to the satisfaction of an assessor (in the early days this was primarily the responsibility of the author).

A pass–fail assessment was only suggested to the candidate after satisfactory delivery of the core components of a three-day training course; little advance warning was provided about these assessments wherever possible. The testing situation was made stressful, and assessors often took an active role in the training course by sometimes adopting an adversarial approach (especially asking difficult questions).

A training system

It was recognized early in the development of the training courses that staff training was necessary but not sufficient on its own to effect behaviour change (Cullen, 1992). An emphasis was placed on the development of policies and procedures in organizations that received the training (see McDonnell et al., 1991a) and specialist consultancy for individuals who presented with severe challenging behaviours.

Services were also audited in terms of their physical interventions usage and adoption of low arousal approaches. Studio3 staff often helped service leaders to amend their policies and in some case chaired policy days when mediation was required. Specialist clinical consultancy and advice was also provided to services in which individuals were deemed to be challenging the accepted syllabus of the Studio3 systems. The need for consultancy was particularly high in services which had previous exposure to training that used the more rational prone restraint holds. In many cases Studio3 staff worked directly with the front-line support staff to ascertain risks and the effectiveness of strategies employed by them. In the vast majority of cases few modifications to physical intervention training were required. The training of trainers in organizations also helped the dissemination of knowledge to aid the development of specific crisis support plans. Regular seminars on issues surrounding restraint and on human rights issues have also been provided to services involved with the training to increase awareness of these issues.

Summary

This chapter has described the development of a core training course in the management of violence and aggression. The aim was to produce staff training in crisis management that concentrated on both physical and non-physical components. An emphasis was placed on developing effective, safe and socially valid methods to manage challenging behaviours. This training course was originally developed for intellectual disability services; however, modification to the course has led to its use in autism, mental health services for adults and services for children, adolescents and older adults. Chapters 4–8 of the book will examine the application of this approach to these care settings.

4

Managing Aggressive Behaviour in Services for People with an Intellectual Disability

Jane is a 23-year-old woman with mild intellectual disabilities. She lives in a semi-independent flat with one other person on the outskirts of a small town. Jane has had a history of challenging behaviours with episodes of aggressive behaviours. Jane receives additional support from two part-time behavioural workers. They have on several occasions had to restrain her in her house to prevent harm to the other service user. Jane is very clear that she wants this practice to stop and her support workers to leave her house. Because of this her specialist support multidisciplinary team is facing a dilemma, as removing her support may place people at risk of harm, although she has never assaulted a member of the public.

Challenging behaviours have remained a major topic of concern for many years in services for people with learning disabilities. Physical aggression can generate fear among care staff who are often expected to manage such behaviours in their day-to-day work (Singh, Lloyd & Kendall, 1990), and furthermore, it can generate strong emotional reactions in staff (Bromley & Emerson, 1995). A meta-analytic review of 86 studies on challenging behaviours has identified risk markers of challenging behaviours (McClintock, Hall & Oliver, 2003). Risk markers have been identified for a number of presenting problems. In the case of aggression these include a higher prevalence of males with a diagnosis of autism and deficits in expressive communication.

Aggressive behaviours have been implicated in the breakdown of family placements (Rousey, Blacher & Hauneman, 1990), placement in more restrictive settings such as institutions (Borthwick-Duff, Black, Cohn, Small & Crites, 1985; Hill & Bruininks, 1984) and breakdown of community placements and subsequent readmission to hospital services (Allen, 1999; Lakin, Hill, Hauber,

Managing Aggressive Behaviour in Care Settings: Understanding and applying low arousal approaches
By Andrew A. McDonnell © 2010 John Wiley & Sons, Ltd

Bruininks & Heal, 1983). Aggressive and violent behaviours result in injury to carers and peers (Hill & Spreat, 1987) and may in some circumstances be associated with high staff turnover and lower job satisfaction (George & Baumeister, 1981; Razza, 1993). These behaviours may furthermore result in injury to clients when attempts are made to restrain them and thus may provoke physical abuse from carers (Rusch, Hall & Griffin, 1986). This may reflect a subjective interpretation of the importance of aggressive behaviours to staff that work 'on the front line'. The need for advice and training on how to manage these behaviours and for carers to defend themselves non-violently, while also ensuring client safety, has been acknowledged (Allen, MacDonald, Dunn & Doyle, 1997; Rusch et al., 1986).

Two studies have reported data on complete populations through the use of state registers. Jacobson (1982a, 1982b) reported data from the New York state register, which contained records on over 30,000 individuals living with their families and in community residences and hospitals. The register included data on both children and adults. The overall prevalence of relevant behaviours included 10.9% for physical assault, 4.3% for property destruction, 1.4% for coercive sexual behaviour, 8.1% for actively resisting supervision and 5.9% for being verbally abusive to others (Jacobson, 1982a).

Higher prevalence of relevant behaviours can be found in dually diagnosed clients (Jacobson, 1982a, 1982b) and recently admitted or re-admitted clients. Jacobson (1982a) reported complex relationships between degrees of learning disabilities and the topography reported above. Thus, the prevalence of the category 'physically assaults others' rises monotonically from 5.5% to 17.3% for adults with mild to profound learning difficulties. Property destruction in adults showed a similar trend, ranging from 1.8% to 6.89%. However, 'verbally abusive to others' showed a trend in the opposite direction, ranging from 9.5% to 2.7%. Higher-prevalence figures are often reported for externalizing behaviour disorders in males compared with females, including people with learning disabilities (e.g. Harris & Russell, 1989; Sigafoos et al., 1994). These findings have not always been replicated in other studies (Tutton, Wynne-Wilson & Piachaud, 1990). This failure in replication may be the result of variations in patterns of differential admission and discharge.

High prevalence of aggression and violence can be found in institutional residents who have been admitted repeatedly (Hill & Bruininks, 1984; Lakin, Hill, Hamber, Bruininks & Heal, 1983). In a study of incidents in a psychiatric ward it was observed that fewer than 20% of incidents appeared to have been reported (Lion, Snyder & Merrill, 1981). However, one could speculate that physical aggression is more likely to be reported than verbal aggression, as it is extreme and memorable; although no published data currently exist to verify such a hypothesis. The literature also identifies that aggressive behaviours tend to be associated with other forms of challenging behaviours (Harris &

Russell, 1989; Sigafoos et al., 1994). Aggressive behaviours are also thought to be relatively stable over time (Kiernan & Alborz, 1996; Lowe & Felce, 1995). A number of studies have investigated violent incidents using global categories such as physical violence (Tutton et al., 1990), physical assault and aggression towards others, defined as 'striking another person' (Spengler, Gilman & Laborde, 1990). There are very wide individual differences in the topography of challenging behaviours.

The Need for Crisis Supports

Over the last decade there has been a substantial move away from interventions based on consequential punishment to those based on reinforcement contingencies (Donnellan, LaVigna, Negri-Schoulz & Fassbender, 1988; LaVigna & Donnellan, 1986; Lerman & Vorndran, 2002). Positive behavioural supports is a development of applied behaviour analytic interventions. There is an emphasis on avoiding punitive consequences to behaviour (Carr et al., 1999, p. 4).

In a major review of 216 articles which included positive behaviour supports from 36 journals published between 1985 and 1996 (Carr et al., 1999) 109 studies were included and 107 were excluded. Carr and colleagues (1999) concluded that positive behavioural supports are widely applicable to a variety of care settings and that stimulus-based interventions are becoming more commonplace than reinforcement-based procedures. They concluded that 'modest to substantial increases in positive behaviour are typically observed following the application of positive behavioural supports' (Carr et al., 1999, p. 4).

Despite the increasing improvements in positive behavioural support technology, incidents involving physical aggression are likely to occur for a significant proportion of individuals with a learning disability. Crisis intervention is a critical component of community supports for people with a learning disability who present with aggressive behaviours (Hanson & Weiseler, 2002; Lakin & Larson, 2002). For the purposes of this section the term 'crisis intervention' will apply to short-term strategies which attempt to manage behaviours with the minimum of harm caused to the individual or others.

Carr and colleagues (1994) argued that without an educational component behavioural change cannot be achieved by crisis management procedures alone. While this view is clearly correct the need to manage behavioural crises that involve physically aggressive behaviour has also been acknowledged by the same authors. Carr and co-workers (1994) maintained that crisis interventions are needed and that 'it is a mistake to think that once an intervention is underway, you no longer need to worry about serious outbursts and the necessity for crisis management' (Carr et al., 1994, p. 14).

Physical Restraint

Physical restraint has been defined as 'actions or procedures which are designed to limit or suppress movement or mobility' (Harris, 1996, p. 100). The physical restraint of people who present a danger to themselves or others may well be socially undesirable but may at times be a necessity.

Usage of physical interventions in services for people with intellectual disability has received some attention in the literature. A study of aversive procedures in Minnesota found that physical restraint, especially manual restraint, is the most commonly used management procedure in community settings (Nord, Wieseler & Hanson, 1991). Emerson and colleagues (2000) in a survey conducted in the United Kingdom and Ireland of 500 people who were labelled as having challenging behaviour reported that 23% of the sample had experienced physical restraint. A similar survey of disability services in Canada reported that 13.3% of a sample of 625 service users had physical restraint as a component of their intervention plan (Feldman, Atkinson, Foti-Gervais & Condilliac, 2004).

The vast majority of the research conducted in this field is predominantly anecdotal in nature (McDonnell & Sturmey, 1993). Physical restraint is not in itself an aversive or non-aversive procedure. Studies have shown that restraint can act as a positive reinforcer in some instances (Favell, McGimsey & Jones, 1978). It may also suppress aggressive behaviour and be a form of punishment.

Physical restraint procedures may be used on an emergency basis to protect the individual or others from harm (LaVigna & Willis, 2002; McDonnell & Sturmey, 1993a; Willis & LaVigna, 1985) and may furthermore be systematically used as part of a behaviour therapy programme as either contingent or non-contingent restraint (Favell, McGimsey & Jones, 1978; Griffin, Williams, Stark, Altmeyer & Mason, 1986). Physical restraint has been used as part of a treatment package for a wide range of problems, which include pica (Paniagua, Braverman & Capriotti, 1986; Singh & Baker, 1984) self-injurious behaviour (Favell et al., 1978; Singh, Dawson & Manning, 1981) and hyperactivity (Singh, Winton & Ball, 1984).

It is difficult to draw firm conclusions about practices such as physical restraint, as the standard of research on them is relatively poor, with the majority primarily consisting of anecdotal evidence. Sailas and Fenton (1999) in a Cochrane review of physical restraint and seclusion research in mental health settings cited 2155 studies. None of these studies met the basic methodological inclusion criteria.

Not only may physical intervention training lead to reductions in staff and service user injuries, but also to increases in these behaviours. Staff training in physical interventions can lead to increases in post-training staff injury rates (Parkes, 1996) as well as reductions (Allen et al., 1997). An area that has been relatively overlooked by researchers is the potential for injury in training courses. Hill and Spreat (1987) reported that 30% of staff injuries in a university-operated residential facility for people with learning disabilities were due to the use of physical restraint. Injuries to staff were much more likely to occur during emergency physical restraint, whereas planned, mechanical restraint appeared to be much safer. Williams (2009) in a U.S. study analysed the use of restraint with 209 individuals with intellectual disabilities over a 12-month period; he reported that the overall rate of injuries during restraint was 0.46 injuries per 100 instances of restraints. The low injury rates in this study may reflect best practice or be an artefact of the recording.

The national evidence would indicate that many of these injuries are minor in nature. In sum the processes which lead to staff and service user injuries when implementing physical interventions are still poorly understood.

There is a potential for abuse when staff use restrictive procedures. In the United Kingdom a BBC undercover documentary which depicted physical abuse of adults with intellectual disabilities had a significant impact on service standards. Baker and Allen (2001) highlighted that high-risk service users may be at risk of abuse from staff using physical interventions. Injuries may be intentional or unintentional. Leadbetter (2002) distinguished between an injury caused by the employment of an ad hoc or unsafe technique by an untrained member of staff and a similar injury caused by a technique which has been directly taught to staff as part of an approved training programme. There are documented cases in the United States in which deaths have been associated with the use of physical restraint (Weiss, 1998); there were seven cases of which two involved people with a learning disability in California (Morrison, Duryea, Moore & Nathanson-Shinn, 2002).

In the United Kingdom a recent survey reported 12 cases of deaths associated with physical restraint between 1979 and 2000 (Patterson, Miller & Leadbetter, 2005). The expression 'positional asphyxia' has been used to describe restraint-related deaths (Patterson, Leadbetter & McComish, 1998). Causation is difficult to ascribe in many cases. Prone holds would appear to be implicated in a large number of deaths (Leadbetter, 2002). Other factors such as obesity, cardiac problems, anti-psychotic medication and cardiac abnormalities also appear to be associated in a number of these cases. A U.K. survey of psychiatric nurses in the experiences of behaviour management reported that 67% of their sample had been taught prone holds in training courses (Lee et al., 2003).

There is only limited evidence on the relative safety of specific physical interventions (Leadbetter, 2002). Physical interventions may also inflict pain (Leadbetter, 2002). In the United Kingdom there has been a debate about the use of pain in managing aggressive behaviour. The control and restraint system which has been developed in the United Kingdom to manage violence in prison populations does include techniques which involve the application of pain (Allen, Doyle & Kaye, 2002; Tarbuck, 1992; Topping-Morris, 1995). The recent code of practice in physical interventions advocated the use of physical techniques which do not inflict pain (BILD, 2006; Code of Practice)* by stating that 'morally and ethically BILD is opposed to the use of touching, guiding, or holding techniques that might or are known to cause pain or discomfort, or techniques that are designed to use pain as affective component to gain compliance, and believes the presumption must be that they are not to be taught' (p. 21). In a national consultation exercise there was considerable support for not teaching techniques which inflict pain on individuals (Harris, 2002b). The subjective experience of pain is notoriously difficult to define. Determining the safety of specific physical interventions is a complicated task, especially in the absence of hard empirical evidence (Leadbetter, 2002). An evidence base which demonstrates effective outcomes (reductions in staff and service user injuries) may help to move the debate forward. Evidence may not always inform the debate. Proponents of specific physical interventions may have specific commercial interest in continuing to teach particular techniques (Harris, 2002a).

Techniques which involve the abnormal rotation and flexion of joints do appear to be designed to inflict pain to control aggressive behaviours (Allen, Doyle & Kaye, 2002). Applying pressure to wrists and using holds such as the swan neck or the gooseneck hold are still taught in the United Kingdom. The evidence base for these intrusive physical interventions is at present wholly inadequate, and there is a particular need for high-quality, independent research into the biomechanics and physiological sequelae of controversial physical holds (Allen, 2007).

Mechanical Restraint

The use of mechanical restraints in learning disability services predominantly appears to focus on self-injurious behaviours (Oliver, Hall, Hales, Murphy & Watts, 1998). These behaviours evoke powerful emotional and behavioural responses among carers (Oliver, 1993). A recent survey of 557 adults and children with intellectual disabilities in South Wales identified severe self-injurious behaviours for nearly one third of their sample (adults = 29%, children = 42%). There was a significant association between self-injurious behaviours and a diagnosis of autism (Lowe et al., 2007).

Mechanical restraint usage has been reduced through the use of relatively simple behavioural measures such as staff feedback (Sturmey, 2002). A quantitative analysis of behavioural research on the treatment of self-injurious behaviour over the past 35 years reported that the treatment was generally effective, although the authors acknowledged the persistence of self-injury (Kahng, Iwata & Lewin, 2001). Despite advances in behavioural interventions it is rare for these behaviours to be eliminated in entirety (Emerson, 1992; Lowe et al., 2007).

*BILD Code of practice for the Use of Physical Interventions, 2006; Reproduced with permission of BILD, Kidderminster.

Extreme life-threatening forms of self-injury have also been subjected to intrusive and controversial interventions such as mild electric shock (Duker & Seys, 1996).

There have been some studies which have addressed the side effects of the use of mechanical restraints. Prolonged use of mechanical restraint such as arm splints can lead to medical complications such as bone demineralization (Griffin et al., 1986). Damage to limbs including shortage of tendons has also been reported (Fisher, Piazza, Bowman, Hanley & Adelinis, 1997). Information about the use of these forms of restraint in services is quite rare (Jones, Allen, Moore, Philips & Lowe, 2007).

The restriction of movement may also be subtle in nature. Consider the example of a six-year-old boy with learning disabilities, who showed high occurrences of hand-to-head hitting. Wrist weights (2 lb per arm) were placed on him. A vibrating micro-switch which he could independently operate was introduced into the sessions. Levels of self-injurious behaviour practically reduced to zero with the use of weights and an electronic toy (Hanley, Piazza, Keeney, Bakely-Smith & Worsdell, 1998).

Guidance about the use of such intrusive methods is lacking in the field (Jones et al., 2007). Spain, Hart and Corbett (1984) recommended guidance that was similarly advocated by more recent researchers (Jones et al., 2007). This guidance included not leaving people unattended in mechanical restraints and an individual functional analysis of the self-injurious behaviour (Iwata et al., 1982). The person should be able to engage in activities, and strategies for fading out the use of restraint should be in place.

Mechanical restraint for people with intellectual disabilities is an under-researched area (Jones et al., 2007), and its use is rather controversial. Nevertheless, mechanical restraints do appear to be used primarily for self-injurious behaviours and not for aggression.

Organizational Approaches to Restraint Reduction

A recent study in the United Kingdom reported that better service-quality outcomes for people with a learning disability appeared to be more commonplace in services with a more positive organizational culture (Gillett & Stenfert-Kroese, 2003). There is even some limited evidence that certain organizational cultures may actually increase service user vulnerability to abuse (White, Holland, Marsland & Oakes, 2003).

In a survey of 44 agencies which supported people with challenges, in the state of Oregon, USA, the authors compared six variables (namely organizational stability, administrative leadership, staff structures, staff training, measurement systems and behaviour systems; Baker & Feil, 2000). Using a regression analysis they found that administrative leadership predicted staff structures, measurement and behaviour systems but not staff training. Staff training was associated with staff structures which included procedures involved in recruiting staff, maintaining performance and building the team and encouraging teamwork. The implications of this survey for staff training in organizations are that structural variables are necessary as setting events for staff training.

Organizational factors may also act as establishing operations for staff training. Organizational cultures may have a powerful mediatory effect on staff-training outcomes (Patterson, Miller & Leadbetter, 2005). Early studies in institutional settings in the United Kingdom reported clear effects of service culture on the implementation and delivery of behavioural programmes (Moores & Grant, 1976; Woods & Cullen, 1983). In a classic study, Woods and Cullen (1983) examined three behaviour programmes conducted by staff in an institutional setting. At follow-up the most successful programme (room management) had been discontinued by staff and the least successful programme (toilet training) was still being maintained.

Sturmey and McGlynn (2002) reported data on a pre-post design (one-month baseline and seven-month interventions) implementation of a restraint reduction programme in a state school for people with learning disability in the United States. The programme included staff training in restraint reduction by teaching alternatives to restraint and role-playing redirection techniques. They reported 57% reduction from baseline in mechanical restraint after seven months of implementation. There were also reductions in emergency (unplanned) mechanical restraint of 45% from baseline. Personal restraint was less clear; there was a 23% reduction from baseline at seven months but a 63% increase over baseline in emergency (unplanned) restraint.

A second study examined an organizational behaviour management approach to restraint reduction with 22 adults having intellectual disabilities. They reported at three-year follow-up that 3 service users were restraint free for at least a quarter of the year, and 16 service users had at least a 50% reduction in physical restraint. The implication of this relatively small study is that organizational approaches can be effective in reducing the use of physical and mechanical restraint. A replication of these findings on a larger sample in a variety of health care settings would be useful in helping to identify key factors in organizations, which may maintain the use of such interventions. Staff leadership and feedback would appear to be important factors in the reductions of intrusive interventions (Deveau & McDonnell, 2007).

The Views of Consumers

Behavioural psychologist Montrose Wolf (1978) originally used the term 'social validity' to describe a subjective method of measurement in which applied behaviour analysis could 'find its heart'. Wolf (1978) questioned the validity of research to society and stated that research had to include the viewpoints of society. He considered applied behaviour analysis to have focused too much on objective measurement.

Wolf (1978) argued that three dimensions were important in understanding the concept of social validity. First, are goals or objectives 'socially significant'? That is to say do they achieve what society wants? Second, are procedures or methods 'socially appropriate'? Literally, do the ends justify the means? Finally, are consumers satisfied with the results?

The social validity of behavioural technology is a dimension which has been increasingly scrutinized by researchers (Storey & Horner, 1991). It could be argued that in the absence of compelling research data to suggest that either approach is more effective, a construct such as social validity will be just as important in the selection of interventions (Allen, 2001). The social validity of interventions includes a number of factors such as the social importance and appropriateness of goals, procedures and outcomes (Wolf, 1978). In a recent study, students were presented with a variety of behavioural intervention vignettes that varied in both aversive and non-aversive approaches and the outcome of the programmes (Bihm, Sigelman & Westbrook, 1997). It was found that successful programmes were judged to be more acceptable than the unsuccessful ones. Positive intervention programmes were viewed as more socially acceptable than punitive alternatives. This study requires further replication with a variety of professional and carer groups. However, it does reflect a trend or 'zeitgeist' that demonstrates the power of such dimensions in the decision-making process (Carr et al., 1999).

Behaviour management technology would require the same degree of scrutiny as behaviour change strategies. The move towards community care (Emerson & Hatton, 1996) may well increase public awareness about the management of aggressive behaviours. This is simply because more people may witness behaviours which previously occurred only within large institutions. The public view of behaviour management strategies is an important factor in determining the choice of the strategy adopted by staff in public settings. Therefore, the social validity of procedures such as physical restraint may well become a more widely debated issue as people encounter its usage in public settings.

Consumer satisfaction is a major component of judgements of social validity. Wolf (1978) stated, 'It seems to me that by giving the same status to social validity that we now give to objective measurement and its reliability, we will bring the consumer, that is society, into our science, soften our image and make sure our pursuit of social relevance' (p. 207). Furthermore, in the case of physical interventions the views of service users with learning disabilities are an area that is under-researched (Baker, 2002). In a follow-up study of 25 people with mild intellectual disabilities and challenging behaviours 16 service users reported their experiences of being restrained. All of the participants reported negative feelings about the procedures (Murphy, Estien & Clare, 1996). This is a promising area of research, especially as the technology for accessing the views of consumers has greatly improved in recent years (Kroese, Gillott & Atkinson, 1998). In a seminal study in the United Kingdom, the views of five women with learning disabilities, who had experienced physical restraint procedures, were gathered using an interview format; the responses were classified into physical pain, anxiety, feelings of anger and some concerns that the procedure was a form of punishment from staff (Sequeira & Halstead, 2001). The relatively small sample size of this study made it difficult to extrapolate its results to the views of people with disabilities as a whole.

A recent study reported investigating consumer views of physical restraint procedures (Cunningham, McDonnell, Sturmey & Easton, 2002). In the study, 24 undergraduate students, 21 residential care staff and 18 service users from community settings rated videotapes of three physical restraint procedures. Two of the methods involved restraining an individual on the floor, and a third method involved restraining an individual in a chair. The participants answered two open-ended questions to rate the methods of restraint and rated the methods on a five-point scale of satisfaction (Flynn, 1986). The participants also rated the three restraint methods by a forced-choice comparison. Restraint was rated negatively by all the participants. However, both the satisfaction ratings and the forced-choice methods rated the chair method of restraint as most acceptable for all three groups of participants. Consumers consistently rated restraint more negatively than the other groups.

Staff and consumers may have different views about the use of physical interventions. A survey of staff and service users in a secure facility found real differences between these groups. Staff reported the main reasons for use of restraint was to prevent harm, while service users tended to report that restraint was used as a form of punishment (Fish & Culshaw, 2005). Hawkins, Allen and Jenkins (2005) in a qualitative study of staff's and service users' views of physical interventions described both groups as experiencing stress caused by the implementation of restraint procedures. A study of staff attributions about physical interventions in a health service facility in the United Kingdom reported high satisfaction with the physical interventions that were used to manage crisis situations. No data for service users were reported in the study (Dagnan & Weston, 2006).

Judging by the quantity of research in the field of learning disability, the views of consumers is an important area of investigation in the physical management of behaviours. This may be partly attributable to the vulnerability to abuse of people with intellectual disabilities (Baker, 2002). The discrepant views of groups of staff and service users (Fish & Culshaw, 2005) may represent issues because of which convergence of views will be an extremely difficult goal to achieve.

Staff Training in Behaviour Management

The behaviour of staff can have powerful effects on the behaviour of people with a learning disability (Hastings & Remington, 1994a). Mediators (Allen, 1999) exert an influence on the behaviour of others and should be included in behavioural analysis. Staff behaviours are often the antecedents and consequences of challenging behaviours (Hastings, 2002; Hastings & Brown, 2000; Hastings & Remington, 1994). Staff's contingent attention can also have direct effects on the frequencies of challenging behaviours (Taylor & Carr, 1992). Challenging behaviours are often followed by staff responding to behaviours (Thompson & Iwata, 2000). Given the importance of staff behaviour it is not surprising that researchers have acknowledged the importance of training staff who work with people with learning disabilities.

There is a small body of research which examines the efficacy of staff training in physical interventions for people with intellectual disabilities. Patterson, Turnbull and Aitken (1992) evaluated a 10-day training course in control and restraint in the United Kingdom. They reported improvements in the use of physical interventions and disengagement strategies using a role-play format. McDonnell (1997) reported increases in confidence and knowledge of behavioural principles of 21 staff in an adult disability service, after a three-day workshop in the management of challenging behaviours. Allen, MacDonald, Dunn and Doyle (1997) reported reductions in restraint usage and emergency medication and the decommissioning of seclusion in an adult service for people with intellectual disabilities. Increases in confidence were also reported when comparing trained staff with untrained staff (Allen & Tynan, 2000). A two-day training course in a school for children with intellectual disabilities reported increases in de-escalation skills at six-month follow-up, and 82% of participants indicated an increase in confidence. Major incidents did not decrease significantly pre and post training (Perkins & Leadbetter, 2002). Studies do not always report reductions in the usage of physical interventions. Baker and Bissmire (2000) reported outcomes of a two-day training course for 17 staff in a 10-bed unit for adults with intellectual disabilities. There was a small reduction in the total number of untoward incidents after training. The proportion of incidents requiring physical intervention increased after training.

There are several themes to staff-training research. First, the research is at best crude (Allen, 2001). Second, the majority of empirical studies in the learning disabilities field are UK based. The majority of intervention studies do not meet basic scientific requirements of scientific rigour (McDonnell, Sturmey, Gould & Butt, 2007). Third, the relative utility of teaching physical interventions is still unknown. Finally, training in de-escalation strategies is often evaluated as a component of staff training in physical interventions, and there is little understanding of the relative effects of physical interventions training and de-escalation methods.

A Low Arousal Case Study

Lenny was born in 1985. An examination of his early medical records indicate that from the age of three it was observed that he was developing at a much slower rate than his peers. He was labelled as having mild to moderate intellectual disability with autistic traits and had acute episodes of epilepsy from three to seven years of age. Until 2002 he was progressing well at home and at school. There were behavioural difficulties noted by some of his key workers. Negative phrases such as attention-seeking behaviour and manipulation were relatively commonplace. Lenny was furthermore labelled by some staff a having 'pseudo-seizures'.

In September 2002 his behaviour patterns changed dramatically with him exhibiting severe agitation, hand biting, sleeplessness, bed/clothes wetting, pseudo-seizures and threatening, self-injurious behaviour. Lenny was placed in a group home of a local service provider from where he absconded on a number of occasions. During this time he became well known to the local emergency services. Lenny started showing extreme acts of self-harm culminating in an incident in which he was alleged to have jumped into a river. Six weeks later the provider organization placed Lenny into the care of the state services, which had had no prior contact with him.

Temporary staff were recruited to work with him, with three staff working with him at any one time. He was lodged in a local hotel as emergency accommodation. Despite these high staffing levels Lenny managed to abscond on several occasions. These absences were typified by extreme incidents of self-injurious behaviour. A review of his situation led to the state obtaining a voluntary care order. This changed his staff to experienced mental health nurses. Lenny was then moved to another hotel as his notoriety spread. Lenny's mother was concerned about the restrictions placed on her son, and she took his case to a district court on five occasions. The state was then ordered to provide a range of therapeutic interventions delivered by professional staff.

In 2003, Lenny and his three mental health nurses were moved into a privately rented home. Initially, a significant improvement in Lenny's functioning was noted. After one year in the state services, Lenny moved to long-term care in a nursing home for people with acquired brain injury. This home had an elderly population, none of whom had a learning disability. Lenny's behaviour and mental health deteriorated markedly during this period, and he eventually absconded. Lenny was returned to a state service community house with his previous team of mental health nurses. During this period there were high levels of staff assault and prone holds for restraint, primarily employed to prevent him from absconding. Although record-keeping was poor, interviews with staff from this time and evidence provided by Lenny indicated that physical restraint was often a daily occurrence.

In January 2004, a local disability agency primarily having experience of autism and challenging behaviours took over the community home, and Lenny joined the service with a view to the other residents joining him. A low arousal model was adopted in which staff were encouraged to reduce demands and requests to Lenny in times of crisis. It was stressed that staff should behave as his friends rather than gaolers. Emphasis was placed on staff responses to his challenging behaviours being as different as possible than his former team of psychiatric nurses. Sanctions were to be avoided.

All staff received training in de-escalation techniques and physical interventions. The staff to user ratio was reduced from 3:1 to 2:1. It was also agreed by his staff team that the service would adopt a non-restraint policy. If Lenny absconded from the house, staff were to follow him at a safe distance. This was rapidly changed to Lenny being given a mobile telephone so that he could contact staff if needed. The general strategy involved Lenny being told to take control of his life and his behaviour and break the vicious circle of absconding. After an initial 'honeymoon period' of two weeks Lenny's behaviour rapidly deteriorated. Two months later the service leaders rented a bungalow nearby to provide a single-person occupancy service for him. The staffing ratio was reduced primarily to 1:1.

In May as a result of property damage and the neighbours' complaints Lenny was evicted from his home. He returned to his original community home on a short-term basis. In June a bungalow next door to the community house was purchased as a single-person unit for Lenny. His support worked with him on a one-to-one basis. These initial six months witnessed absconding almost as a daily occurrence, once culminating in visits to emergency services. Lenny would often telephone these services and state that he had a seizure or had taken paracetamol. Verbal aggression and property destruction occurred with high frequency, although there were no instances of physical aggression towards staff. Several extreme behaviours occurred at this time, which these included eating broken glass, gate-crashing a wedding at a local hotel and cutting his forehead with glass, standing in front of traffic and lowering himself into the local canal at least twice, culminating in the involvement of emergency services.

Regular liaison meetings took place with the police and emergency services. Requests to prevent him from leaving the house were made but were declined by the team responsible for Lenny. It was determined that Lenny's visits to hospitals did not seem to be maintained by the responses of staff towards him in those places. Some medical staff were quite understanding and positive towards him, while others saw him as a nuisance and at times could be extremely aggressive towards him. The team determined that Lenny might be suffering from a form of panic anxiety, possibly caused by his extremely traumatic negative life events. His hospital visits served the function of temporarily reducing this anxiety. The staff team were encouraged to avoid confrontation with Lenny about these visits but to stress that they were his 'friends'. The next six months witnessed declines in his use of emergency services and absconding behaviours. For the majority of 2006 there were few incidents of aggression or self-harm. Throughout the entire period there was only one minor incident of aggression towards staff. According to Lenny this contrasted dramatically with his previous care packages.

In 2007, up to the time of writing the book, Lenny has requested to move into a group home setting, as he stated that he wanted to live with other people. There have been some episodes of absconding, but the majority of these are viewed by his staff team as relatively minor in nature.

Staff Training in the Management of Challenging Behaviours: A Case Example

In Chapter 2 the development and outline of a three-day training course was described. This case example reports early data gathered in the mid 1990s from studies which investigated the effects of staff training over a series of training courses. This section will examine an evaluation of 15 training courses on the confidence and knowledge of care staff in adult disability services in the United Kingdom and Ireland.

A total of 275 care staff participated in 15 separate training events; the mean age was 34.4 years, with a standard deviation of 10.6 years. There were 182 female staff and 93 male staff. The staff were selected from a wide range of community residential establishments for people with an intellectual disability in the United Kingdom; 10 of these services catered for less than 10 residents, and 5 involved services with more than 10 residents. All of the services had individuals who presented with aggressive behaviours. In all 15 establishments training had been requested as a response to crises with specific individuals.

Two measures were developed to evaluate the training course. The first was a 15-item challenging behaviour confidence scale. The second measure was a 20-item multiple-choice knowledge test. The confidence scale contained 15 items relating to managing challenging behaviours in caring environments. The questionnaire was divided into three categories: the first five contained behavioural statements about 'potentially violent' people; items 6 to 10 contained behavioural statements that would be carried out during a violent incident; and items 11 to 15 contained statements about physical interventions.

The scale was subjected to a principle components analysis (PCA). The PCA method was used to extract all factors having an eigenvalue greater than 0.

A three-factor solution, accounting for 70.8% of the total variance was found. These factors were then rotated using the varimax rotation procedure. Factor 1, with an eigenvalue of 6.53, loaded highest on items that were concerned with physical interventions during a violent incident. Factor 2, with an eigenvalue of 1.57, loaded most highly with those items that contained behavioural statements about what would be carried out during a violent incident. Factor 3, with an eigenvalue of 1.55, loaded most highly with those items that contained behavioural statements about 'potentially violent' people (McDonnell, 1997). The 'confidence' questionnaire produced a Cronbach's alpha reliability coefficient of .92 for the entire scale, indicating a high degree of internal reliability between the 15 items comprising the scale. The knowledge test contained 20 items which were selected to cover key areas of the training course. These included legal issues (two questions), behavioural knowledge (six questions), strategies for defusing incidents (four questions) and descriptions of responses to the physical management of challenging behaviours (eight questions). All responses were in a multiple-choice format.

A role-play test was similarly used to evaluate the competence of course participants. Each course participant was asked to demonstrate the physical restraint procedure taught on the last day of the training course. This procedure was developed as an alternative to prone and supine holds (McDonnell, Dearden & Richens, 1991). The method also has high levels of acceptability from professionals (McDonnell & Sturmey, 2000), young people (McDonnell, Dearden & Sturmey, 1993b) and services users (Cunningham et al., 2002). A course facilitator attempted to mimic aggressive behaviours which would require the course participant to ask a colleague for assistance to restrain the facilitator. Attempts were made to make the role-plays as realistic as possible. Each role-play lasted approximately five minutes. All role-plays were videotaped. The physical restraint procedure was task analysed into nine key steps (McDonnell, 1997). Two observers were asked to independently rate 45 of the role-play videos. The two scores of the observers were compared by dividing the number of agreements by the number of agreements plus the number of disagreements and multiplying by 100. This produced an inter-rater reliability coefficient of 96%.

To ensure that there was consistency between training events, the training courses were task analysed into 21 key units. The trainers had to indicate that each component had been completed on a course checklist. There was 100% agreement between the 14 course checklists. Two training courses were monitored at random throughout the three days by an independent observer to check that each course module accurately reflected the information presented on the checklists. There was moreover 100% agreement between the course trainer and the independent assessor.

Six months later, the initial training managers in the 15 services were contacted and asked a series of questions about consumer satisfaction. The four days selected to make telephone contact were chosen at random. The interviewer described the purpose of the interview and requested the two senior managers who attended the workshop to provide responses to five short questions. A total of 27 (2 senior managers in each of the 12 services responded, and in the rest 3 services only 1 manager responded) senior staff were asked the following questions: (1) How useful have you found the training course in the management of challenging behaviours? (2) What areas of the training course were the most helpful? (3) What areas were the least helpful? (4) To your knowledge have you had to use any of the physical procedures taught on the training course? (5) How effective are these procedures? (6) What changes (if any) do you think that the training has brought about in your work practice? (7) Do you feel that the training has made your staff more or less confident in managing challenging behaviours, or has there been no change at all?

The main results of the two 'pre' and 'post' measures were reasonably predictable. Knowledge measures were subjected to a two-way analysis of variance (ANOVA). There was a significant difference in the pre- and post-knowledge training course ($F[1, 253] = 94.8, p < .01$). There was also a significant effect in terms of between-course scores ($F[14, 253] = 8.77, p < .01$). An analysis of the data using Scheffes multiple comparison procedure indicated that nine courses demonstrated statistically significant increases in mean scores at the 1% level ($p < .01$) and one course at the 5% level ($p < .05$). One course showed a decrease ($p < .01$). There was no effect of sex on pre- and post-training scores ($F[1, 253] = .01, p > .05$) or the between-course scores ($F[14, 253] = 0.94, p > .05$).

The confidence scores were also analysed using a two-way ANOVA. There was a significant effect in changes of scores before and after training ($F[1, 253] = 45.97, p < .01$). There was a significant effect of confidence scores compared between the courses ($F[14, 253] = 2.63, p < .01$). There was no effect of sex on pre- and post-training scores ($F[1, 253] = 0.01, p > .05$). There was no effect of sex on the between-course comparisons ($F[14, 253] = 1.42, p > .05$). Scheffes multiple comparison test produced significant increases at the 1% level for six training courses ($p < .01$); three courses produced significant changes at the 5% level ($p < .05$). One course had a significant reduction in confidence ($p < .05$).

The role-play scores were calculated for all 275 course participants. A score of eight on the nine steps was required to achieve a pass criterion. All participants achieved a pass (181 participants achieved an 8/9 pass, and 94 achieved a 9/9 perfect pass score). No course participants reported injuries to the facilitators at the end of each training course.

27 senior managers agreed to be interviewed (2 staff each from 12 training courses and 3 from the remaining services). 23 interviewees reported the training to be useful; two respondents were undecided; and two respondents reported the training not to have been useful. The second question asked participants to rate 'what areas of the training they found to be most useful'. Fourteen

respondents reported the strategies suggested for defusing incidents (low arousal approaches) as the most useful. Ten respondents reported physical restraint as the most useful component. Two participants reported the role-play practice as useful. And two people did not respond to this question. To the question that asked what they found least useful about the training, 15 respondents could not specify a response. Seven managers indicated the role-play components as least useful. Four people reported 'legal issues' as the least useful. One respondent stated that 'it was all pretty useless'.

Twenty-three managers reported that some of the physical skills taught on the training course had been used in their residential services to their knowledge. Eighteen of these respondents reported the methods as effective; three were unsure; and two respondents reported that the methods were ineffective. To the question 'What changes were required to the training courses?' 21 respondents reported that no changes were necessary. Four requested that the training course should be longer in duration. One person felt that the restraint procedure required changing, and one respondent stated that the entire course needed changing, as it was 'too soft on people with mental retardation'. Finally, 22 respondents reported that in their opinion their staff were more confident in managing behaviours after the training course. Five respondents reported no change in the confidence of staff.

This research study demonstrated statistically significant increases in knowl-edge and confidence scores for the vast majority of training events. These results further replicate the findings of an earlier published study (McDonnell, 1997). However, the scores of knowledge and confidence did not increase in all train-ing courses, and one group had significant decreases in both scores. Anecdotal information indicates that the participants clearly indicated that the training was 'too soft' and would not work on the people in their service. It is important to note that not all training will have desirable outcomes (Cullen, 1992). High staff turnover can also affect the impact of training (Campbell, 2007).

Increases in confidence are important, especially as aggressive behaviours can invoke powerful responses in carers (Oliver, 1993). It would appear to be a reasonable working hypothesis that carers who report that they are more confident in dealing with challenging situations may in some instances manage behaviours more effectively (McDonnell, 1997). It is interesting that the vast majority of the managers interviewed in the telephone survey reported that their staff were more confident since the training had taken place. Although such an assertion may have some face validity, further research is needed to empirically demonstrate whether confidence is a critical variable in the management of challenging behaviours.

Increases in the knowledge scores were perhaps a little less surprising, as the items reflected the material presented to participants over the three days. Participants could demonstrate improvements in this measure over a relatively short period of time. Whether knowledge increases would directly effect staff behaviour is a debatable point. Knowledge of behavioural principles does not always have an effect on staff behaviour (O'Dell, 1974). Further research would be needed to answer this question with regard to this training.

The satisfaction responses of service managers at six-month follow-up would appear to provide some limited insight into the effectiveness of the training. However, care should be taken when evaluating the responses of individuals, as their opinions may not necessarily reflect the working practices in these residential services. It would appear at face value that the training did have an impact in these services. It is also important to note that the staff team that reported significant decreases in knowledge and confidence scores also supplied the most negative management feedback. It is interesting that this staff team appeared to find the training 'too soft'. Particular reference was made to the notion of low arousal approaches which sometimes can involve reinforcing behaviours in the short term to manage crises and reduce confrontation (McDonnell et al., 1998). It has been documented that a problem with such strategies is that staff may feel that they are 'giving in' to people who present management difficulties (McDonnell et al., 1998). This particular staff team expressed the view that they believed that these approaches would make the behaviour of their residents worse. In direct contrast, over 50% of the managers surveyed specifically named low arousal approaches as the most useful component of the training course. Given that the research into the effectiveness of behaviour management strategies has been relatively crude (Allen, 2000; McDonnell & Sturmey, 1993), more research is needed into both staff perceptions of behaviour management strategies and their relative effectiveness.

It is difficult to analyse which components of the training were the most effective. The majority of managers reported using low arousal approaches (McDonnell et al., 1998) and the physical restraint method (Cunningham, McDonnell, Sturmey & Easton, 2002; McDonnell et al., 1993) as the most useful components of the training. 23 managers reported that physical skills had been used in their services, although the authors were unable to assess the frequency of usage. It is important to examine outcomes in this field, as training may not always achieve the desired result. One training group showed decreases in both knowledge and confidence measures. There were also some training courses which showed no statistically significant increases.

Training staff in 'safer' physical interventions use is only an initial step towards the reduction and in many cases the eradication of such methods. In a recent paper Sturmey (2009) made a clear and unequivocal statement about what can be achieved in this area:

> Researchers have thoroughly documented the problem of excessive use of restrictive behavioural practices and their negative effects. They have been amply documented in special education, community residential and day programmes and institutional settings. We must now move towards the safe elimination of restrictive behavioural practices.

Conclusion

Let us return to Jane's story, which looked at Jane being restrained by support staff in her home. This poses moral dilemmas about empowering staff to carry out these practices in these situations. At present Jane may be exposed to a variety of different restraint holds depending on the staff-training model that is in use in the service. It is also possible that her staff might have received no training in physical interventions. If Jane becomes angry she might receive low arousal approaches or a whole range of methods, depending on the training of her staff. Services are increasingly becoming community based in their focus. Supporting adults who present with challenging behaviours in these situations is a major challenge for service providers. Effective crisis management strategies such as low arousal approaches will hopefully enable staff to engage people in activities and develop appropriate social networks.

5

Managing Aggressive Behaviour in Individuals with Autistic Spectrum Disorders

Sheila is a 24-year-old woman with a diagnosis of autism. She has been described as having 'Kanner-type' autism. She lives in a group setting with several other individuals who have also been diagnosed with autism. Her difficult behaviours tend to occur at busy times of the day in the house, especially mealtimes and bedtimes. It was reported by her family that her rituals surrounding eating were very repetitive; where she sits, in what order she eats her food, the type of cutlery she uses can all have an effect on this routine. It takes Sheila approximately 45 minutes to eat her meal in this manner. When her rituals are interrupted she screams and covers her ears. She has also been known to be physically aggressive with other service users and staff. Sheila's behaviours can present major difficulties for her carers, and they have all identified that attempting to change her rituals can be extremely stressful. Sheila's story is not that untypical. In this chapter the low arousal approach will be applied specifically to meet her needs.

The term 'autism' was first used by Kanner (1943), who described 11 case descriptions of young children. The children were described as 'aloof' and distant, with limited facial expression. Routine and structure appeared to be important with these individuals. At almost the same time in Europe, Asperger (1944) described people with very similar behaviours. Asperger's syndrome is now used to describe people with autistic traits who have normal and above intelligence (Wing, 1981). In this chapter the term 'autistic spectrum disorders' (ASDs) will be used to describe people with autism and Asperger's syndrome.

The whole autistic spectrum is defined by the presence of impairments affecting social interaction, social communication and social imagination (Wing & Gould, 1979). The autistic spectrum is very broad and reflects a

Managing Aggressive Behaviour in Care Settings: Understanding and applying low arousal approaches
By Andrew A. McDonnell © 2010 John Wiley & Sons, Ltd

wide range of individual behavioural presentations, ranging from individuals who appear detached from the social world of others to people who are observed to possess appropriate interactional skills (at least on the surface) but view the world very differently. There are three prominent cognitive theories of autism: theory of mind (TOM) (Baron-Cohen, 1995), weak central coherence (Frith, 1989, 2003; Happe, 1996) and executive dysfunction (Ozonoff, Strayer, McMahon & Filouz, 1994). Critics of cognitive deficit models argue that they attempt to provide a universal explanation of autism symptoms rather than a collection of multiple deficits (Rajendran & Mitchell, 2007).

Difference or Deficit?

Autism can be viewed as a collection of deficits or impairments (as is the case with the triad of impairments) or as characteristics which exemplify difference. There are accounts of differences in perception experienced by people on the autistic spectrum (Grandin, 1992a, 1992b; O'Neill & Jones, 1997). Some individuals do not view autism in terms of deficits but regard themselves as different. Sinclair (1992) described this view: 'There are many ways in which it is difficult or impossible for me to meet standard definitions of normalcy. Some of these relate to impairments or deficits in functions that come easily to most people'. Sinclair poignantly describes his experiences of perception as qualitatively different from other people. He also clearly describes the difficulties in social understanding experienced by many people with autism, 'Some of my greatest deficits involve my inability to learn and internalize social norms that appear meaningless to me'. Sinclair is very clear that he has strengths and positive abilities which compensates for some of his other difficulties, '... is it possible for me to find, or create, a place in society that allows me to make maximum use of my strengths and to minimize the limitations of the things I can't do?'

Autism, Self-Injury and Aggression

Autism has been identified as a risk marker for physical aggression (McClintock, Hall & Oliver, 2003). A large number of intervention studies with children have focused on physical aggression (Horner, Carr, Strain, Todd & Reed, 2002). People with autism can present with behaviours that challenge their carers. A recent survey of 157 Irish children with a diagnosis of autism identified that 82% of the sample showed some form of challenging behaviour (self-injurious behaviour, stereotypies, aggression), although a detailed analysis which excluded stereotyped behaviours reduced this to five individuals who showed self-injurious behaviour or aggressive behaviours (Murphy, Healy & Leader, in press).

Self-injurious behaviours can evoke strong emotional responses among care staff (Oliver, 1993) and appear to be associated with individuals with a diagnosis of autism (Romanczyk, Kistner & Plienis, 1982). Significant advances have been made in our understanding of the causes and function(s) of self-injurious behaviour (Iwata et al., 1982; Rojahn, Schroeder & Hoch, 2008). Behavioural models would suggest that behaviour may be reinforced by extrinsic sources of positive reinforcement such as attention and negative reinforcement such as escape from demands (Iwata et al., 1982) or that the behaviour may produce intrinsic reinforcement such as sensory stimulation or pain reduction (Rojahn et al., 2008).

In a study of overt signs of pain in a group of 35 people with intellectual disabilities and self-injurious behaviour matched with 35 controls, the group characterized by self-injurious behaviour had significantly more overall non-verbal pain signs relative to the matched comparison group on a global non-verbal pain measure (Symons et al., in press). There is clearly a complex pattern of interactions between the self-injurious behaviour and the experience of pain. For some individuals pain mechanisms may reinforce self-injurious behaviour. There are also many other areas of complexity which need to be considered in the management of self-injurious behaviour. A good example of this is the relationship between self-injurious behaviour, self-stimulatory behaviour and sensory factors (Smith et al., 2005).

Individuals with a severe/profound degree of intellectual disability are significantly more likely to show self-injury and stereotypy than individuals with a mild/moderate degree of intellectual disability (McClintock et al., 2003). There also appears to be a relationship between self-injurious behaviour and stereotypic behaviour. Clinically, the reduction of one type of behaviour can lead to an increase in the other type. Individuals with deficits in receptive and expressive communication are significantly more likely to show self-injury (Bird et al., 1989; McClintock et al., 2003).

Aggressive behaviours occur across the entire autistic spectrum. Difficulties in managing their anger among people with Asperger's syndrome are reported in the literature, although there is little hard data to estimate the size of the problem (Attwood, 2004). Many individuals with this form of autism may not always show good insight into their own emotional states. Misreading of social situations can lead to extreme behavioural responses. The expression 'meltdowns' has been used to describe the extreme states of hyper-arousal in people with Asperger's syndrome (Lipsky & Richards, 2009). Attwood (2007) used the term 'rage' to describe aggressive behaviours in children with Asperger's syndrome. These extreme and intense reactions can present major problems for staff and families. The author has extensive experience working with individuals who may incubate responses to novel situations incrementally over time. In these circumstances it is more appropriate to label the very explosive aggression as a form of 'panic anxiety'. There is a link between these anxiety states and physiological arousal. Unusual sensory experiences can often exacerbate these emotional states.

Sensory Differences in People with ASD

When examining these issues it is important to use language that avoids unnecessary stigma. Some authors use terms such as 'sensory problem'. With motor issues some authors have used the term 'difference' rather than 'problem' (Leary & Hill, 1996). A similar distinction will be made in this chapter; the term 'sensory differences' will be adopted as the preferred term.

Relating sensory experiences to everyday behaviour is not a new phenomenon. Kanner (1943) in his seminal paper described sensory issues in some of the children. He reported the case of Herbert B., who 'was tremendously frightened by running water, gas burners and many other things' (p. 231). Similarly, Frederick W. had a fear of certain objects and the sensation of movement or confinement: 'He is afraid of mechanical things; he runs from them. He used to be afraid of my egg beater, is perfectly petrified of my vacuum cleaner. Elevators are simply a terrifying experience for him. He is afraid of spinning tops' (p. 223).

In the 63 years since this paper our knowledge of information processing deficits has greatly increased. There have been attempts to understand these deficits from a biological perspective. Damasio and Maurer (1978) produced a neurological model for childhood autism. They argued that areas of the temporal area and mesolimbic systems were implicated in autism. Studies have also attempted to identify structural areas of the brain implicated in sensory differences, particularly the limbic system involving the hippocampus and the amygdala (Lathe, 2006). Ornitz (1988) argued that sensory inputs may have had a causal role in the development of ASD. Given the complexity of autism it is unlikely that one factor will have a clear causal role.

There have been attempts to relate sensory processing difficulties as a rationale for challenging behaviours. Dunn (2001) identified a strong relationship between sensory information processing and behaviour: '[P]eople have different thresholds for noticing, responding to and becoming irritated with sensations; reflected in their mood, temperament and ways of organizing their lives' (Dunn, 2001, p. 609). He furthermore distinguished the thresholds of sensory perception (low and high registration) and behavioural responses (sensation seeking and sensation avoiding). There is a rapidly developing literature which would appear to show that these constructs may have some face validity.

Sensory differences in individuals with ASD are increasingly being reported by researchers. A U.S. study of 104 individuals with a diagnosis of autism matched with a control group of individuals without ASD identified differences between the two populations (Kern et al., 2006). The authors used the sensory profile (Dunn, 1999) in their study and found that there were differences in auditory, visual, touch and oral sensory processing.

A study of children with autism showed different responses to a variety of sensory stimuli (Baranek, David, Poe, Stone & Watson, 2006). In a survey of the parents of 75 children with ASD conducted in the United Kingdom, 71% appeared to be hypersensitive to sound, touch, smell and taste (Bromley, Hare, Davison & Emerson, 2004). There appears to be an emerging body of literature which strongly suggests that individuals show abnormalities across multiple domains (Baranek et al., 2006; Leekam et al., 2003).

The sensory measures developed by Dunn (2001, 1997) were also in one study used to compare 42 children with a diagnosis of Asperger's syndrome and 42 non-learning-disabled controls (Dunn, Smyth Myles & Orr, 2002). Differences were reported in 22 out of 23 comparisons, the Asperger's sample reporting both hyposensitivity and hypersensitive responses. However, there are difficulties in interpreting questionnaire studies, as they do not directly report behavioural measures of sensory difficulties. There are of course obvious ethical issues involved in conducting functional assessments using analogue baselines. The use of measures such as galvanic skin responses (Brown et al., 2001) may be a helpful way forward for practitioners, where individuals will tolerate this level of intrusion.

In a survey of parents of children with autism in the United Kingdom, 71% of children were hyposensitive to sound and 41% were hyposensitive to smells (Bromley et al., 2004). Vestibular sensations are also reported to be experiences with both more and less intensity than that experienced by people without a diagnosis of ASD. In a comparison, using Dunn's sensory profile, of 103 persons having autism with matched controls, differences were found between people with ASD in both high and low processing of vestibular sensations (Kern et al., 2007)

There is some evidence for sensory differences reported in the literature, which is based on the personal accounts of people with ASD (Grandin, 1992a, 1992b; Mukhopaday, 2003; O'Neil & Jones, 1997). Considerable caution should always be taken when interpreting such experiences, as we have no way of knowing whether these experiences are common to the ASD population as a whole. O'Neil and Jones (1997) reported the experiences of individuals with ASD and identified sensory perception abnormalities in people with autism; these included hypersensitivity and hyposensitivity, sensory distortion, over-load, multi-channel receptivity and processing difficulties. These have mainly been reported through first-hand accounts. Grandin (1992a, 1992b, 1996) de-scribed several of her sensory differences; she reported, '[S]udden loud noises hurt my ears – like a dentist's drill hitting a nerve' (1992a). She also linked this to challenging behaviours: 'The fear of a noise that hurts the ears is often the cause of many bad behaviours and tantrums' (Grandin, 1996).

In summary, responsiveness to sensory stimuli does appear to be different for populations of people with autism and Asperger's syndrome. The personal accounts of people with ASD (Grandin, 1992, 1996; Mukhopaday, 2003; O'Neil & Jones, 1997; Shore, 2003) are useful but do not constitute strong empirical data. Care should always be taken not to generalize individual accounts to a population as a whole (O'Neill & Jones, 1997). To date there are only a limited number of studies which primarily use checklist-based measures (Brown et al., 2001; Dunn et al., 2002; Kern et al., 2006). More emphasis is required on empirical studies which use direct behavioural observation rather than indirect questionnaires. In sum, sensory processing difficulties would appear to be fairly prominent in people with ASD.

Anxiety/Arousal Difficulties and Their Reduction

In Chapter 2 a low arousal approach has been outlined. Physiological arousal is not a new construct and has long been implicated in ASDs (Hutt, Hutt, Lee & Ounsted, 1964). Two implications of this are that children and adults with ASD are more reactive to sensory stimuli than the normal population and are moreover slower to habituate to stimuli. This is in part supported by laboratory evidence of differences in physiological responses of individuals with ASD compared to non-autistic controls (Althaus et al., 2004; Hirstein, Iversen & Ramachandran, 2001; van Engeland, Roelofs, Verbaten & Slangen, 1991).

There is mixed evidence across the spectrum for increased and decreased arousal in response to predicted stressors. Jansen and colleagues (2006) compared adults with ASD with non-ASD adults in their response to public speaking and found that under the circumstances the individuals with ASD showed decreased heart rate but normal cortisol responses. Goodwin et al. (2006) compared five children with ASD with five non-autistic controls and reported higher baseline heart rates for ASD participants. Hirstein and co-workers (2001) reported unusually high and unusually low baseline skin conductance responses in autistic children compared with non-autistic controls. These differences require replication using larger samples, but these results suggest a considerable variation in physiological reactivity of both children and adults with autism.

There would appear to be considerable practitioner evidence to indicate a link between physiological arousal, autism and aggressive behaviours. The sensory factors discussed in the previous section are likely to be linked in some way to anxiety. Autism has been viewed as an anxiety/stress disorder by some individuals (Morgan, 2006). This view has clear implications for practitioners, especially if knowledge about stress/anxiety reduction is applied to this population. Lazarus and Folkman (1984) described a transactional model of stress, emphasizing interaction between the individuals and their environment. Stress occurs when the demands of stressors outweigh coping responses and when there is a clear interaction between environmental and physiological events. Physiological hyper-arousal has been associated by researchers with childhood autism (Hutt et al., 1964). Sensory over-reactivity has been explained as a possible response to over-arousal (Liss et al., 2006). It has also been suggested that repetitive movements may serve as a 'de-arousing' function (Kinsbourne, 1980). Physiological arousal would appear to be associated with behavioural difficulties. Methods that achieve reductions in arousal may therefore be of significant benefit.

Relaxation techniques to reduce physiological arousal are a significant tool in alleviating sensory processing difficulties, and positive results of training individuals in relaxation techniques have been reported in the literature (Groden et al., 1994). Along with anxiety management techniques (Attwood, 2007; Sofronoff & Attwood, 2003; Sofronoff, Attwood & Hinton, 2005), training in techniques based on cognitive behaviour therapy has also been advocated for people with intellectual disabilities (Dagnan & Jahoda, 2006).

The effects of multi-sensory environments (sometimes known as Snoezelen rooms) appear to indicate that increase in relaxation and reduction in overt signs of anxiety can be achieved (Lancioni, Cuvo & O'Reilly, 2002; Stephenson, 2002). A 10-week observational study which compared the effect of Snoezelen, skills training and vocational skills training reported lower levels of aggressive behaviour and self-injurious behaviour in the Snoezelen group (Singh et al., 2004).

There is limited information which claims better concentration is observed after multi-sensory sessions (Lindsay et al., 1997). A recent single-case study of three adults with a diagnosis of ASD reported fewer prompts required in a preferred activity for two out of the three participants (Kaplan, Clopton, Kaplan, Messbauer & McPherson, 2006).

Sensory rooms may reduce anxiety levels, which may have an impact on behaviour. A study conducted in Hong Kong reported that increase in behavioural relaxation were observed after sessions but no decreases in heart rate (Chan, Yuen Fung, Wai Tong & Thompson, 2005). There are a limited number of studies that imply that lower levels of physiological arousal may be accompanied by reduced frequencies of challenging behaviours. Shapiro, Parush, Green and Roth (1997) described the effects of Snoezelen sessions on stereotyped behaviours and heart rate levels. They reported lower heart rate levels and fewer stereotyped behaviours during such sessions. In sum, there would appear to be a strong association between physiological arousal and sensory input.

Studies have also demonstrated reductions in stereotyped behaviours of people with ASD with increases in exercise (Allison, Basile & MacDonald, 1991;

Kern, Koegel & Dunlap, 1984; Rosenthal-Malek & Mitchell, 1997). The role of physical exercise in managing aggressive behaviour is not as well understood. McGimsey and Favell (1988) found that when severely aggressive and hyperactive service users were exposed to two daily periods of jogging and strenuous activities there was a systematic reduction in problem behaviour for 8 of the 10 participants to levels considered to denote 'not a problem' or only 'an occasional problem'. They argued that physical exercise may offer promise as an effective, benign and practical adjunct to other treatment and management techniques. Physical exercise may have positive effects on reducing physiological arousal.

Physical Interventions

Physical interventions can make individuals more prone to abusive practices (Baker, 2002). The application of physical restraint to people on the autistic spectrum may present significant challenges for service providers. The negative sensory experiences reported earlier in this chapter when applied to the application of physical interventions indicate that some individuals may find restraint aversive, whereas others may find it positively reinforcing.

Service user accounts of the implementation of physical interventions can provide a useful perspective. Blackburn (2006) is a young woman with what she describes as 'high-functioning' autism. In a personal account she described the implementation of a physical intervention which was associated with her compulsion to fold paper, which she calls 'flappies':

> Of course, in hospitals as in most public places the 'flappie racks' are just inside the main entrance and my attempts to procure some flappies in order to line them up on the floor and give myself more security have often been misconstrued as attempts to escape. (p. 87)

She moreover admitted that she had been restrained because of the misconstruction of her behaviours by staff: 'I've been physically restrained often none too gently' (Blackburn, 2006, p. 87).

There are also other narrative accounts of people with autism/Asperger's syndrome about experiences of physical contact. Gunila Gerland referred to light physical contact giving her a feeling similar to an electric shock. Aversion to touch was also identified by parents in 52% of 75 children in a U.K. survey (Bromley et al., 2004). In contrast Temple Grandin referred to the comforting effect of deep pressure contact (Grandin, 1992b). It is possible to speculate that some individuals with ASD may find restrictive physical interventions positively reinforcing, similar to an effect reported with mechanical restraints for people with intellectual difficulties (Favell et al., 1978). However, it is difficult to quantify the numbers of people who may find the experience of restraint either positively reinforcing or aversive.

In the case of individuals who may find immobilizing holds aversive, the increase in physiological arousal may present significant risks to the cardiovascular system. Specific restraint holds that involve holding individuals on the ground may have elevated risks. Prone restraint holds may present an even greater risk of harm. Some experts have even called for a teaching ban on all prone restraint holds in care environments (McDonnell, 2007); other academics refute the claims that these postures are strongly associated with sudden deaths (Paterson, 2007). Incorrect application of methods has been associated with a few restraint deaths among children in care environments in the United States (Nunno, Holden & Tollar, 2006).

Dunn (2001) identified that some individuals may have 'low registration' of sensory stimuli. Low registration of pain may therefore be a significant factor to consider. In these circumstances care staff may apply restraint methods too robustly, as the individual does not appear to show overt signs of distress. A good example involves the teaching of physical restraint skills which can include the hyperflexion of joints. From an ethical viewpoint the deliberate infliction of pain to suppress behaviour raises major ethical concerns. Leadbetter (2002) used the expression 'high-tariff techniques' to describe these types of methods. There are good practical reasons why the use of these methods on service users with ASD should be avoided.

Applying a hold which involves the abnormal rotation of the wrists has additional risks. An individual with low registration may not appear to respond to the painful stimulus. There is considerable evidence from the sensory literature that indicates that some people may respond to painful stimuli with a limited behavioural response. The survey of parents conducted by Bromley and colleagues (2004) reported that 45% of children were hyposensitive to pain. In conclusion, physical intervention methods which involve the infliction of pain may have to be applied very robustly to some people with ASD, who have low registration difficulties, and therefore increase the risk of harm to the service user.

The recent evidence for differences in processing of vestibular stimulation (Kern et al., 2007) also has major relevance for the application of physical interventions. It is possible to speculate that some individuals may find restraint procedures which require movement more effective than immobilization holds. The author would argue that if physical restraint is required to keep an individual with autism safe, there are some guiding principles based on the low arousal philosophy that need to be observed. It would be practical to keep the duration of any hold to a minimum. If an individual has a need for deep-pressure contact, then this could be applied through tight-fitting garments or by staff holding a person in a seated position. Holds that require immobilization on the ground in either prone or supine positions should be avoided.

Intermittent physical contact may represent a safe alternative. There has been evidence that a technique which involves movement, known as the 'walk-around method', can be used with people with ASD (Merrett, McDonnell & Jones, 2009). The use of unexpected movements may operate by overloading the person's sensory system or by increasing vestibular stimulation.

A Case Example

James was a 28-year-old man with a diagnosis of autism and mild intellectual disability; moreover, he was visually impaired. From the age of 12 he had attended a residential school and at 18 was transferred to an adult intellectual disability service which was far from the family home. His 'challenging behaviours' were stated as a reason for his placement in the service. His family visited weekly and expressed the clear wish that he be returned to a placement near his family home.

It took nearly 10 years to identify a placement near his family home. This organization had an established track record in the area of intellectual disabilities. To meet the needs of James and other local individuals with autism, the organization opened a house for five people which they described as 'autism specific'. The staff team was highly motivated, but in reality they had received limited training in the management of aggressive behaviours. The autism awareness training was retrospectively described as mostly theoretical and not tailored to the individuals with autism.

When James arrived at the service he found it difficult to adjust to living with his new peers. Inadvertently, significant pressure was placed on him by both his staff team and his family. The staff adopted what they described as a 'needs-led' approach. This entailed providing James with multiple activity choices. Each day he was encouraged to interact with his peers and take walks in the local area. At the same time his family visits increased to daily. The family began to routinely take him to a local pub, and every effort was made to maximize his community opportunities.

Within three weeks James started to show behaviours which indicated a hyper-aroused state. His sleep pattern deteriorated, and on four occasions he was destructive to property. The duration of most of the incidents tended to last between one and two hours. James began to avoid the communal areas in the house and withdrew to his room. Staff tried to encourage him to come out of his room, but James would often begin to scream when these requests were made. In the fourth week of the scheme James had a day-long episode of destructive behaviours. This culminated in an incident of physical aggression, where he punched a member of staff in the face and kicked another in the groin. The staff team felt that they could not manage this new set of behaviours. Their 'on-call' manager decided to telephone the local police. Four policemen arrived and decided to arrest James after he threw a chair at one of them. The officers held him face down on the floor and applied handcuffs. This appeared to agitate him further. James was screaming, shouting and struggling with the police officers. A staff member had driven to the police station, as she was concerned that he would be more agitated in an unfamiliar environment. Within 10 minutes of his arrival at the police station James visibly began to calm down. This settled period led to the staff member requesting the police to take him back to his group home.

An emergency meeting was called the next day, which involved specialist advisors from the Studio3 organization. The staff team were noticeably in disagreement about what they should do with James. Some were very fearful and suggested that he be placed in a hospital placement; others felt that they should persevere. A crisis plan based on a low arousal model was adopted. There were several key elements, listed as follows:

- All verbal demands and requests by staff were radically reduced; it was noted that staff often requested James to 'calm down', which appeared to agitate him further. Staff were to follow a plan to avoid speaking to James on a routine basis, as this would reduce his confusion and distress.
- Staff were encouraged to speak in a clear and concrete manner.
- If James damaged property, staff were told to avoid verbally responding to these behaviours unless he damaged property in a manner in which the risk of personal harm was elevated.
- Staff were advised that James's aggression and property destruction were an outward expression of 'panic anxiety'. This was used as a key rationale for his low arousal plan. It was explained that the reduction of his anxiety was a key aim of the plan.
- It was discovered that staff had also been attempting to discourage James's stereotypical behaviours, particularly his rocking backward and forward in a seated position or bouncing on his bed. The Studio3 advisors strongly suggested that staff avoid responding to his stereotypies, as the behaviours in essence probably served the function of anxiety reduction.
- His family was requested to reduce their visits on a temporary basis.
- Staff were encouraged to establish a predictable routine for James for every day of the week. Exercise of up to one hour per day was regularly introduced.
- A short-term additional advice line was put in place by Studio3 staff to be used in the event of an emergency.
- Studio3 training was implemented for all staff over a four-week period. The physical interventions described in Chapter 3 were taught on a 'bespoke basis'. (Hair pulling, airway protection and the two-person walk-around method was taught using role-play scenarios.)

- All staff also received specific autism awareness training tailored to James's needs. This training focused on sensory triggers to his behaviours, especially his sensitivity to sounds and sudden physical contact. Positive sensory experiences (walking in the rain, swimming, car journeys) were all increased as part of a 'sensory diet' (Bogadashina, 2003).
- Staff were encouraged to talk about their fear of James in team meetings and to debrief with colleagues after witnessing property destruction or aggression.

Within two weeks of implementing these plans James's behaviour began to settle. Property destruction became less frequent, and there were two incidents of physical aggression. Both of these incidents were managed using the 'walk-around' procedure described in Chapter 3. Although some staff still expressed negative feelings about James, the majority reported that they were more confident in interacting with him. After a month of implementation, James's activity programme was altered, and staff established new activities in the community.

There were many elements which led to the change in staff behaviour. James's key worker stated categorically that 'low arousal works'; she was also worried that some staff still 'did not get him'. There were still debates between staff members, some of whom felt that they were 'giving in' far too much. This observation is often made when adopting a low arousal approach (McDonnell et al., 1998). One member of staff suggested forcibly that James needed strong boundaries, as he was a bully, and that his colleagues were making too many excuses to justify their hands-off approach. This individual was encouraged to work with other individuals in the home.

This case illustrates a combination of factors that can lead to extreme behaviours. First is a lack of understanding of autism and in particular knowledge of sensory triggers (McDonnell et al., 2009). Second, training in managing aggressive behaviours was tailor made. Third, demand reduction and establishing a predictable routine was a key aspect of the approach. Finally, the example illustrates that services which cater to people with intellectual disabilities and adopt a strong activity-based approach may not be appropriate for all individuals who are on the autistic spectrum. The staff had to adapt their approach to take account of James's view of the world and limit their social interaction goals at least in the short term. In essence the service had become much more 'autism informed'. The use of low arousal approaches had a rapid effect on James's behaviours.

An Organizational Approach to Staff Training

This training example describes the implementation of the Studio3 training methods to a service for adults with ASD (see McDonnell et al., 2008). The training covers a 10-year period. Initially, the service catered for 52 service users, 34 of whom resided in communal residences of five or six persons in each group home. Two specialist day services provided support to the majority of service users. By the end of the period the service had expanded its residential places by eight places, which included two individualized schemes for people with severe challenging behaviours. One person had a diagnosis of Asperger's syndrome; another presented with severe challenging behaviours. A specialized home-based day service was provided for one individual with Kanner-type autism.

The referral for Studio3 training arose from a service user injuring a number of staff. Over period of one month all core staff within the service were trained in the core three-day training course (McDonnell, 1997). The training course was not received universally positively by all of the staff who attended. A significant and vocal minority raised concerns about the validity of the training for people with ASD. A post hoc evaluation conducted by the service director revealed four key issues of confrontation. First, a minority of staff raised concerns about the application of the low arousal approach to people with ASD. The reduction of demands in a crisis was interpreted by these particular staff as a 'lack of rule and boundaries'. The approach was considered to be primarily theoretical and aspirational rather than pragmatic. Second, serious concerns were also raised by these staff about the lack of variety of physical interventions taught on the training courses. Some staff were genuinely concerned that the physical interventions may not have been robust enough. Third, concerns were raised that Studio3 trainers were critical of a number of restrictive practices in the service. Key issues were raised by trainers about the use of time-out rooms in the day service, the number of unwritten behaviour management programmes which regularly contained the use of sanctions and withdrawal of privileges. Finally, a number of autism issues, which focused on the philosophy of the organization, were raised by senior staff. It was important to have a 'clear message' about how low arousal approaches interfaced with other elements, such as the application of 'theory of mind' (ToM) research and the use of the picture exchange communication system (Charlop-Christy, Carpenter, Le, LeBlanc & Kellet, 2002) and the TEACCH approach.

Internal debates continued within the service over the next year. A consensus about the service having a number of deficiencies emerged between Studio3 senior staff and the service director. Most notably the lack of the psychology provision had created considerable problems during the implementation of low arousal approaches. The lack of the psychology input provided a tabula rasa for the creation of a new service.

It was decided to train a member of staff who was internally well respected as an in-house trainer. Studio3 also agreed to provide regular psychology support to this individual. The service was viewed as a test bed for low arousal approaches. Several objectives were set for the service. These included reduction of restrictive procedures and a general approach to behaviour management which avoided intensive applied behaviour analytic methodologies. Care staff within the service were actively encouraged to reflect on their own behaviours which might maintain the challenging behaviours of service users. The low arousal approach was to be a central tenet of the service philosophy. This was typified by a person-centred approach to challenging behaviours. Records of incidents were deemed to be lacking in accuracy. An incident-recording system was also implemented in 2000 to help to monitor staff responses to challenging behaviours. Finally, the development of a comprehensive staff training pro-gramme was a major objective.

By 2001 the Studio3 approach was firmly established within the service. The time-out rooms had been abolished in the day centres. All behaviour management programmes needed multidisciplinary approval. There was also a clear reduction in the use of sanctions by staff within the service. The number and frequency of meetings which focused on staff responses to challenging behaviours of service users significantly increased. A systematic series of in-house training in Studio3 methods were delivered to all staff.

In 2000 a service audit indicated that approximately 30% of incidents of challenging behaviour were being accurately recorded by care staff. Between 2001 and 2004 a systematic monitoring and staff support system was put in place. Staff were actively encouraged to record all incidents of challenging behaviours. In addition the checklist of challenging behaviour was used to provide a staff perception measure of challenging behaviours. An analysis of the frequency of physical intervention usage showed a low and consistent use of physical interventions to manage incidents. In 2001 there were a total of 60 recorded incidents with 10 requiring the use of physical interventions. In 2002 there was an increase to 102 incidents of which 16 required physical interventions. In 2003 there were 108 recorded incidents, 8 of which required physical interventions. Finally, in 2004 there were 86 incidents with 12 requiring physical interventions. There were several observations that surrounded these incidents. First, staff reported that the management difficulty ratings as measured by the checklist of challenging behaviours were significantly reduced over the entire time period. There were also consistent comments that the intensity of these behaviours had reduced. Therefore, staff appeared to accept that behaviours still occurred, that they were episodic in nature and that they were managing the vast majority of these episodes successfully.

An analysis of incidents over this time period showed that property destruc-tion had increased. Staff accounted for this by stating that to reduce physical interventions service users were not restrained to protect property. The priority in these situations was to evacuate an area and keep other service users safe. The physical interventions used were of a minimal kind. No prone or supine holds were used. In addition the majority of techniques involved physical disengage-ment strategies, and less than one third involved a two-person escort procedure. There were no incidents that required chair restraint. There were two incidents

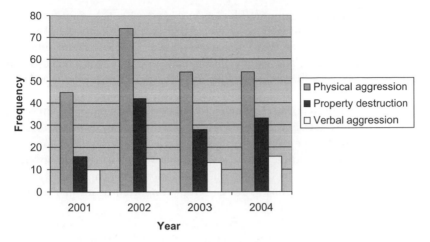

Figure 5.1. Frequency of behaviours.

of non-Studio3 holds being used, and in both instances key staff were retrained to prevent recurrence (Figure 5.1).

In 2004 one new service user accounted for nearly 30% of the incidents involving property destruction. At the same time, the chair restraint method was phased out of the core staff training, as it was deemed unnecessary.

From 2004 to 2006 the in-house training system for all staff was fully established. Core training included the three-day training course in the Studio3 system, training in picture exchange communication system and a standardized induction workshop in low arousal approaches, working positively with people who challenge and understanding autism. In this training, practical approaches to manage and avoid aversive sensory stimuli were also included. Emphasis was placed on the reduction of subtler restrictive strategies. Delaying responses to requests for food and drink were directly targeted, as they were deemed to be a significant cause of negative interactions. The rapid meeting of needs of basic requests by service users had a positive impact. The use of picture exchange communication system symbols for food and drinks helped to provide more control and choice to service users. A new house for six people was opened in this time period. Three of these individuals presented with severe challenging behaviours.

In 2007 a retrospective interview was conducted with the Studio3 training leader and the service director to determine issues raised by 10 years of Studio3 training within the service. Several themes emerged from this interview. In their view the training increased staff awareness and understanding of challenging behaviour, in that staff are now more likely to ask why someone might present with challenges. There had been a culture shift for the whole service; the biggest change had been challenging staff beliefs and biases about the causes of challenging behaviours. Staff were more aware that they may inadvertently cause challenging behaviours. Staff did appear to reflect on their own contribution to a challenging situation. The training also applied to staff in that it had brought about a change in the hierarchical structure of the service. Prior to the training the management system was typical of many health care services in Ireland with a psychiatrist at the top. This had now changed, with the front-line staff being considered the experts, as they were the people who lived and worked with the service users. Rather than simply presenting staff with a programme for a service user and asking to implement it, staff were now asked to agree on how they would implement it among themselves. Thus, training had empowered staff to consider their job and responsibilities as being as important as any management position.

Another effect of the training was that the intensity of challenging behaviours had decreased. The majority of untoward incidents tended to be minor and episodic in nature. Few service users had consistently been challenging throughout the time period. Staff were also using less intrusive physical interventions, which was a very positive step. Restrictive holds such as prone and supine restraint were in effect eradicated from the service.

The lack of in vivo practice of physical interventions did present a problem. Staff confidence in using physical interventions actually lowered, as they no longer used the skills learned in physical intervention. This necessitated the staff completing refresher courses in this area. Low arousal training is about giving the service users control over their own lives. The intervention stops when the behaviour stops, not when staff decide it has to. The fear level of staff prior to the introduction of the training was very high. There was no debriefing after an incident in which control and restraint had been used; therefore, another benefit had been the staff support in the form of debriefing. Training also involved teaching staff not to catastrophize events and how to avoid thinking in terms of 'what if' and instead to deal with the situation as it had actually occurred. In addition, training had reduced paperwork in the offices, as there were far more face-to-face meetings. The in-house trainer routinely met staff informally or formally if they were experiencing difficulties with a service user. One of the difficulties which the training officer had encountered was the length of time it would take for staff to change their outlook, especially with regard to the motivation behind a service user's behaviour.

New staff in the service appeared to accept the low arousal approach much more readily. There was a problem that many staff members did not have as much experience of intense physical aggression. Two incidents typified this training problem. First, two members of staff were working with a young adult with autism, who had, in their words, 'a bad week'. It was unclear why this was deemed a bad week. During this time both staff members had their hair pulled very hard. Both staff also admitted that they knew what to do, but they froze because the behaviour was so unexpected. The training officer for the service was presented with a real training dilemma. Should staff regularly practice physical interventions which are quite rare? Should we accept that staff will sometimes freeze in these experiences, especially if the behaviour is of a low intensity? In this case the service retrained these two individuals but discouraged staff from having too much practice of physical interventions. This also communicated the message that staff training in these methods can never eradicate risks.

This service has developed a national reputation for excellence in managing challenging behaviours and understanding autism. The demands for external training have significantly increased. These positive changes have also greatly assisted in the recruitment of staff to the service.

We started this chapter with a discussion of the needs of Sheila. It could be presumed that her rituals and routines help her to make sense of her world and cope with anxiety. From the perspective of her staff they are interrupting these rituals to help her, although the approaches adopted are not based on good evidence-based practice. Currently, there is limited experimental evidence to advise staff about altering rituals and obsessions (Matson & Dempsey, 2009). The attempts to alter Sheila's rituals have probably led to increases in anxiety and overtly distressed behaviour.

A low arousal approach would avoid altering Sheila's behaviour directly but would focus on accommodating her rituals and obsessions. These behaviours are likely to serve the purpose of anxiety reduction and should be viewed as 'coping strategies' rather than behaviours that have to be modified per se. Low arousal approaches focus on a person-centred approach to managing the behaviours of people with autism. In this example accepting these behaviours and focusing on supporting Sheila to eat meals on her own or at quieter times may be helpful. The behaviour management approach needs to concentrate on managing both Sheila's and her staff team's behaviour and needs to have a strong person-centred focus. Sinclair (1992) described the key elements of such an approach: 'If you would help me, don't try to change me to fit your world. Don't try to confine me to some tiny part of the world that you can change to fit me'. He argues that we need to view autism as a communication problem, where we have to learn to understand that person rather than change them. He says 'Grant me the dignity of meeting me on my own terms – recognize that we are equally alien to each other, and that my ways of being are not merely damaged versions of yours. Question your assumptions. Define your terms. Work with me to build more bridges between us.'

6

Applying Low Arousal Approaches to Children and Adolescents in Residential Care Services

Sarah is a 14-year-old girl who currently lives in a care home for children who have 'emotional and behavioural difficulties'. She was taken away from her family after a court ruling stated that she needed to be in a safe place. During the previous three years Sarah's aggressive behaviour had significantly deteriorated. Her behavioural episodes were also associated with intense episodes of self-harm (involving cutting her wrists and thighs). She had been excluded from several schools including one specialist residential school. Her social workers investigated her family circumstances. During this investigation both Sarah and her mother disclosed that she had been repeatedly sexually abused by her father in the family home.

The Orchard, Sarah's care home, consists of five other young people, all of whom present with aggressive behaviours. Like Sarah, nearly all of them have been victims of sexual, emotional and physical abuse. When she first arrived at the care home the staff found it increasingly difficult to manage her threatening and physically aggressive behaviours. They were uncomfortable about using physical restraint methods in these circumstances. Fights would break out fairly routinely between the children, and it was not uncommon for Sarah to be involved in some way. The staff found her cutting episodes to be particularly distressing to manage. In some services Sarah would have been secluded or physically restrained; it is fortunate that she had been sent to a service which had a minimalist approach to restraint and a non-seclusion policy. This chapter will outline some of the issues faced by staff in children's residential services.

Managing Aggressive Behaviour in Care Settings: Understanding and applying low arousal approaches
By Andrew A. McDonnell   © 2010 John Wiley & Sons, Ltd

Violence and Aggression in Services for Children and Young People

Significant numbers of young people live in care environments. In the United States over 100,000 young people reside in residential programmes (Child Welfare League of America ([CWLA], 2005). However, the effectiveness of child residential placements has been questioned. Lyons and Schaefer (2000) suggested that extremely violent and dangerous individuals may receive the greatest benefit from residential treatment. Conversely, some of the research has described residential treatment as only somewhat effective (Lyons et al., 2001).

There are a wide range of presenting problems catered to in these services (O'Malley, 1993), with children receiving a wide range of interventions for emotional and behavioural difficulties. Conduct disorders (CDs) account for a significant number of the difficulties presented by children within residential placement. Cathcart Shabat, Lyons and Martinovich (2008) investigated a sample of 457 children and adolescents with and without CDs in 50 residential treatment facilities and group homes across Illinois. In the study, multidisciplinary teams rated measures of mental health and other factors within 30 days of admission, about seven months after admission and at discharge. While both the CD and non-CD groups initially responded similarly to treatment, the CD group performed better relative to the non-CD group over the full course of treatment, showing healthier change on five outcome variables and more significant improvement.

Vulnerability of Young People to Abuse

Serious abuse in families can take many forms. Sinclair and Bullock (2002) randomly selected 40 'serious review' cases in the United Kingdom between 1998 and 2001. The sample consisted of 31 deaths and 8 serious injuries along with one case in which the child's behaviour had led to a prison sentence. The researchers identified common precipitating factors such as mental health problems in parents and domestic violence. They found that in some cases there appeared to be a lack of predictability, whereas other cases were described as 'waiting to happen'.

There is a growing body of literature which indicates that children are vulnerable to a wide range of abuse and trauma. In a survey of 4039 school students in Sweden 65% of the girls and 23% of the boys reported having experienced some form of sexual abuse (Priebea & Svedin, 2008). Of the girls who reported experiencing sexual abuse 10% reported non-contact abuse; 69.2% reported contact abuse without penetration; and 20.8% reported penetrating abuse.

Non-contact abuse was reported by 18.4% of the boys who reported sexual abuse, while 57.3% reported contact abuse and 24.3% penetrating abuse. These figures would appear to indicate that abuse in this population may be more widespread. A significant problem with this type of abuse is that it is associated with the development of difficulties in adulthood, such as sexual difficulties and dating aggression (Fiering, Simon & Cleland, 2009). There are always significant difficulties with interpreting retrospective studies that have investigated negative effects. Nevertheless, despite this negative picture many victims of child sexual abuse appear to overcome their difficulties in adulthood (Noll, 2008).

The long-term negative psychological effects of physical abuse are now better understood by researchers. Miller-Perrin, Perrin and Cochur (2009) in a retrospective study of college students found that individuals who were exposed to the severest forms of childhood violence demonstrated poorer psychological outcome compared with respondents who reported experiencing no violence or corporal punishment.

Abusive practices are also known to occur in residential services. In the United Kingdom the so-called pin-down inquiry highlighted the negative effects of using seclusion as punitive procedures (Levy & Kahan, 1991). A total of 132 children, aged nine and older, experienced what came to be called a 'pin-down' between 1983 and 1989. Pin-down was little short of a system of solitary confinement for large periods of time. Isolation was employed as a punishment for such activities as running away from care or school, petty theft, bullying and threats of violence. Children in residential care environments may also be vulnerable to sexual abuse from their carers (Bloom, 1992). Kendrick (1998) argued cogently that inquiries and public notoriety has led to a breakdown of trust between some consumers and care providers. An area of concern is the use of restrictive practices in these environments.

The Use of Restrictive Procedures in Childcare Services

Restraint and seclusion occur in residential facilities for children and young people, and there are both proponents and opponents of the methods (Day, 2002). In the United Kingdom figures were recently published for secure training centres that house young offenders, which identified significant variation in restraint usage. One third of all reported restraint use over a 21-month period occurred in only four centres. As an example the Oakhill facility catered for 80 people and reported 1493 uses of restraint, which would average approximately 71 restraints per month (Ahmed, 2008).

A study conducted by the CWLA (2004) reported high levels of injury rates to children during the application of crisis management strategies. Injury occurred during 3.8% of all reported emergency physical interventions, 4% of seclusion incidents, 3.5% of physical restraint incidents and 8.8% of mechanical restraint incidents. These injury rates did not appear to be significantly reduced by a variety of staff training programmes. Of the children involved in restraint or seclusion incidents 55% were between the ages of 5 and 12. These figures would appear to indicate that many young children are involved in incidents of emergency safety intervention.

Seclusion appears to be a practice that is also used in adolescent psychiatric services. Fryer, Beech and Byrne (2004) in a study of an 11-bed Australian youth facility analysed rates of seclusion over a one-year period, involving 105 separate admissions of 78 young people. There were 98 episodes of seclusion over the time period. An analysis of case records revealed that the reasons for seclusion use involved physical aggression towards person or property (67 incidents) and verbal abuse/aggression, threats or harassment. These data are somewhat a cause of concern, as a significant number of incidents did not involve actual physical harm.

There is some limited evidence that females prior to admission to residential facilities present more risk factors than males and moreover that, when in care, females are often perceived as being more difficult to work with than males (Handwerk et al., 2006). A study of Japanese female juveniles in secure settings identified that 33% of the sample met the criterion for post-traumatic stress disorder (PTSD). In addition to this, 77% of the female juvenile offenders had been exposed to trauma. The offenders with PTSD showed significantly high psychiatric co-morbidity.

The use of restraint and seclusion practices with female adolescents is not well understood. Leidy, Haugaard, Nunno and Kwartner (2006) investigated restraint usage in a U.S. facility for female adolescents. They examined 1059 incidents of physical restraint, involving 155 adolescents. The length of the restraints ranged from 1 minute to 98 minutes, with the average being 11 minutes; 38% of adolescents experienced restraints, out of which the average number of restraints equalled eight restraints. However, restraints were not evenly distributed even among the adolescents who were restrained. About 48 of the 155 adolescents who were restrained were restrained eight or more times while in placement. These 48 adolescents accounted for 76% of the facility's physical restraint.

Larson, Sheitman, Kraus, Mayo and Leidy (2008) reported an unusual alternative to mechanical restraints in a 360-bed state psychiatric hospital for adolescents. They described a 'padded room' as a safer alternative to mechanical restraint usage, the use of which led to decrease of 93.7%, from 21.2 to 1.3, in mechanical restraint events per 1000 patient days in their study. The authors argued that a padded seclusion room may offer a safer, albeit a less-than-desirable, alternative to mechanical restraint. This study identified a clear distinction between safety and social validity (Wolf, 1978) of restrictive practices – replacing mechanical restraint with seclusion in a padded area could be considered as a 'Hobson's choice'. There are cases in which mechanical restraint can be significantly reduced without the need for such alternatives.

The experiences of staff while applying restraint methods are also of significant interest to researchers and practitioners. Bell (1996) in a qualitative study analysed 14 incidents of restraint of young people in Scottish children's services. The majority of the children (9 out of 14) were described as having had multiple previous restraints. Three clear antecedents to the implementation of restraint were described by childcare workers: first, when the child refused to enter, engage in or disrupted the daily routine; second, situations in which the child was a danger to self, others or property; finally, situations in which the child was distressed/angry about something that they had been told. Out of the 14 workers 12 felt that the restraint had been entirely appropriate. '7 out of 14 workers said that they did not believe the restraint had had a significant effect on the child. Three others felt that the important positive effect of restraint was that it had helped to set "limits" for the child' (Bell, 1996, p. 44).

This quotation illustrates the view that physical restraint may have a therapeutic value in terms of setting limits. The alternative view is that restraint should not be regarded as therapeutic in the management of aggression (Leadbetter, 2002; Mohr, Mahon & Noone, 1998; Mohr, Petti & Mohr, 2003). Practices such as restraint may be used by staff and carers more to enforce control than to reduce the risk of immediate harm per se. Another area of concern involves the use of restraint as part of a therapeutic intervention. Mercer (2002) identified at least four approaches that claim to use restraint with children as a component of therapy. While there is very little evidence for these methods (Mercer, 2001), education for individuals who intend to use such methods is needed.

Restraint-related deaths for children also appears to be an issue of major concern in U.S. services. Nunno, Holden and Tollar (2006) in a descriptive study examined 45 child and adolescent fatalities related to restraints in residential (institutional) placements in the United States from 1993 to 2003. Male children and adolescents were over-represented in the study sample. 38 of the fatalities occurred during or after a physical restraint, and seven fatalities occurred during the use of mechanical restraints. 28 of the deaths occurred in a prone (face down) restraint position. In 25 of the fatalities, asphyxia was the cause of death. Significantly, for the 23 cases in this study where information is available, none of the behaviours or conditions that prompted the restraint would meet the standard of danger to self or others, the commonly accepted criteria for the use of a restraint. This study identifies the possibility that restraint may not always be the last resort.

Tragedies can lead to changes in the practice by increasing public awareness of these issues. In the United Kingdom two notable cases of death in the youth care system were those of Gareth Myatt and Adam Rickwood. These deaths highlighted many issues for service providers about the safety of specific restraint methods. These fatalities led to a full review of training in children's secure facilities in the United Kingdom. A major recommendation was the establishment of a mandatory national accreditation system for training that includes physical interventions (Smallridge & Williamson, 2008).

Training Staff in Childcare Settings

Training staff to manage the behaviour of children and adolescents has been a high-profile area. Another major observation from previous research is that following training, the confidence of staff increases (Nunno et al., 2003; Perkins & Leadbetter, 2002; Titus, 1989). There is an assumption that increases in staff confidence should lead to better behaviour management practices, but the evidence for this assumption appears to be somewhat limited (see Chapter 9 for a fuller explanation).

Fear also seems to be a principal feature of staff training; it is not unreasonable to expect a person confronted by an angry individual to experience fear. Coping with fearful situations would appear to be a crucial aspect of self-protection (McDonnell, McEvoy & Dearden, 1994). How a threat is perceived is integral to staff response (Whittington & Wykes, 1996) and can lead to aggressive responses if a member of staff feels under personal threat. It is therefore important for staff to acquire skills to cope with fearful situations.

Titus (1989) in a Canadian study reported data on the implementation of a training programme. Sixteen care staff were trained by qualified therapeutic crisis intervention (TCI) trainers to become trainers themselves. Following this, these newly qualified trainers over a 17-month period trained the remaining 150 staff at Kinark child service facility in TCI methods. Direct service workers and managers reported that the number of physical restraints had been reduced after training; this was supported by the physical restraint summaries which also conveyed a reduction. Staff answered that they felt that less injuries occurred to themselves and the children residing at Kinark. The study claimed that TCI provides staff with a safe way of physically restraining a child, which helps to reduce injury to staff and children. However the number of injuries to both staff and children actually increased during the assessment period.

Staff reported that the time that they restrained children was reduced as a consequence of training. However physical restraint summary forms contradicted this and instead showed an increase in time of restraint over the assessment period. Similar explanations were used for this finding; possibly incidents were severer, requiring physical restraint to be longer in time and staff were becoming more accurate at recording incidents. Staff felt that there were two main issues which restricted them from utilizing the TCI training.

The first was that there was not enough staff per shift to deal with situations in the manner in which they were trained. The second was that staff turnover was very high and, consequently, staff were often working with untrained staff and therefore could not use the techniques correctly. It would be hoped that as few people as possible would be required to restrain an individual, as having large numbers of staff around, as research has shown, often provides the stimulus for a person to continue to challenge (McDonnell, 1997). Titus (1989) concluded that confidence increased as a side effect of training. This is important, as studies have shown that increased staff confidence correlates with a reduction in the use of physical restraint (McDonnell, 2005).

Nunno, Holden and Leidy (2003) also evaluated the effectiveness of TCI staff training. Their study focused on a residential facility in North America with the help of the Cornell University Child Care Project, which agreed to implement Cornell's TCI programme and evaluate its impact. Again as with Titus's (1989) study a major flaw of this study was the lack of information provided about the course content and teaching methods used, which makes it difficult to evaluate and attribute possible causal variables to outcomes and findings of the study.

The service consisted of four separate units: Unit A, meant for children with serious emotional disorders, housed 11 children aged 6 to 12. Unit B served as an emergency shelter and assessment unit; the emergency shelter section catered for children 12 to 18 years of age and the assessment part for children between the ages of 5 and 18. A total of 295 children were included in the study from this unit. Unit C was designed for 28 children between the ages of 14 and 18, who had been placed in the home by the courts because of neglect/delinquency. All residents had emotional or behavioural problems. Unit D was a group home for youths ranging from 14 to 18 years in age, who were recovering from addictions. The number of children included in the study from this unit was 18.

All staff who worked directly with children at the facility received TCI training ($N = 62$); the study spanned an 18-month period and consisted of a pre-implementation phase in which incident data were reviewed, confidence measures taken, knowledge levels tested, staff interviews conducted and needs of the service discussed. Following this an implementation phase occurred, where four supervisors agreed to complete a five-day course to become TCI trainers themselves (the 'train the trainer' programme). They then disseminated TCI training to the remaining staff. TCI training occurred over a four-day time span. Again, incident data were reviewed during this period. The post-implementation phase consisted of reviewing incident data and taking staff interviews, staff knowledge levels of training and confidence measures.

It was found that staff's knowledge increased after training. This was measured by a multiple-choice test which assessed the content of the training course given before and after training with correct responses increasing from 49.97% (pre-training) to 83.39% (post-training). As the knowledge test was based on testing staff's knowledge of the training course it is not surprising that there was a large increase during the post-training period. Twenty-three staff who completed the test after a nine-month period only incurred a 5% decrease in knowledge. This provides support to the fact that the 'train the trainer' programme, which is integral to the implementation of TCI training, does increase staff's knowledge, and knowledge is largely maintained over a nine-month period.

Confidence scores also increased after training; however it should be noted that the questionnaire used had poor reliability with a Cronbach's alpha figure of .52. As with knowledge scores and confidence scores the lack of clear statistical analysis makes interpretation difficult. Supervisor interviews were generally very positive, focusing on increased staff skills as a result of training, specifically staff offering alternatives to physical restraint and the implementation of a consistent approach which can be transferred to all of the units. This is quite positive, but caution must be taken when interpreting these findings because of the reliance of the responses on subjective perceptions.

Central to the study was the intent that training would decrease the amount of restraints used. This occurred in unit B, showing a significant reduction of 66%. In units C and D no significant increase or decrease occurred after training. Unit A data were omitted from the study for reasons of lack of staff, support and structure of this unit. Unfortunately, as already mentioned, there is often a lack of staff and structure within the caring services, and training programmes need to be able to be implemented effectively in difficult circumstances.

Perkins and Leadbetter (2002) evaluated the impact of a training programme on aggression management and physical intervention in a Scottish special school. This training model views aggression as an interaction between individual pathology and the environment. It promotes an approach to behavioural control based on the analysis of the underpinning functions of behaviour and assumes that an organizational approach involving clear policies and staff development is required. It includes a five-level system of physical intervention training based on non-aversive principles. No clear description is provided for the specific content of the training course, again making it difficult to compare and evaluate training styles.

It was expected that after training, staff stress would be reduced; confidence would be increased; attitudes would be in line with the course attitudes; and the number of major incidents would decrease. A pre ($N = 14$), post ($N = 13$) and six-month follow-up study ($N = 12$) was conducted, providing useful follow-up data. Indeed analysis of incident logs showed that at the six-month follow-up stage a significant increase in the use of verbal de-escalation techniques when dealing with challenging situations had occurred (a rise from 33% to 75%).

No significant change in staff attitudes before and after training was reported. Staff knowledge of physical restraint gathered through questionnaire responses showed mixed responses. At follow-up interviews 8 out of the 12 participants interviewed felt that a level-four 'figure four' restraint was suitable for relocation of a child; however this is not the case and does produce concerns that the physical restraint procedures are not being implemented correctly.

Adequately controlled studies are a rarity in the field. A U.S. study has provided some data that may challenge the notion of the effectiveness of staff training in this area. A three-year project, evaluating the impact of a variety of training in five residential sites which catered for children with behavioural difficulties, reported a reduction in seclusion and mechanical restraints (CWLA, 2004). In the first year of the study over 300 days of support were provided to help services to establish training programmes. The rate of seclusion per 1000 patient days fell by 29%, from 16.7 incidents in 2002 to 11.9 incidents in 2003. One site eliminated seclusion, and another reduced its use by 99%. Mechanical restraint was used in one site only. Over the period of the study the use of mechanical restraint was reduced by 61%, with a total of 922 mechanical restraints being administered in 2002, which dropped to 361 in 2003. Physical restraint reductions were less impressive. One site managed to reduce physical restraint by 49%; the remainder managed to 'decrease their numbers of physical restraints marginally or experienced increases' (CWLA, 2004, p. 12).

This important multi-site study shows relatively modest effects of training programmes in reducing restrictive practices. Training may be necessary but not sufficient to achieve reductions in these practices. A follow-up of these programmes would provide more robust data. It is also difficult to evaluate the multiple components of training programmes in this study. Little information was provided about the specific content and emphasis of the programmes.

Training Staff in Low Arousal Approaches

Thirty-five care staff participated in the study of a childcare organization that provided residential placements for approximately 12 young people; this consisted of five homes in the community.

Two groups of care staff took part in the study: group one (consisting of three staff teams from three care homes for young people) received Studio3 training first, as it was deemed that this group was in more need of training because they were experiencing crisis situations more frequently with the young people they were caring for compared with group two. They completed 'fear', 'confidence' and 'perception of control' measures immediately before the training course and on completion of the course. At the same time as training group one attended the course a number of care staff from training group two completed the questionnaire measures and served as a 'waiting-list' control group.

The second group received Studio3 training three months after training group one, and again they completed the questionnaire measures immediately before and after the training course. At the same time a number of staff from group one completed the questionnaires again to provide the three-month follow-up data. Three months after group two had completed their training a number of staff also completed the measures to provide follow-up data for group two.

Three main measures were used in the study: a staff confidence scale (McDonnell, 1997); a 20-item measure of staff fear (Butt, 2004), which asks staff to rate specific physical behaviours in terms of their subjective fear; and the controllability belief scale (Dagnan, McDonnell & Grant, 2005), which is a 15-item scale examining carers' views about how much an individual is in control of their behaviour.

The result indicated that there was a significant inverse relationship between participants' confidence scores and their fear scores – as confidence scores increased fear scores decreased. No relationship between the confidence measure and the controllability belief scale was found. Likewise there was no relationship between the fear measure and the controllability belief scale.

An analysis of the intervention group scores indicated that staff acquired increased confidence immediately after training and that this affect was maintained at the three-month follow-up period. Similarly, staff fear was decreased as a consequence of training, which was again maintained at the three-month follow-up stage. Post-training participants also attributed less personal control to young people in reference to their challenging behaviour; however this was not maintained at the three-month follow-up stage. Surprisingly, group one's pre-training confidence scores when compared with the waiting-list control group scores showed that group one's scores were significantly lower. Further unpredictably, group one's post-training confidence scores compared with the waiting-list control group's scores illustrated no significant difference.

Twelve participants agreed to take part in an informal semi-structured interview at the three-month follow-up, focusing on what they could remember about the Studio3 training course, what techniques they had used since the course and how they thought the training could be improved. The staff interviews conveyed that the most remembered aspect of the training course was the role-play that took place at the end of the course (26%). This was followed closely by the walk-around technique (21%), along with the non-confrontational philosophy of managing challenging behaviour (21%).

Staff did appear to use low arousal approaches since the implementation of training. Praise, reward and distraction were the most frequent answers accounting for almost 50% of the total. Debriefing after incidents accounted for 20% of participants' responses, and not becoming confrontational when a young person is already angry also accounted for 20% of responses. Other techniques that had been used were discussing incidents when young people were calm (10%) and being aware of body language (5%).

Participants were asked if they had been required to use any of the physical interventions since attending the training course. The majority (79%) answered no to this question. Of the remaining 21% answered that the most frequently used technique was a simple blocking skill (75%), followed by grab releases (15%) and release from hair pull (10%).

The increases found in the confidence scores and the decreases found in the fear scores after training are consistent with previous research findings (Nunno et al., 2003; Perkins & Leadbetter, 2002; Titus, 1989). The explanation of this increase may be attributed to the Studio3 training that staff received, which provides further evidence (McDonnell, 1997) that Studio3 training can increase staff confidence levels, and with the increase in confidence a decrease in fear occurs. The maintenance of increased confidence and decreased fear levels may be credited to the training course; this enhances previous research (Perkins & Leadbetter, 2002) that also conveyed increases in confidence but did not specify if confidence levels were maintained at the follow-up stage. It may be that confidence and fear levels were retained because of the relatively short follow-up period. In addition it is noted that a number of staff left the service; subsequently it may be that the remaining staff were the more confident and consequently the less fearful members of staff.

The likely reason why the pre-training confidence scores of participants in group one were significantly lower than the waiting-list control group scores was that the needs of group one participants were considered priority prior to training, as they were experiencing increased crisis situations and more diffi-culty in managing challenging behaviour. In addition, group two was identified as experiencing less challenging situations; speculatively this may support the fear–confidence relationship found in this study. Staff may have been experi-encing less fearful situations and therefore had higher confidence levels and vice versa.

Low Arousal in Childcare: A Narrative Case Study

This case study is an unusual format, as it describes the experiences of a female staff member trained in the low arousal approach. She worked in a residential setting with a 15-year-old young man called Alan who showed very intense aggressive behaviours. He was physically a large and imposing young man. He had been moved to a children's home in the country hundreds of miles from his urban home. He had been expelled from many schools and had been involved in minor criminal activity. He had been moved from several children's homes because of his intense physical aggression and absconding. He had a negative relationship with his stepfather, and their arguments had led to physical violence in the past.

The narrative style of this case study is different from some of the case studies described in other chapters in this book. A member of staff submitted this study to a colleague of the author and said that she would, if possible, like it to be included in this book. The study is told in the first person by the team leader who realized how distressed and angry this young man was and that he posed serious risks to the staff team. His arousal levels were incredibly high when he arrived at the service. His verbal aggression and threatening behaviour were seen on an hourly basis. Physical aggression occurred daily and sometimes twice a day. Staff found that when they tried to hold him in an upright position such as the walk-around method (see Chapter 3) he would drop to the ground and almost place himself into a supine hold position. In these circumstances the staff would back off. The team leader's priority was to create a low-demand environment based on the low arousal philosophy. There was a major emphasis on developing a positive and trusting relationship with the young man. Critical to the approach was the strategy of avoiding the use of physical interventions.

Alan and Me

I remember the first day I met Alan, my handshake, my greeting, his urban street gear, his strength, unspoken aggression and swagger. He walked to the window and asked, 'Where are the streets, tall buildings? All these trees, fields – it's not right. Get me out of here'. He was definitely a kid who was used to urban life, a 'street-wise kid'.

Little by little in between the threats, damage and intimidation he started to give us small pieces of information. He was not important; it did not matter what happened to him. He knew the score as sure as birds fly and the tide goes in and out – threats, staff response, intimidation, staff response, more intimidation, staff response, physical threats, restraint and finally the floor, pinned down by three, sometimes four, staff and then nothing. A painful and perpetual circle that would never end. Sometimes he felt good with the predictability of his life despite the pain.

The depth of his knowledge of everyday matters sometimes shocked staff. He liked to discuss religion, his Catholic faith and his mother whom he loved to bits. But with disclosure came more anger and streams of verbal aggression; this was nearly always about his mother and would culminate in him targeting staff. In previous placements three or four staff sometimes had to pin him to the floor, across his chest, across his legs, arms out, arms in. It didn't matter – he still bit, spat, fought, swore, until he and they could take no more.

He was her own 'flesh and blood'; so why did she choose her new husband – a man who more often than not beat her in front of him – over him? He knew that he would never do this to his mother; he wanted to protect her, to love her, to care for her, to hurt the man who hurt her. With the confusion came emotions he didn't understand, a warrant to hate his mum, more confusion, more anger, more intimidation and, ultimately, more physical restraint.

He told me to telephone his social worker to get him out. He stepped not just close to me but right into my face. He stood close to me and threatened to get a knife and stab me. I couldn't break eye contact (even though I was trained to). I saw a very frightened young man where anger, aggression and more confusion were the only expectations. Slowly, calmly, I tried to explain that it wouldn't be easy to simply move him. I didn't touch him, even though I didn't want to lose him, and I didn't want to let him down. I wanted to show that I respected his feelings, that I cared, that I wouldn't give up.

I would often just quietly stand there. When I did not back away, threaten him with the police or call for help he slowly turned and faced the window. I saw his eyes fill with tears. He couldn't show me he was about to cry. All he would repeatedly say was 'Where's the city? Where's the city?' Chairs were banged but not thrown, a bit of face saving before he walked out, maybe choking back tears. I just let it go; he didn't expect that. I hadn't won; he hadn't lost; and we were still talking.

Next came the fire extinguishers – pretty good for putting out fires and damaging staff! Again I knew he was really angry. I looked in his eyes and could see him burning inside. I told him I knew that was what he was feeling but not why. If I tried to take the extinguishers off him I would cause a reaction; we would be 'out of the frying pan and into the fire'. But I felt he wouldn't follow through and hit me with it. So I waited and told staff not to intervene, not to restrain him. 'Back off! back off!' I would tell them. Better the window broken than bones broken. It became obvious that Alan did not seem to want to hurt us, but our approach did mean that he broke things in the house. In some way it almost helped him to calm down.

And over time restraint became the final hurdle. He expected it, needed it, maybe even welcomed it, but that's no way to live your life. We talked more and more, and I knew that my no restraint choice was the right choice. He told me how he felt that all his life had been worthless, how staff in other children's homes always took the easy option and restrained him rather than tried to understand him, how he had learnt to intimidate and push boundaries and how other's negative responses would justify his actions. He talked about being respected and trusted and of his difficulty in learning how to respect and trust.

Over time the physical restraint stopped being an option at all. I promised him that we would keep him safe and that we would not physically restrain him. Our increasingly positive relationship was working. I won't pretend it was always easy – he was still angry but never physically threatening. He destroyed quite a lot of things, but he always showed me respect; my office door was never locked, and he never entered without being asked even when he was angry. I smile when I remember him pacing outside when I was on the phone and recognized how he struggled but succeeded in waiting. We would sit in my office and have open and honest discussions. I was not afraid to be left alone. He told me that this was the first place that has ever shown him any respect and trust and had helped him break the vicious circle of aggression and restraint. He talked of the time he had to reflect and not just seethe about being restrained. Over time he began to understand the concept of choice and self-determination for better or worse. We all make decisions that may not always make sense to others or even ourselves – staff choose to restrain or not restrain, a mother chooses a husband even though he abuses, a young person decides to start talking or keep quiet.

I always told him to remember that he 'is a very important young man and that for young people to begin to trust anyone, they have to be shown respect and not simply be controlled or restrained because often young people don't learn anything from this. We are the adults. He is the damaged child. And it is our job to help him.'

Ultimately he had no real control over his life; nobody respected him; nobody thought his life was that important. Despite his size and aggression he was too easy to control and had never been given the chance to really change. I think we helped in a little way to change this. He cried the day he left and said he didn't want to go.

This case highlights a number of important issues when considering the behaviour management of children in care environments. First, there are clear implications that the reduction and avoidance of physical interventions is achievable with individuals who show extreme distress and physically aggressive behaviours. The young man in this example had been exposed to a variety of 'hold downs' in previous services, all of which eventually failed. In this real-life example physical interventions became the last resort. Alan was not restrained for property destruction or threatening behaviour. Therefore, staff were really only holding him using the Studio3 methods if he was directly aggressive with staff or other service users.

Second, there is a clear focus on the development of a positive relationship with the young person. A key element of this relationship involved trust, which is evidenced by the statement 'He told me that this was the first place that has ever shown him any respect and trust'. Third, the staff member had a person-centred and positive outlook about the young person. It is clear from the description that the staff member understood the young man's trauma. Fourth, staff were encouraged to withdraw from situations and reduce demands, exemplified by 'Back off! Back off! Better the window broken than bones broken'. In the author's view this really encapsulates the philosophy of a low arousal approach. The statement 'People matter more than property' is a central tenet of the approach. Fifth, staff showed some tolerance to behaviours such as property destruction and verbal abuse. Finally, the use of rules and boundaries (which are demands in themselves) were kept to a minimum. It is important to note that in this example there were some rules in place (knock on the office door, wait to be seen); the strategy of demand reduction, described in Chapter 2, should not be viewed as the eradication of all demands but as merely a reduction in these practices.

Conclusions

At the beginning of this chapter we described the case of Sarah. What can we say about the experiences of Sarah in a residential environment? The studies described in this chapter would appear to indicate that she could be exposed to practices such as restraint and seclusion (or mechanical restraint in the United States). The case of Alan does illustrate that in the right positive environment she could be in a position in which she could safely express her negative feelings in an atmosphere that actively encourages choice and empowerment. An understanding of negative life experiences and a tolerance of verbal aggression and property destruction are critical to an approach in which the development of positive trusting and empowering relationships are critical.

The management of Sarah's self-harm would present significant challenges to residential care staff. Madge and colleagues (2008) profiled females who primarily cut and did not take overdoses or attempt to kill themselves by other means. 'Among females, self-cutters were less likely than others to say they wanted to die or show how desperate they were feeling, but were more likely to say they wanted to punish themselves' (p. 674).

Staff might even consider the radical step of helping Sarah to harm in a safer and more controlled manner. In some situations this might involve applying ice cubes to her skin or making her pinch herself hard through to getting her to make small surface cuts with clean implements.

In conclusion, Sarah and many young people in her situation require staff to respond in a manner conducive to a low arousal approach. In Chapter 2 trauma-informed services were described as a critical element of the low arousal approach. Sarah is a victim of sexual abuse, and an understanding of her traumatic experiences will have a significant impact on behaviour management practices.

Developing Alternatives to Coercive Behaviour Management Approaches in Psychiatric Settings

Michael walks down his local high street muttering under his breath. He is well known to the people in his local community. Michael drinks alcohol in binges and has been known to regularly use cannabis. He has been detained in secure psychiatric services on two occasions totalling 18 months in the last 10 years. During these acute psychotic episodes he experienced hallucinations and episodes of aggression towards psychiatric staff. People in the neighbourhood perceive him as strange and eccentric. The public perception of psychiatric services is often influenced by powerful media imagery. In his book *One Flew Over the Cuckoo's Nest*, Ken Kesey portrayed the classic stereotypes of psychotic individuals as potentially violent with the indomitable nurse Ratchett behaving like an authoritarian concentration camp guard. The public stereotype of mental illness is strongly associated with violence. The killing of Jonathan Zito, an innocent member of the public, in 1991 by Christopher Clunis, a man with a history of psychiatric illness, shifted the emphasis from protection of people with mental illness to the safety of the public in the United Kingdom (Laurance, 2002). Managing Michael's behaviour presents significant challenges to mental health services, especially when he experiences an acute psychotic episode. This chapter will review the use of coercive practices primarily in hospital care settings and will provide evidence for low arousal approaches to manage these behaviours.

Mental Illness Diagnosis and Crime

A survey of 1444 U.S. citizens reported that people with alcohol or drug problems or schizophrenia are the ones most likely to be violent towards others

Managing Aggressive Behaviour in Care Settings: Understanding and applying low arousal approaches
By Andrew A. McDonnell © 2010 John Wiley & Sons, Ltd

(Pescosolido, Monahan, Link, Stueve & Kikuzawa, 1999). Most crimes are actually committed by people who are mentally well rather than those with a mental illness (Turgut, Lagace, Izmir & Dursen, 2006). A risk within a population is not the same as a risk to the population in general. Taylor and Gunn (1999) examined U.K. homicide rates recorded by the Home Office between 1957 and 1995. There was little fluctuation in the number of people with a diagnosed mental illness committing homicide; overall there was a 3% reduction over the time period. A review of the literature has indicated that individuals with schizophrenia may show an increased risk, especially if they are abusing substances or experiencing acute psychotic symptoms (Walsh, Buchanan & Fahy, 2002). Command hallucinations, especially voices which instruct a person to be violent, do appear to increase the risk of aggression (McNeil, Eisner & Binder, 2000). In sum, people with a mental illness should not be perceived as presenting an elevated risk to the general population as a whole. Specific behaviours such as acute psychosis, substance abuse and previous history of violence do elevate the risk of violence.

Rates of Violence and Aggression towards Mental Health Staff

Establishing the rates of aggression and violence has a number of methodological difficulties. Studies that tend to report verbal aggression tend to report higher rates than those that focus on physical aggression (Paterson & Leadbetter, 1999). Nurses are often exposed to verbal abuse in their day-to-day work (Paton, 2004). Verbal aggression is more common than physical violence (Duxbury, 2003; Paton, 2004). Around 80–90% of mental health nurses experienced verbal aggression over the period of one year (Nijman, Bowers & Oud, 2005).

Many studies use different definitions and different time periods (Nijman et al., 2005). A review of the literature concluded that general nurses were four times more at risk of assault than workers in general (Wells & Bowers, 2002). A U.K. survey of 74 psychiatrists and 301 mental health nurses indicated that the latter group were more likely to have experienced violence in the previous 12 months of work (Nolan, Dallender, Soares, Thomsen & Arnetz, 1999). The authors argued that the difference may have reflected the fact that nurses spend more of their day-to-day time with patients. A survey of 87 Irish mental health nurses reported that 80% of their sample had experienced non-threatening aggression and that 54% had experienced threatening aggression in the previous month at work; 38% of the sample reported mild physical violence (McQuire & Ryan, 2007). Great care should be taken when interpreting this study, as it had a low response rate of 31%, which would imply the possibility of response bias. Duxbury (2002) in her survey of psychiatric wards in the United Kingdom reported that 30% of incidents involved physical assault. Nursing staff do appear to be at an increased risk of physical aggression from people with mental illness in hospital settings. Quantifying the size of the risk is more difficult. Ryan and Bowers (2006) in a survey of incidents in a U.K. psychiatric service for adults found actual assaults on nurses to be relatively low in comparison with attempted assaults.

Physical Restraint

Ryan and Bowers (2006) investigated 403 restraint requests for a response team over a one-year period in a psychiatric service in the United Kingdom. Acute admission wards accounted for 46% of the incidents. Actual manual restraint occurred in half of the incidents; 52% of the responses involved reactions to sudden ward disruptions, and 48% of incidents appeared to be planned. The authors indicated that nearly half of the crisis responses were successfully resolved without manual restraint. Only two reports contained information on the duration of restraint (1 hour and 90 minutes). Oral or intramuscular medication was given in 51% of episodes. The main reasons for restraint were challenging behaviour (63%), agitated and chaotic behaviour (50%) and incidents involving people attempting to escape from the ward (26%).

Physical restraint is in use in psychiatric services (Whitington, Baskind & Paterson, 2007). Leggett and Silvester (2003) reported data about a 65-bed medium-secure psychiatric facility in the United Kingdom, where all physical restraint forms were reviewed over a four-year period. A total of 557 restraint forms were completed by 58 care staff. The mean length of a restraint episode was 12 minutes (range = 1–195); 58 incidents involved seclusion.

Injuries while participating on training courses for physical interventions do occur. A postal survey in U.K. secure facilities showed that a staggering 29% of nursing staff reported receiving injuries while participating in training courses, with 7% requiring medical attention (Lee et al., 2001). Another U.K. survey reported that 18.8% of staff reported injuries, with one in six requiring medical attention (Gournay, 2002). Leggett and Silvester (2003) reported 18.3% incidents of restraint involving minor physical injury (bruises, abrasions, small lacerations) to staff and 17.6% involving minor physical injury to patients. There were two incidents involving serious injury to patients and two involving injuries to staff. These were defined as large lacerations, fractures, loss of consciousness, need for special investigations and death.

In the United Kingdom the debate about the respective dangers of specific restraint holds is very prominent. Many training systems in the United Kingdom use 'floor restraint' methods (Leadbetter, 2002), and a potential hazard of this is 'positional asphyxia', where the person becomes unable to breathe, which causes respiratory and cardiac problems (Reay, Fligner, Stilwell & Arnold, 1992). The death of David 'Rocky' Bennett in 1998 in a secure psychiatric facility focused public attention on the problem in the United Kingdom. Mr Bennett was held for over 20 minutes in a prone position. This led to an inquiry which identified institutionalized racism as a factor which contributed to his death. The authors also recommended restriction of the use of prone restraint holds to a maximum of three minutes (Sallah, Sashidharan, Stone, Struthers & Blofeld, 2003). This recommendation was rejected by the U.K. Department of Health.

The argument about the specific dangers of restraint holds is coloured by a lack of research in this field (Allen, 2001). The Millfields Charter is a U.K. protest website which calls for a ban on the use of prone restraint holds in care environments. Its supporters argue for a ban on primarily moral and ethical grounds (McDonnell, 2007). Its critics have argued that bans on specific restraint holds do not address the key organizational factors which lead to restraint, and thus an emphasis on banning methods is primarily a reductionist argument (Leadbetter, 2007; Paterson, 2007).

Riley, Meehan, Whittington, Lancaster and Lane (2006) conducted a cross-sectional survey-design study, and data were obtained from a violence and aggression audit form completed by staff within 72 hours of an episode of patient aggression or self-harm. The survey found that prone restraint was significantly associated with the reports of the patient's imminent violence and high-intensity observation after the incident. Supine restraint was significantly associated with the patient being withdrawn and/or refusing to communicate prior to the episode and with a high severity incident rating after the incident. It was recommended that training programmes should create a sense that controlled descent to the floor is not inevitable.

Use of Seclusion

Rates of seclusion vary considerably from country to country (Whitington et al., 2007). A survey of acute-ward seclusion practices in Italy, Greece and the United Kingdom over a two-week period revealed that 5% of patients were secluded in the United Kingdom, 0% in Italy and 0.5% in Greece (Bowers et al., 2004). Meehan, Bergen and Feldsoe (2004) surveyed 29 inpatients and 60 nursing staff about the use of seclusion in an acute ward of a medium-secure facility in Australia. Both patients and staff agreed that seclusion had to be used some of the time. Only 4% of patients and 60% of staff believed the procedure to be beneficial. Furthermore, 68% of patients believed that refusal to take medication could result in seclusion being used, but 78% of staff believed that this would never be the case. The entire staff reported that seclusion had a calming and positive effect, compared with only half of the patients. Moreover, 2% of staff and 22% of patients reported that they wanted seclusion discontinued.

Child psychiatric services also report more positive views on seclusion from staff than from young people (Lebel et al., 2004). In a survey of a 65-bed medium-secure facility, females were found to be more likely to be secluded than males; however no clear rationale for this process was provided by the authors (Leggett & Silvester, 2003). In another study, 18% of emergency responses in incidents in a psychiatric service for adults in the United Kingdom resulted in seclusion (Ryan & Bowers, 2006).

It was found that in a child and adolescent psychiatry service in the United States 61% of children had experienced the process over a two-year period; many of the children who experienced seclusion were under 11 years of age (Donovan, Plant, Peller, Siegel & Martin, 2003a). To summarize, seclusion is a practice that is in regular use in adult and child psychiatric services around the world.

Mechanical Restraint

Mechanical restraint was defined by Sailas and Wahlbeck (2005) as the use of belts, handcuffs or any other device which restricts movement. The use of mechanical restraint in adult mental health services is a controversial subject. Mechanical restraint is not in regular use in U.K. services (Davison, 2005). During the Victorian era the United Kingdom led the world in initiatives to reduce the use of mechanical restraints in asylums: Robert Gardiner Hill abolished their use in the Lincoln Asylum; John Connolly introduced non-restraint to the Hanwell Asylum in 1839; claims were also made for the success of a non-restraint initiative at the Northampton Asylum by Thomas Prichard (Haw & Yorston, 2004).

There is considerable evidence that mechanical restraint is in use in a large number of countries. A recent review of coercive practices (Whittington et al., 2007) identified restrictive practices in 21 countries around the world, with 18 nations reporting the use of mechanical restraint either occasionally or widely in their services. Only three nations, namely Thailand, Iceland and Ireland, were believed not to use these practices. The reliability of this information may be questioned, as the authors classified the U.K. services as occasionally using such methods, which does not appear to reflect current practice.

There are cross-cultural differences in the day-to-day use of mechanical restraints across cultures. A study of seven German and seven Swiss psychiatric hospitals investigated the use of mechanical restraint over a one-year period. Mechanical restraint was defined as 'the use of belts to fix a patient to a bed'.

They reported that 6.6% of Swiss admissions and 10.4% of German admissions had experienced mechanical restraint. One Swiss hospital from the same study used no mechanical restraint (Martin, Bernhardsgrutter, Goebel & Steinert, 2007).

In the United Kingdom there is less acceptance of the use of mechanical restraints than in other European countries. Bowers and co-workers (2006) surveyed psychiatric nursing professionals in the United Kingdom, the Netherlands, Finland and Australia about their attitudes towards coercive practices including mechanical restraint. They found that U.K. nurses rated the use of mechanical restraint as less acceptable than their counterparts in the Netherlands and Finland. Mechanical restraint as a method of behaviour control remains controversial in day-to-day practice. In the United Kingdom there has been a call to reopen the debate about its usage in psychiatric services for adults by leading academic figures in psychiatric nursing (Batty, 2007). This has produced two main responses: the first cautiously makes the case to hold a public debate (Duxbury, 2007); the second describes this as a knee-jerk response by others (Bowers, 2007).

Staff Attitudes to Coercive Practices

The role of staff behaviour in the maintenance and cause of aggression has been investigated in this field. Morrison (1999) proposed a model of aggression and violence in psychiatry, which emphasized that people are more aggressive and violent when they are being 'controlled' by care staff. Whittington and Wykes (1996) interviewed psychiatric nurses within 72 hours of an assault: 86% of assaults appeared to have been preceded by aversive stimulation from nursing staff; 60% of incidents were preceded by staff approaching the person or initiating physical contact; 51% were the result of frustrating a person in their goals or refusing a request; 38% included requests to the person or demanding that they do certain activities. A review of the research of staff attitudes has highlighted that the majority of studies tend to focus on surveys rather than direct observations of behaviour. There is also a lack of valid measures (Jansen, Dassen & Groot Jebbink, 2005).

Duxbury (2002) investigated the views of 80 inpatients, 72 nurses and 10 medical staff about responses to aggression and violence over a six-month period. Using an attributional framework it was reported that there were clear discrepancies between the views of staff and patients. Nursing staff appeared to want practices such as seclusion to continue, whereas a significant number of patients did not. It was inferred that many of the nursing staff interviewed did not view the way they interacted with people with mental illness as contributing towards aggression. Inpatients viewed staff behaviour as having an effect on ward-based violence. Duxbury and Whittington (2005) in a survey of 80 inpatients and 82 psychiatric nursing staff reported that nurses tended to attribute the causes of aggression to mental illness rather than negative interactions.

Illkiw, Lavelle and Grenyer (2003) interviewed both staff and consumers in an psychiatric service for adults in Australia about their views on the causes on incidents. There were clear discrepancies between the groups about how aggression could be reduced in their wards. Improved handling of conflicts was identified as important by 64% of consumers and only 32% of staff. In contrast, 46% of staff and only 4% of consumers identified improved medical management as important. Furthermore, 32% of staff and 4% of consumers identified sufficient and appropriate medication as important. It would appear in these studies that the views of consumers and staff may differ considerably in terms of the management of aggression. The dilemma for practitioners and researchers is to achieve a balance between these views to help to develop more effective behaviour management strategies.

Spokes and colleagues (2002) interviewed 102 staff working in psychiatric acute admission, intensive care and low-secure units. Of the respondents 69% felt that some staff were assaulted more than others; 84% of respondents identified that their colleagues had weaknesses in managing violence. Interestingly, more than 80% respondents identified that their colleagues had contributed to an incident.

Nijman, Campo, Ravelli and Merckelbach (1999) described a model of inpatient aggression in which the consumer's psychopathology is exacerbated by environmental and communication stressors. The understanding of their own role by psychiatric staff in decreasing and increasing aggression is critical to the development of non-confrontational approaches. The evidence here suggests that there may be a need to assess the views of both staff and consumers about behaviour management practices.

Staff Training in the Management of Aggression

Control and restraint training was developed in the United Kingdom in 1981 in the prison service; this system has been expanded to cover health care establishments as well (Wright, 2003). The term 'control and restraint' is often used to describe specific training systems and is sometimes used as a collective term for a variety of systems (McDonnell & Gallon, 2006).

McDonnell and Gallon (2006) have described systems as either progressive or traditional. Progressive systems attempt to reduce the volume and type of physical interventions and also include emphasis on de-escalation. A survey conducted among U.K. psychiatric nurses about their experiences of training courses in managing violence that predominantly included control and restraint methods found that less than 21% had training in verbal 'defusion' skills (Wright et al., 2002). Traditional control and restraint training often uses a 'kitchen sink' approach (McDonnell & Gallon, 2006); that is to say large numbers of physical interventions are taught to staff to cater for a wide variety of situations. Anecdotal information strongly suggests that many staff have difficulty recalling the majority of these physical interventions.

There is a view that there is a good evidence base for control and restraint training (Wright, 2003; Wright, Gray, Parkes & Gournay, 2002). These claims would appear to contradict the established reviews in the field. Sailas and Fenton (1999) in their review of studies of physical restraint could find no properly controlled studies. The evidence base for staff training in physical interventions in general is relatively weak (Allen, 2001; McDonnell, Gould, Adams, Sallis & Anker, 2009; Morrison & Carney Love, 2003).

There are few training studies which examine the management of aggressive behaviour in psychiatric settings (Morrison & Carney Love, 2003). Many training studies do not report behavioural outcomes such as reduction in restraint usage (Delaney, 2006). A review of staff training which contained physical interventions identified 25 such studies in the adult psychiatric field (McDonnell, Gould, Butt & Sturmey, 2007). The majority of these studies had been conducted in North America. Nine of these studies made the limited criterion for an extended review. The only randomized control trial of staff training using a version of the control system in Switzerland produced no significant impact on ward-based violence (Needham et al., 2005). Increase in staff confidence after training was reported in some studies (McGowan, Wynaden, Harding, Yassine & Parker, 1999) but not in others (Hurlebaus, 1994; Hurlebaus & Link, 1997). Staff who received aggression management training reported lower rates of injury in the workplace, as well as lower assault rates (Infantino & Musingo, 1985), when compared with staff who had received training in emergency first aid (Carmel & Hunter, 1990). In contrast, assault rates actually increased after training in one study with high staff satisfaction with training at a 16-month follow-up (Rice, Helzel & Varney, 1985).

Philips and Rudestam (1995) reported a detailed observational analysis in which staff who received no training in physical interventions were compared with two groups that had been given either aggression management training or the same training with physical interventions. The authors found competence in physical interventions to be higher for the latter groups. Judges rated the participants' fear during a role-play test and found an inverse relationship between their ratings of physical competence and the observed fear in staff participants. It was also noted that staff who had received training in either aggression management or aggression management plus physical interventions reported 23% fewer incidents.

Interpreting literature with relatively poor levels of experimental control can produce a confirmation bias. It should be assumed that these studies represent research that had positive results; we have no way of knowing about studies with negative examples. To demonstrate this effect we have selected a recent study which would appear to present positive findings. However, closer scrutiny reveals a different perspective.

A study of three psychiatric units in the United States reported significant reductions in the rates of restraint usage (Jonikas, Cook, Rosen, Laris & Kym, 2005). Two elements of the programme included interviews with consumers to help to determine individual crisis plans and training in aggression management. Over a two-year period restraint was claimed to have reduced in all three areas: adolescent psychiatry (98%), general psychiatry (99%) and a clinical research unit (98%). This study typifies some of the difficulties in assessing the impact of training. First, it is difficult to assess the effects of the independent components of training. Second, there was no adequate control group. Third, the rates of restraint usage were measured by the quarterly number of hours spent in restraint and the number of patient days. It is possible that without adequate comparison with other services the relative decrease and therefore the size of the effect may be quite small. Finally, no clear description was provided of the training. While uncontrolled studies in our view should not be ignored, great care should be taken to negatively weigh such findings.

Most of the training described in this section tends to focus on both theoretical aspects of aggression management and physical interventions. There is some evidence that only training in defusion skills can reduce the risk of assaults on staff. Whittington and Wykes (1996b) reported on a one-day training course for psychiatric staff that emphasized the verbal and non-verbal behaviour of staff. This staff group showed a 31% reduction in reported assaults. Another study (Whittington & Wykes, 1996a) showed that in a particular psychiatric hospital, 86% of assaults on staff were preceded by something aversive such as a demand to or a perceived attack by the consumer. The implications of this research are that defusion skills should be a core component of any training system, as they appear to have the potential to dramatically reduce incidents.

Training courses can attempt to alter staff attitudes. Middleby-Clements & Grenyer (2007) in a pre–post design evaluated the impact of two training programmes in the management of aggression. The courses were identical except one training group emphasized zero tolerance to aggression. Both training courses showed improvements in confidence and skills. The zero-tolerance group reported lower tolerance levels to aggression and more rigid attitudes after training. This study would have been greatly enhanced by behaviourally observing staff interactions in situ. This study is significant, as it emphasizes the subtle negative impact that training could have on participants. A Swiss study compared the attitudes of 29 nurses who attended a five-day workshop in the management of aggression with 34 controls. No changes in attitude were found between the two groups (Hahn, Needham, Abderhalden, Duxbury & Halfens, 2006). These studies indicate that caution should be exercised when assuming that attitudes can be changed by staff training in the management of aggression. Attitudes and capabilities of trainers on training programmes in the management of aggression may have a significant impact on outcomes.

Studies of the outcomes of staff training present a grim picture of the current state of knowledge. Practices would appear to evolve not from a scientific evidence base but from a practitioner perspective. Paterson (2006) maintained that local values and cultural tradition accounted for the variation in restraint usage across European psychiatric services. There has been a lack of outcome evaluation among training organizations (Beech & Leather, 2005). The worrying conclusion is that staff are trained in methods based on crude evidence (McDonnell et al., 2007).

Reducing Coercive Practices

The reduction of practices such as restraint and seclusion in psychiatric services has been a goal of both researchers and practitioners. The poor quality of living environments can lead to overcrowding among potentially distressed and traumatized individuals. There is a modest association between overcrowding and aggression in psychiatric services for adults (Nijman & Rector, 1999). There is little evidence in the literature that examines changes in living environment in any detail. Better-quality standards in living environments are acknowledged to be important (Huckshorn, 2004). A more immediate strategy to reduce restraint, seclusion and other coercive practices involves an organizational approach.

A good indicator that organizational culture can have an effect on these practices has been reported in a study conducted in Australia (Daffern, Mayer & Martin, 2003). Two acute wards reported dramatically different rates of seclusion despite the similarity of the populations. This study raises important issues about the 'postcode lottery' in psychiatric services (Whittington et al., 2007). Curie (2005) outlined the role of organizational culture in the reduction of seclusion and restraint: 'Success begins with a change in culture from one of power to one of empowerment from coercion to caring and from hopelessness to hope' (p. 1139).

There is a growing body of evidence which is identifying the themes common to organizational programmes for the reduction of restraint and seclusion. Highly effective and visible leadership has been identified as a key component, much as good-quality measures and individualized seclusion and restraint reduction plans are (Huckshorn, 2004). Observation of individuals may also be a factor in reducing the need for restraint and seclusion (Whitington et al., 2007).

D'Orio, Purselle, Stevens and Garlow (2004) described a restraint and seclusion reduction approach in a U.S. psychiatric emergency hospital. A multidisciplinary safety committee was organized to develop a reduction plan and increase hospital compliance with seclusion and restraint procedures. The approach included monitoring of restraint and seclusion usage, improved crisis communication, staff training in the management of violence with an emphasis on verbal de-escalation skills and an increase of video surveillance. Improved compliance with restraint and seclusion methods was reported along with a reduction of restraint and seclusion usage by 39% over a two-year period.

Donat (2003) analysed a five-year restraint and seclusion reduction programme in a public psychiatric hospital in Virginia. In the first year of the programme restraint and seclusion usage averaged 1244 hours per month; the average monthly figures dropped to 314 hours during the final year. The strategy consisted of five components: First, the criterion for case review were changed from six applications or 72-hour duration within a monthly period in the first year to two applications or eight-hour duration in a week by the end of the project. Second, changes in the membership of a review committee were made. Third, a behavioural consultation team was developed. Fourth, behavioural assessment and plans were enhanced. Finally, staff consumer ratios were increased. A regression analysis revealed that the most significant factor implicated in the reduction process was the process for reviewing and monitoring cases.

Restraint reduction programmes can also have side effects. Donovan and colleagues (2003) reported a prevalence study over a two-year period in a U.S. psychiatric hospital for children. The total number of incidents decreased by 26% and their duration by 38%. The authors noted that staff injuries did not increase, whereas patient injuries did. As needed medications also increased over the period of the study. This study identifies that a broad range of variables require measurement to evaluate the effectiveness of reduction in coercive practices. It is possible that reductions in one method may be inversely correlated with increases in others.

Systematic attempts to reduce restraint in statewide child psychiatric services have also been reported (Lebel et al., 2004). One such multi-layered approach involved the development of individualized crisis prevention plans, increased monitoring of the levels of restraint and seclusion, raising awareness of the programme by means of structured discussions and conferences and the development of their own strategic reduction plans by individual services. Data were gathered using a one-year baseline and a 22-month intervention period. Incidents of restraint and seclusion in services for children (aged 5–12 years) decreased from 84.03 to 22.78 episodes per 1000 consumer days (72.9%), in adolescent units from 72.22 to 37.99 episodes (47.4%) and in mixed child/adolescent units from 73.37 to 33.08 episodes (59%).

Behavioural interventions may also have an impact in the reduction of restraint and seclusion. There has been an emphasis on the use of behavioural programmes to enhance treatment efficacy in psychiatric services (Corrigan &

Liberman, 1994). Two key factors are the improvement of staff knowledge of behavioural interventions and the creation of an environment that enhances the application of skills (Donat, 2005). The individual application of functional analytic approaches can have significant impact in this regard. Bisconer, Green, Mallon-Czaijka and Johnson (2006) reported the implementation of a behavioural intervention plan using an 'AB design' on a 40-year-old man with a history of aggression towards others and self. A functional assessment indicated that his behaviours served multiple functions, which included avoidance of staff, peers or tasks, perceiving that peers were bothering him and an inability to communicate his thoughts or needs. Target behaviours included more positive communication, completing daily activities and asking for breaks from activities. He received additional reinforcement for achievement of goals. All staff received training to help them to recognize and reward target behaviours. There was a three-month baseline which was followed by a 33-month intervention period. Reductions in aggression and the application of restraint were reported, although the behaviour was not completely eradicated.

In conclusion, it is difficult to establish the specific effects of the elements of restraint reduction initiatives. The review of cases and the application of behavioural technology and programme leadership would appear to be strongly associated with positive outcomes. The next section will describe a single case study which identifies the role of non-confrontational strategies in the management of difficult behaviours in an adult with a psychiatric diagnosis.

A Low Arousal Intervention

Alice was 46 years of age. She had a confused mixture of diagnoses including depression and borderline personality disorder. She had resided at a psychiatric hospital for over 14 years. Prior to her admission Alice had been married and had lived with her partner for eight years. They had one child, Serena. The relationship was tumultuous, and at times her husband was both physically and sexually violent. During this time Alice was admitted to a psychiatric unit, apparently suffering from a 'nervous breakdown'. She received primarily drug-based treatment during this time.

After seven months Alice returned home, where the relationship with her husband still continued to deteriorate. At this time Alice began to suffer from a variety of illnesses, and on a weekly basis she would attempt to get herself admitted to a general ward at the local hospital. She would often present with a variety of complaints including upset stomachs, a rapidly beating heart and elevated temperature. The causes of these problems were difficult to determine. Staff reported that she visibly relaxed after admission to a general medical ward. As the admissions became more frequent, staff at the hospital began to become more aggressive with Alice. This did not appear to decrease her rate of presentation. Within two months Alice's complaints became more extreme in nature. She began to tell staff that she had taken overdoses, usually of pain relief medicine. This escalated to her burning herself on the wrists and arms. Alice also began to swallow objects such as cigarette lighters and household keys to get admitted. Exasperated by her behaviour some of the local hospitals banned her from their premises.

Social workers began monitoring seven-year-old Serena. Her attendance at school was erratic, and she was prone to illnesses, particularly stomach upsets. A multidisciplinary meeting decided that there was a real risk that her mother was making her daughter unwell to gain access to medical services. The term 'Munchausen syndrome by proxy' was used at the meeting, but it was agreed that this should not be recorded directly in her notes. These professionals were concerned that they did not have enough evidence to overtly make this diagnosis.

Three months later Alice was readmitted to a secure psychiatric facility after swallowing a large quantity of detergent. Serena was placed in a foster facility, where she remained until adulthood. Over the years the relationship between mother and daughter had become strained. Serena was uncomfortable with the stigma that her mother was a psychiatric inpatient at an infamous local psychiatric hospital. On one occasion her mother turned up at her place of work to find out why she was not contacting her. Phone calls to Serena at work from Alice persisted. This led to an argument between the two in front of Serena's office staff, which ultimately led to Serena changing jobs.

Alice stayed at the psychiatric hospital for nearly 14 years. Her attempts to be admitted for surgery were still occurring on a weekly basis. Alice, who was a heavy smoker, set fire to her nightdress, which culminated in severe burns to her body. Her multidisciplinary team could not determine whether this was a deliberate or an accidental act. An attempt was made to place her in a community psychiatric hostel environment on three occasions. All of these attempts were unsuccessful. Alice's hospital admissions increased to daily occurrences, culminating in her readmission to a general psychiatric ward. It was noted by staff at this time that her self-care and general domestic skills had deteriorated so that she did not wash regularly or prepare basic meals. Her team concluded that Alice was becoming more and more institutionalized.

There was a lack of provision of individualized community services in the field of adult mental health. Alice was referred to a community-based service which catered for individuals with intellectual disabilities and dual diagnoses. This service had considerable success developing individualized services for people with severe challenging behaviours. After an initial assessment period it was determined to place Alice in a group situation with people with borderline intellectual disabilities. Alice would receive 24-hour one-to-one staffing. At first she would be living in the house on her own, and over time three other individuals would be moved in. The central premise was to get Alice to interact with other individuals.

All staff were trained in low arousal approaches and received monthly group supervision which primarily focused on a person-centred approach to the management of Alice's behaviour. In these sessions staff were actively encouraged to problem-solve and express their own anxieties about working with this woman. The primary emphasis was for staff to develop a positive relationship with Alice. Her need for admission to the hospital was deemed to serve the following functions: First, Alice had genuine health-related problems primarily caused by years of smoking and neglect. Staff speculated that there were times when she admitted herself to the hospital because she genuinely believed herself to be seriously ill. Second, Alice appeared to show symptoms of PTSD. Her abusive history and unresolved issues from her past made her sleep pattern erratic. It was noted that Alice often sought hospital admission either late in the evening or at night. Third, a series of punitive consequences had been used with her by a variety of hospital services; all of these had appeared to be unsuccessful.

Alice's behaviour management plan involved the minimization of reactions by staff to her requests to go to the hospital. Staff were told to stress that they would meet her request and that she was not to get anxious. Where necessary, staff would attend the visit with her and stay with her if she were admitted. Staff were encouraged to actively engage Alice in positive non-health-related behaviours on a daily basis. It was stressed to her staff team that this was not 'giving in' but creating a new approach from Alice's perspective.

Within two weeks of attending her service Alice told a staff member that she had swallowed a lighter and needed to be admitted to the hospital. The staff member took her to the hospital, where Alice requested to be admitted to a general ward. Alice returned home two days later, and it was explained to her that the next time she felt that she needed to go to the hospital she should tell staff who would meet her request without any need for her to harm herself. The staff team also stressed that it understood her need to feel safe. Staff also decided to visit her local psychiatric hospital as part of a structured routine in the hope that this would help to break the pattern of only visiting the service after claiming to be ill.

Alice continued to attend hospital services almost on a daily basis for approximately two weeks. Each time, she requested admission. A breakthrough occurred one night when Alice returned in a taxi to her home. This pattern has continued for the last five months. Alice's frequency of hospital attendance has reduced by over 50%, and the duration of her stays averages three to four hours. There have been few overnight stays. We have also noted that Alice perceives her small staff team as her support staff, and she appears to understand that their role is to advise her and not to use coercion.

Her staff team have reported significant positive changes in their relationship with Alice. A key facet of the approach has required their willingness to resist attempting to control her or use punitive consequences to manage her behaviour. Staff members have reported that sometimes they do feel that they are giving in to Alice, which is not uncommon when adopting a low arousal approach (McDonnell et al., 1998). At the time of writing, Alice was continuing to make progress.

A Staff Training Approach

Can low arousal strategies be applied in mental health settings? A health care trust in the United Kingdom reviewed its control and restraint training programme and decided that this management technique was too stringent for the majority of the service users. It was deemed unsuitable for individuals with enduring mental illness and services for older adults. A number of staff had raised concerns about their previous training experiences in a variety of control and restraint training courses. There were many reservations about the physical interventions taught on standard training courses within the service. Key criticisms of the physical interventions that had been previously taught included the following: many physical interventions required the deliberate infliction of pain to achieve behavioural control; the methods were potentially open to abuse; and additionally, the issues of skill retention and a lack of emphasis on defusion skills were present. A training course using Studio3 methods, originally developed for people with learning disabilities, was considered for adaptation to mental health services (McDonnell, 1997).

This training was required for a unit called the Watermill Unit. It was composed of three acute admission wards (each with 25 beds), a ward for people with challenging behaviour (12 beds), an assessment ward for older people with organic mental health problems and day therapy staff. Before a course could be put together, various factors needed to be taken into account. These were the existing courses, the type of challenging behaviours encountered and their frequency and the problems with current control and restraint training.

In June 1994 a three-day course in managing challenging behaviour was attended by members of the mental health service to determine whether the approach could be developed for their services. This course was aimed at people with learning disabilities and was run by Studio3 training systems. The mental health staff feedback was positive. From March to July 1995 two practice development workshops were carried out with staff from the Watermill Unit. Approximately 20 multi-disciplinary staff including nurses, occupational therapists, physiotherapists, doctors, commissioners and trade union representatives attended each of these workshops. Within these workshops a survey was conducted to establish the types and frequency of challenging behaviours typically encountered. This revealed that approximately 70% of assaults were a punch or a slap to the head/face; 10% were a kick to the legs; and 20% were a push or strike to the chest or trunk.

Themes emerged from the workshops. Control and restraint was regarded by the majority of staff as being 'over the top', on the basis of on the pain caused and openness to abuse. Too many physical intervention skills were often taught (the kitchen sink approach), which are unlikely to be remembered after a brief course (McDonnell & Gallon, 2006). Other factors discussed were the number of injuries received in the control and restraint training, Home Office approval for certain methods, litigation and deaths. Based on this information a training course was produced that catered to Watermill's service needs.

The training course

From May 1996 to April 1997, the three-day training courses on the management of challenging behaviours were attended by staff. All nursing and occupational staff were invited to attend the training courses, and two consultant medical staff were also included. There were follow-up days from August to December 1997 and in June 1998. The content of the three-day course was as follows: an introduction to the law in relation to the health care services, qualitative differences in challenging behaviour, an introduction to the causes of challenging behaviour, defusing violent behaviour and low arousal approaches (McDonnell, McEvoy & Dearden, 1994). This involved staff analysing persistent areas of confrontation, reducing staff demands in a crisis, reducing other environmental demands wherever possible, examining cues and triggers that staff may be inadvertently using (touch, speech, space), challenging staff beliefs about the causes of challenging behaviour and developing reactive plans, coping with the trauma, debriefing staff and behaviour management versus behaviour change. This refers to the fact that it is often the safest option to not try and change people's behaviour in the short term and instead manage their behaviour safely and see behaviour change as a long-term goal.

On the second day of the training course non-violent physical skills were taught to staff which included hair pulling, airway protection, giving assistance to other staff members who are having their hair pulled or are being slapped and punched. Trainers combined the low arousal approach with non-violent physical skills using role-play scenarios. The course trainers portrayed a person who presented with verbal and physical aggression, and the staff trainees applied both verbal de-escalation and physical skills. The final day of the training consisted of teaching restraint skills. There was an introduction to a two-person chair restraint as an alternative to prone or supine holds (McDonnell, Sturmey & Dearden, 1993). All staff had to pass a restraint role-play at the end of the training course. Moreover, the social validity of physical restraint procedures was discussed.

Outcomes

Three measures were used to evaluate the outcomes of the training course. A 15-item confidence scale (see McDonnell, 1997), which measures the staff's perception of their ability to manage challenging behaviour, was administered both before and after training. A six-item follow-up questionnaire was administered after one-day follow-up training, which occurred approximately one year after the initial training. This included questions about the usefulness of the training and the use of physical techniques. Along with this, the incident levels in the service were examined.

A scale to measure the confidence in managing challenging behaviour that was developed in services for people with intellectual disabilities (McDonnell, 1997) was administered. Over six courses there were 108 staff members (76 female, 32 male) who filled out the scale before and after training. All showed statistically significant improvement after training ($t = 3.75$, $p < .05$, $df = 107$). Males reported higher confidence levels than females both before and after training. Finally, no staff injuries leading to time off work by course participants were reported on any of the training courses.

There were 59 questionnaires fully completed and returned. The majority of the staff reported that the course was useful in their day-to-day work. The parts of the course that they saw as being most useful in everyday work were information about the causes of challenging behaviour (97%), the low arousal approach (98%) and reactive planning (76%). Other areas such as debriefing (64%) and the law (47%) were also deemed as being useful. Theoretically this supports the value of a course that teaches more than just physical skills, as staff regard these practices as useful in their day-to-day work.

Few of the 59 staff had to use any of the physical interventions after training (being punched in the face = 14 cases; being strangled from the front = 1 case; hair pulling = 4 cases; being strangled from behind = 1 case). The most commonly used skill was a defence from a punch to the face, although most of the skills did not need to be used. A total of 64% of staff reported that they had to use a physical intervention procedure, the majority of which involved a two-person escort technique; 73% of staff reported that the chair restraint method was a viable alternative to more traditional prone and supine holds; 80% of the staff reported that the training course was a viable alternative to control and restraint training.

It had been identified at the practice development workshops that 70% of reported assaults at this unit were a punch or slap to the head or face. As expected, the most commonly used physical skill was the response to being punched in the face. Nevertheless, the majority of responses showed that most people had not had to use most of the skills trained (countering being punched in the face, being strangled from the front and having hair pulled from the front and airway protection).

The restraint procedure taught to staff was a chair restraint. The majority of staff felt that this was a practical and acceptable solution, with 73% stating that they thought that the chair restraint could be used on a psychiatric population. However, 3% said it could not be used, and 22% said they did not know how to use it.

The incident levels at three years and nine months after training were analysed in a service audit. Despite teaching far fewer physical interventions there were no significant increases in assault, with minor injuries to staff reported after training. Minor assaults without injuries showed a modest decline. Major assaults also remained low throughout the period. Threatening behaviour initially increased and then decreased below baseline levels over the time period.

There were no reported injuries during the training courses. There is evidence that staff have been injured on training courses (Lee et al., 2001) and in the workplace when using restraint techniques (Leggett & Silvester, 2003). This result is very positive, especially as the training was conducted in a non-matted area. The lack of increase in staff injuries in the workplace is important, as the there were nearly 60% fewer physical interventions taught to care staff compared with their previous training. Because of this there was a real fear that equipping staff with fewer physical interventions could lead to an increase in staff injuries in the workplace. Finally, the rates of using breakaway skills were extremely low. This may call into question the merits of teaching these procedures.

Conclusions

This chapter described the case of Michael, a man who may well be detained again at some time in the future. Contrary to public stereotypes his mental illness only slightly increases the likelihood of aggressive behaviour. His abuse of both alcohol and cannabis significantly increases the risk of aggressive behaviour. It also increases the likelihood of an acute psychotic episode which could lead to an admission to a secure psychiatric facility. Once he arrives at a facility Michael may be at risk of physical restraint, seclusion and even mechanical restraint. His behaviour management will depend on numerous organizational factors, most importantly the service ethos and attitudes of staff to coercive practice. Training in non-confrontation and the adoption of low arousal strategies are possible to deliver in psychiatric services.

8

Low Arousal Approaches in Care Environments for Older Adults

Dorothy was 84 years old and resided in a residential care home called Happy Acres. She had her own room and hated being placed in the day area with other residents whom she viewed as having far more problems than she did. Dorothy used to be a head teacher, and she was accustomed to being in control of her environment. She liked things to be done as quickly as possible, and she loathed being made to wait.

Many of the younger staff did not particularly like working with Dorothy because she had an offhand manner. Dorothy often made patronizing comments and showed verbally aggressive behaviour such as swearing and criticizing staff. Younger staff found this difficult to deal with in a calm and professional manner. Dorothy complained about many things, such as her tea being cold and her room not being cleaned. It was not unusual to have 10–15 complaints in a typical working day. When she got angry she started to swear and insult staff. On one occasion she slapped a staff member across the face.

Dorothy's case is not unusual. In the Western world there has been a consistent increase in the older adult population. In the United States alone people over 65 years of age are the fastest growing group of the population (Stevens et al., 1999). There are increasing demands on resources for the care of older adults.

Older adults are a vulnerable population, and acts of abuse in care homes and other settings do happen. In 1999 28-year-old Simon Hack, a care worker in the United Kingdom, was jailed for four years after admitting to a series of abusive acts towards older adults in his care in the 1980s and 1990s. Abuse may not necessarily be physical; a recent study in Germany highlighted that the regular use of chairs, tables and side rails was both a human rights and an abuse

Managing Aggressive Behaviour in Care Settings: Understanding and applying low arousal approaches
By Andrew A. McDonnell   © 2010 John Wiley & Sons, Ltd

issue (Bredthauer, Becker, Eichner, Koczy & Nikolaus, 2005).This chapter will examine the application of low arousal methods to this population. We will examine the following areas: the nature and frequency of aggressive behaviours in elderly populations, the issues surrounding the use of mechanical restraints, the reduction of restrain usage and the use of person-centred approaches. Staff training in behaviour management will be examined with both a group-based and an individual case example.

Aggressive Behaviour in Services for Older Adults

There is evidence which specifically focuses on aggressive behaviour among older adults. There are a number of studies which report associations between organic brain damage and aggressive behaviour in older adults (Pulsford & Duxbury, 2006).

People with dementia in care homes can present significant challenges to staff, and behaviours such as aggression, screaming, restlessness, agitation and wandering are a frequent reason for referral to specialist mental health services for older people (Turner, 2005). Aggressive behaviours in older adults are difficult to accurately estimate in terms of prevalence (Pulsford & Duxbury, 2006).

A study in Norway monitored aggressive behaviour using the Staff Observation Aggression Scale–Revised (SOAS-R) in two nursing homes and two geriatric psychiatric wards for a period of three months. During the study period 32 out of the 82 patients were reported to be violent. The majority of the incidents were caused by a small minority of the patients. Physical injury to the staff as a consequence of the aggression was extremely rare. Situations in which the client was denied something were the most provocative ones. The authors concluded that personal care situations appeared to be a positive risk indicator (Almvik, Rasmussen & Woods, 2006).

In Australia a study of 11 nursing homes using two common screening tools identified both aggressive and non-aggressive populations. Aggression was associated with younger males in the sample. Psychotropic medications, such as benzodiazepines, and neuroleptic medications were extensively employed (Shah, Chiu, Ames, Harrigan & McKenzie, 2000). In another study conducted in a secure facility for older adults, people on lower levels of antidepressants were associated with lower physical aggression scores (Ryden et al., 1999).

In a cross-sectional study conducted in a sample of 1322 demented patients living in 59 special care units for dementia, Zuidema, Derksen, Verhey and Koopmans (2006) estimated the prevalence of neuropsychiatric symptoms among dementia patients in Dutch nursing homes. Symptoms were observed by licensed vocational nurses during regular caregiving in a two-week observational period: More than 80% of these individuals presented agitation/aggression, apathy and irritability; 85% of the patients showed at least one symptom of agitation, of which general restlessness was observed most frequently (44%). Other frequently observed symptoms with prevalence rates of 30% were swearing or verbal aggression, constant requests for attention, negativism and repetitive sentences, mannerisms, pacing and complaining. Physically aggressive symptoms such as hitting, kicking and biting occurred less often (in less than 13% of the cases). Testad, Aarsland and Aarsland (2007) studied 211 older adults in four Norwegian nursing homes. Of their sample 79% had a diagnosis of dementia, and weekly ratings of agitation occurred in 75% of the entire sample. Agitated behaviours which include aggressive behaviours would appear to be a significant problem in services for older adults. The severity of cognitive decline is strongly associated with agitated behaviours (Beck et al., 1998). The decline of cognitive functioning and the associated behavioural difficulties do demonstrate a clear need for effective behaviour management strategies.

Mechanical Restraints

Problems of definition

Studies in the care of the elderly often confuse the use of mechanical and physical restraint (Gallinagh et al., 2002). In the United States the use of limb and vest restraints are more common than in the United Kingdom (Minnick, Mion, Leipzig, Lamb & Palmer, 1998). The use of cot sides is included in some studies and not others. Studies in this chapter tend to focus on mechanical restraints. It is difficult to ascertain the nature and usage of physical restraint in services for older adults. These definitional issues can have an impact on interpreting studies. In their naturalistic survey the areas in which lowest restraint use was reported did not take into account tray, table, tub chairs and beanbags (O'Connor et al., 2004).

A 24-month audit of restraint and seclusion in five inpatient units for older adults in Australia reported significant variation from service to service in monthly figures ranging from 0 to 59.1% (O'Connor et al., 2004). In their naturalistic observation study, seclusion was not used on two out of five wards, and monthly seclusion rates varied from 0 to 13.8 episodes.

A Norwegian study defined mechanical restraints separately from other forms of restraint and included bed rails and being strapped to beds and chairs in its definition (Kirkevold, Sandevik & Engedal, 2004). The use of mechanical restraint was investigated over a seven-day period by interviewing staff on 222 wards. In their sample of 1362 people 23% had received mechanical restraints in regular elderly units. The rate was 14.4% in special care units. In a postal survey of 285 directors of Australian services, which supported 16,397 older adults, 15.2% of the sample admitted to being restrained. The most commonly used restraints included restraint vests (25.3%), restraint belts (18.9%), bed rails (17.2%), lap trays (14.4%) and geri chairs (10.5%) (Retsas & Crabbe, 1998). In their sample of 116 residents who were rated as aggressive in a secure unit in North America, Ryden and colleagues (1999) found that 47% of participants had been restrained.

A small cross-cultural survey of 39 nurses from the United Kingdom and 11 nurses from Greece (Molasasiotis & Newell, 1996) indicated that mechanical restraints appeared to be an accepted practice in both countries. All of the Greek sample and 43% of the U.K. nurses reported using such restraints. In the U.K. sample, cot sides/bed rails accounted for the vast majority of restraint usage. Usage of these devices in general hospitals in the United Kingdom has been reported to be between 14.5% and 61.3% (Mildner, Snell, Arora, Sims & Wales, 2003). All of the Greek nurses and 22 of the U.K. sample reported that there was no increase in injury to people to whom restraints had been administered (Molassiotis & Newell, 1996). In an eight-country cross-cultural survey which investigated trunk, limb and chair restraints considerable variation was reported. Participants from Japan, Denmark and Iceland reported that less than 9% of their sample had been restrained; 15–17% of the users had been restrained in France, Italy, Sweden and the United States; and the Spanish services reported the highest figure at 40% (Ljunggren, Philips & Sgadari, 1997).

A larger observational study conducted in four rehabilitation wards in Northern Ireland reported that 68% of the people observed were subjected to mechanical restraints, the most commonly used form being side rails (Gallinagh et al., 2002). In sum, there would appear to be good evidence for relatively high uses of mechanical restraints in several international studies (Ljunggren, Philips & Sgadari, 1997; Molassiotis & Newell, 1996; Retsas & Crabbe, 1998).

If mechanical restraint is in common use in services, what are the factors which have an impact on its use? There are a number of characteristics that are common among residential homes which are reported to have high mechanical restraint usage. An observational study of residential homes in California revealed three key findings. First, residents in high-restraint homes were observed to be in bed in the day more than the people in low-restraint care homes. Second, higher usage of bed rails was observed in high-restraint homes compared with low-restraint homes. Third, staff helped less with feeding in high-restraint homes (Schnelle et al., 2004).

Karlsson, Bucht, Eriksonn and Olof Sandman (2001) in a Swedish study investigated factors which appeared to determine restraint usage. The authors only included procedures which restrict movement, and therefore they excluded cot sides from their analysis. They classified wards as 'restraint free', 'low use' and 'high use'. Overall, 24% of their sample had been subjected to restraint in the previous week. Environmental characteristics and staffing ratios did not appear to predict restraint use. Two variables did appear to account for low usage of restraints. First, the dependency level of the person was associated with restraint use. People who required more help in terms of dressing and self-care skills were more likely to be in the high-restraint category. This is consistent with cross-cultural research in which the level of cognitive impairment and physical dependency predicted restraint usage (Ljunggren, Philips & Sgadrai, 1997). Second, the knowledge levels of staff about restraint were higher in restraint-free wards. Finally, physically abusive behaviour was more common in the high-restraint-use wards. It is not possible to test whether restraint usage is causal in this instance, but the association appears to be quite strong.

A common rationale for using restraints is to prevent older adults from hurting themselves by falling. One U.S. estimate claims that nearly half of the residents in care homes will experience a fall at some time in their lives (Hill-Westmoreland & Gruber-Baldini, 2005). However, there are studies which appear to indicate that falls may actually increase after restraint is implemented (Shore et al., 2002).

Overt signs of distress do appear to be associated with restraint use. Rateau (2000) observed five people who had been mechanically restrained after hip surgery for six 20-minute time periods over a maximum of three days. She observed confusional states marked by behaviours such as slurred speech, dis-orientation to time and forgetfulness. The author implied that the application of restraints might have heightened these experiences. The lack of a control group makes it difficult to conclude that the confusional states were exacer-bated by mechanical restraints, although there would be appear to be a strong association between the two.

Reducing restraints

There is some evidence that the use of restraints is being reduced in care settings (Strumpf, Evans, Wagner & Patterson, 1992). Educational programmes have been the major target of intervention strategies. Using a pre–post design and a half-day educational programme two facilities developed their own restraint reduction plans. A key component of these plans was to target specific individuals for whom there was high usage of restraints. In the design, post-test data were collected one year after implementation, and 118 out of 144 people were found to be completely free of bed and chair restraints at the post-test stage (Ejaz, Folmar, Kaufmann, Rose & Goldman, 1994). In a U.S. service 90% reduction in restraint usage was reported over a two-year period after the imple-mentation of a staff education programme (Dunbar, Neufeld, White & Libow, 1996).

A two-year restraint reduction programme in a 226-bed long-term residence in the United States reported zero restraint usage. Significant reduction in falls was also reported over the same time period (Battar & Nichols, 2004).

What can be concluded about the use of mechanical restraints? Great care should be taken when making recommendations for the use of any restrictive procedure, as restraint-free services are the desirable goal (Dunbar et al., 1996). Other authors argue for their need in restricted circumstances: 'Restraint and seclusion can be applied constructively for a limited period under regular clinical and statutory review as a means of promoting safety and recovery' (O'Connor et al., 2004, p. 797). In sum, older adults are exposed to restrictive procedures on a frequent basis in a variety of settings and in a number of countries. The safe and effective reduction of these methods is an important goal for service providers.

Behavioural and Psychosocial Interventions

There has been emphasis in the literature on behavioural approaches to the management of agitated behaviours (Pulsford & Duxbury, 2006). A review of outcome studies of behavioural interventions for wandering, disruptive vocalization, physical aggression, other agitated behaviours and a combination of these behaviours produced generally positive outcomes (Spira & Edelstein, 2006). The authors noted that the literature contained numerous design flaws and methodological issues.

Kovach, Kelber, Simpson and Wells (2006) surveyed 54 nurses in 14 U.S. nursing homes for the elderly. Half received training in serial trial assessments which adopted a staged approach to the treatment of behaviours characteristic of dementia. The system involved physical assessment, affective assessment, non-pharmacological interventions and pain management. The approach required a structured approach to assessing the needs of an older adult. The intervention group received seven hours of instruction in the method, and the controls received more generic training over a similar time period. Daily records of nursing were examined to gather evidence for the use of the approach over a 20-day period. Nursing responses in the study were classified as dismissive (no treatment provided), reactive (treatment provided without prior assessment), static (using the same treatments over a 24-hour period) or comprehensive (multiple interventions and systematic use of treatment). Dismissive reactions were experienced by 13 residents, and it was furthermore found that reactive responses were employed for 87 residents. In a regression analysis static and reactive responses were found to predict recurrence of behavioural symptomatology. Systematic and structured approaches to care from nursing staff can have an impact on the behaviour of people with dementia (Kovach, Noonan, Schildt, Reynolds & Wells, 2006).

Reality orientation has been a popular approach in the management of dementia. Reality orientation has been described as an approach in which the individual is prompted by staff when they appear disorientated or suffering from memory problems (Holden & Woods, 1982). The approach can be divided into classroom-based sessions or 24-hour staff-based approaches (Twining, 1988). The approach is clearly behavioural in nature. This approach was popular in the 1980s and is now experiencing a resurgence especially in continental Europe (Woods, 2002). A review of 43 studies including six randomized controlled trials indicated evidence for the effectiveness of the approach (Spector, Davies, Woods & Orrell, 2000). To conclude, the evidence for the effectiveness of psychosocial and behavioural interventions with confused and agitated older adults does show some promise (Pulsford & Duxbury, 2006). When the highly intrusive and risky nature of restraint is considered, it is all too apparent that the present evidence base is wholly inadequate and that there is a particular need for high-quality, independent research into the biomechanics and physiological sequelae of controversial physical holds (Pulsford & Duxbury, 2006).

Person-Centred Approaches to Managing Aggressive Behaviour in People with Dementia

In the United Kingdom there has been an increasing move towards person-centred approaches in care settings for older adults (Stokes, 2001). This was greatly influenced by the work of Tom Kitwood of the Bradford Dementia Group. A central part of such approaches is to focus on celebrating an individual's life, a process that is called validation (Kitwood, 1997). Interacting with a person who has dementia by talking about the more distant past of which they are more likely to have intact memories is a major facet of this approach.

Kitwood (1997) proposed a theory which described from a social psychological perspective how staff and environments can have a negative effect on an older adult's behaviour. This theory is about how poor practice combines with neurological damage to make the dementia worse. Kitwood suggested that older people with neurological damage are very vulnerable to the effects of 'malignant social psychology' (MSP), a term that refers to a collection of damaging interactions which add up to make the person's social world psychologically dangerous. MSP is caused by negative attitudes and practical methods in health care, which are damaging to people's self-esteem and capabilities. It is not usually done on purpose; more often than not it is a matter of unthinking approaches and bad habits.

Kitwood (1997) defined personhood as 'a standing or status that is bestowed on one human being, by others, in the context of relationship and social being. It implies recognition, respect and trust'. He believed that protection and enhancement of personhood leads to higher-quality care. Kitwood maintained that our focus should be on who the person is, how they understand and experience their world and what they need in order to maintain their sense of self. A review of behaviour management approaches concluded that although person-centred approaches appeared desirable there was little research evidence for their efficacy (Pulsford & Duxbury, 2006). In sum, communication approaches that focus on the interaction between the nurse and the patient are an essential component of care for older adults (Conlin Shaw, 2004; Killick & Allen, 2001).

Person-centred approaches to managing aggressive behaviour in older adults would have a number of key components. First, behaviour management may require methods which divert a confused individual. For instance a person who is confused and agitated and is looking for an object or a relative may be distracted by a staff member asking questions about a person's childhood where memories are likely to be more accurate. Second, the avoidance of restraints wherever possible would be a valid goal. Third, training staff to understand and manage behaviours would be critical. In the next section we will review the evidence for staff training in behavioural management. We will then present a case study which typifies low arousal strategies in older adult populations.

Staff Training in Managing Aggression

Staff training in the management of aggressive behaviours is based on the rationale that the modification of staff behaviour by increasing knowledge and understanding of behavioural difficulties should help to reduce negative interactions. There have been attempts to increase staff knowledge and understanding of aggressive behaviours (Maxfield, Lewis & Cannon, 1996; Mentes & Ferario, 1989; Shah & De, 1998). Training staff to specifically understand and manage challenging behaviours is less common in this field. A British study reported the outcomes of a 15-hour training course, which examined the causes of challenging behaviour, person-centred planning and communication strategies (Moniz-Cook et al., 1998). The sample consisted of two local care homes. Two houses received training, and one house acted as a control. Staff rated residents' interactions using the problem behaviour inventory at baseline, post-training, and at a 13-month follow-up. Problem severity and frequency did not decrease, but staff ratings of management difficulty did improve.

A study in Canada evaluated the impact of training in crisis prevention intervention for 48 staff in a service which catered for older adults with dementia. The training included both physical and non-physical components. No clear outcome data were reported, although the authors acknowledged the usefulness of the role-play methods (Martin, 1999).

In a quasi-experimental pre–post design, which looked at the effect of staff training on the use of restraint in dementia in four nursing homes in Stavanger, Norway, data were collected immediately before and after the training had taken place (Testad, Aarsland & Aarsland, 2005). Intervention consisted of a six-hour seminar focusing on dementia, aggression, problem behaviour, decision-making process and alternatives for the use of restraint. Each group was then given guidance for one hour every month for six months. At follow-up the use of restraint was significantly lower in the intervention group compared with the control group. The number of restraints had been reduced by 54%. In conclusion there is some limited evidence that staff training in behaviour management techniques may have an impact on work practice. More research is needed to investigate the specific variables that lead to the reductions in restraints and other restrictive procedures.

A Staff Training Low Arousal Intervention

A three-year study was conducted in an internationally renowned private care agency in Scotland. The organization was concerned that new national be-haviour management guidelines in Scotland would lead to greater emphasis on training for their staff in physical interventions. Local inspectors had already suggested that control and restraint training might be required for all of their staff. The senior managers of the organization were concerned that their rates of physical interventions were quite low and that too much emphasis on training in this area might lead to an increase in injuries for both staff and service users.

A series of internal meetings led them to conclude that training that con-tained the minimal number of physical interventions would be required. Staff at Studio3 Training Systems were requested to develop a short workshop based on the low arousal philosophy (see Chapter 2). A series of staff interviews were conducted to ascertain the levels of aggression encountered by front-line staff. In addition service records which reported the frequency of physical interven-tions were closely examined. It was rapidly established that the rates of physical aggression were low across the majority of the care homes and that the majority of incidents tended to occur when staff provided personal care to older adults who were confused and agitated. Verbal aggression, especially the use of abusive and threatening language towards staff, was quite common.

A two-day workshop using Studio3 principles of low arousal was adapted from existing training courses developed for people with ASD (McDonnell et al., 2008) and people with intellectual disabilities (McDonnell, 1997). The training course contained modules for the following fields: human rights law, understanding the causes of dementia, low arousal approaches to the management of confused older adults, physical disengagement skills and a two-person escort procedure.

The training took place in three phases. The first phase involved teaching 140 staff the two-day workshop. The second phase identified in-house trainers who were judged to be suitable candidates to be trained as trainers. In the third phase in-house trainers were trained to a standard at which they could independently deliver the training. The pass standard of the training was to deliver a two-day workshop while being observed by an independent assessor. Approximately 70% of candidates achieved the satisfactory training standard.

There were a number of positive outcomes of the training. There was high staff satisfaction with training, and a corresponding reduction in physical interventions usage was reported at the end of the study. Staff also considered the low arousal model to be useful with this client population. Finally, the training continues to be popular with staff and is maintained internally by in-house trainers. The success of the programme has led to it being extended to services in the United Kingdom.

An Individual Case Example

The following example took place several years ago: Peter was a 79-year-old man. He lived on his own in a two-bedroom house on the edge of a small Northern town in the United Kingdom. His wife, Edith, had passed away 12 years ago. Peter had held a variety of manual jobs in the past, including 12 years as a coal miner.

Peter was very well known to the local police and had been bound over to keep the peace on several occasions in his younger days. The most recent occasion was six months ago when he smashed a neighbour's window with a rock. Peter claimed that the neighbours were deliberately throwing rubbish in his front garden and that he felt threatened by them. The police officers mediated between the neighbours and Peter, and no formal charges were made after Peter agreed to pay for the window.

There was also some indirect evidence that he had been physically aggressive towards Edith. These episodes of violence were usually associated with bouts of drunkenness. In the last five years Peter had started to show signs of cognitive decline. His short-term memory was particularly poor. He had difficulties with his right hip, and now he required the used of a walking frame to move around his house. There were times when he appeared very confused, and this was often when he became aggressive towards people.

In the last 10 years Peter's physical health had deteriorated, and in addition to requiring a walking frame he required assistance in bathing. Peter had a team of staff who provided practical support in his home on a regular basis. The local agency found it difficult to get staff to work with Peter, as he was abusive and threatening, especially to black workers. Racist insults were commonplace. Several staff in the support service refused to work with him until his racist language was dealt with. The agency employed a range of workers for a short period of time so that each staff member worked with him only for a short period. Jean and Sheila were two workers who had worked with him for more than six years. His behaviour was much better when either of these women visited his house.

One month he was visited by two social workers and the director of the local staff support agency to discuss his racist comments. They had decided to visit as a group because they felt that this would be safer. He was told by the agency representative that all support would be withdrawn if his racist behaviour persisted. The main consequence of this withdrawal of support would be that he would be likely to be placed in a local authority care home. Upon hearing this Peter became verbally abusive and threatening, and he threw a mug of coffee which hit the representative of the local support agency on her head, resulting in stitches.

After this incident an emergency multi-disciplinary team met to consider options for his care. They ruled out compulsory placement orders, as they were difficult to obtain. His social workers Jean and Sheila felt that he should be given another chance. They stressed that Peter had forgotten about the incident. Other staff disagreed with their view and reported that he was deliberately not telling the truth. His team decided that his care could not be withdrawn without the agencies appearing negligent. The duty of care required that support should continue. The people at the meeting also agreed that specialist training would be needed to help staff work with Peter and that this should be provided rapidly. One social worker agreed to approach Studio3 Training Systems to provide some practical advice and training about the matter.

Staff who worked directly with Peter attended a two-day training within two weeks of the referral. This course consisted of legal aspects of care, debriefing and understanding the causes of challenging behaviour with specific emphasis on dementia. The course included practical advice on working with older adults with memory difficulties, including focusing the conversations with Peter on his memories of the distant past (Kitwood, 1997). In addition staff were trained in the concept of low arousal approaches to aggression. This low arousal model was used to examine previous challenging incidents the staff had experienced and to develop alternative less intrusive strategies for the future. The second day of the training course concentrated on non-painful, physical disengagement strategies, which are described in Chapter 3. Peter had punched a staff member in the face; so special attention was given to teaching staff the methods to deflect punches by placing their hands in front of their bodies with their open hands towards Peter. Finally, the Studio3 two-person walk-around procedure was taught for extreme circumstances in which a staff member might need help. Role-play practice of both diversionary low arousal tactics and physical strategies took place for all participants. At the end of the training course staff reported feeling more confident and produced the following reactive plan:

- One low arousal strategy was to remove triggers for aggression. In this regard, non-preferred staff were identified as triggers. Therefore, in order to remover non-preferred staff, the two preferred staff, Sheila and Jean, worked with him for more shifts than previously.
- One low arousal strategy to reduce staff distress, the arguments between staff and Peter and the potential for abuse from staff was to provide them with another forum to air their complaints. In this example, staff who reported that it was too difficult to work with Peter with regard to his racist comments were given regular staff support sessions from their managers to help them to talk about how they felt and to express their own anger at being insulted. Managers were coached to reinforce to staff that they were to refrain from arguing with Peter and remain calm in the face of insults.
- If Peter was judged to be aroused to the level that he might present the threat of assault, two staff were assigned to work with Peter, rather than one. In circumstances in which they genuinely believed that there was a risk that he could cause harm to them, the two-person walk-around method could be used to physically contain him.
- Another low arousal strategy was to encourage alternative acceptable behaviour. When working with Peter, the staff were encouraged not to respond to his verbally abusive behaviours and to talk about other topics. They used two strategies. First, they distracted Peter with the items that he preferred, such as cups of tea or sandwiches. Second, if Peter started to get angry over something that had to do with his memory, such as when he would say, 'I've lost some money' or 'I can't find my shoes', staff would ask him questions that related to his past, such as 'Did you or your wife use to buy your shoes and clothes?'
- Another example of removing triggers is related to having conversations with Peter when he was verbally aggressive or physically threatened staff. Staff were coached to talk about his distant past. Peter's staff were also coached to maintain at least a 3-foot distance between them and him in these situations. This was done both to remove the trigger of their proximity to him and to ensure their safety.
- One low arousal strategy which was used was to reduce the verbal demands placed on Peter. For example, many arguments between staff and Peter were related to cleaning up his own dishes. On a number of occasions arguments with staff escalated, with the result that Peter took the dirty dishes, smashed them and told the staff to pick them up. Staff had rules that Peter should

wash his dishes every day and that they should do only minor clean up. When training staff, the two preferred staff members revealed that they washed Peter's dishes for him. After a vigorous discussion between all staff, they agreed to do the dishes for him. This resulted in staff no longer asking him to clean his own dishes.

- A final example of removing triggers related to instances in which Peter threatened physical violence to staff. When this occurred, staff were to leave the house immediately and call their duty supervisor.

Prior to the intervention Peter had made approximately four physical assaults in the previous six months. These had resulted in staff injuries, including sutures around the eye of a staff. Two staff had taken time off from work after injuries. The case was followed up at one year. Staff reported that Peter had no major incidents of actual physical assault for the entire year. Staff never had to use restraints with him. No staff had been injured, and no staff had taken time off from work because of his aggression. Staff also reported that they felt confident in managing his behaviours. The reports from the service managers indicated high satisfaction with the plan. At one-year follow-up, his team did not wish to place him in a nursing home. Staff also reported that Peter's verbally aggressive behaviour had greatly decreased. They also reported that although he continued to be a challenging client, he was much easier to work with than before.

Three years later Peter died at home of natural causes. He had spent the last three years of his life in his own familiar environment with fewer overt signs of agitation and distress and with staff who were comfortable and confident working with him.

There were a number of key learning points in this case example. First, emphasis was placed on keeping Peter in his own home. This was a key personal goal for Peter. This was also the goal for many staff and administrators who were concerned about keeping Peter in his home for his own comfort and independence and to reduce the need for admission to a nursing home. Second, the staff were trained thoroughly in how to manage his aggressive behaviours. Third, the variability and inconsistencies in responding to Peter's aggressive behaviour were greatly improved by achieving consensus and agreement about management strategies in the two-day training courses. Fourth, it was acknowledged that Peter's racist comments were extremely distressing but were difficult to modify. Therefore, coping strategies for staff were more important. Fifth, staff viewed diversionary strategies, such as changing the subject and talking about his past, as deceitful. After training most staff accepted that the strategies were effective and rapidly calmed him down. Finally, few rules were placed on Peter about his behaviour. For example, one staff member stated, 'Maybe we expect too much of him. He is very set in his ways.'

Conclusions

This chapter has a number of sobering conclusions. Older adult populations in residential care settings encounter restrictive procedures with a relatively high frequency (Galinagh et al., 2002; Kirkevold et al., 2004; O'Connor et al., 2004). The levels of mechanical restraint usage would appear to be far higher than physical restraint or seclusion. We are unclear whether the use of such devices on such a scale would be deemed acceptable in other populations such as younger people or people with intellectual disabilities. A more positive message is that physical and mechanical restraints can be reduced by staff training and organizational feedback approaches (Battar & Nichol, 2004; Ejaz et al., 1994). The low arousal case study reported in this chapter involved keeping an individual in his own familiar environment despite his level of aggression. This was a laudable and positive goal. The Scottish training example indicated that staff can be trained in a person-centred manner, which leads them to be more confident in difficult situations. Training staff to manage disruptive and aggressive behaviour would therefore appear to be a useful and cost-effective strategy (Moniz-Cook et al., 1998).

We started this chapter by describing Dorothy who had a number of risk factors, which could lead to her being either mechanically or physically restrained. Her forgetfulness demonstrated evidence of cognitive decline. Dorothy was starting to become physically more dependent and to require more personal care. Sadly she was perceived by staff to be disruptive and aggressive. The evidence presented in this chapter makes it clear that staff responses to Dorothy will dictate how her behaviour will be managed in the future. Dorothy's future is likely to be decided by the level of competence among staff and their understanding of her behaviour. In addition good-quality staff training in behaviour management and the development of a positive service culture will also be important. Finally the ethos of the service with regard to restrictive interventions is a crucial component. In our view Dorothy's staff will need to develop better strategies based on low arousal approaches to manage her behaviour.

Evaluating the Outcomes of Crisis Management Training

The Need for Evidence-Based Practice

There are a large number of training organizations which train staff in behaviour management which includes physical interventions. In the United Kingdom there *is* a marketplace for these interventions (Harris, 2002). However the evaluation of training approaches is fraught with methodological difficulties. The integrity of the independent variable (Peterson, Homer & Wonderlich, 1982) can be particularly problematic, as a training course would always have to be delivered in a similar manner to be evaluated. The impact of training can also be difficult to evaluate in organizations. How do we know that training was the major factor in the apparent change in the behaviour of staff or families? What other changes in the work environment could have occurred that could have produced the same result?

Staff Training Research: A Process Full of Paradoxes

Training staff in a variety of skills would appear to be an efficient method of disseminating information. Although it should be acknowledged that staff training is important in transmitting skills to the front-line staff (Smith & Cumella, 1996), there are many limitations to the approach (Cullen, 2002; Reid & Parsons, 1992). In care environments, staff who may require specific training may often not attend the training (Campbell, 2007). Furthermore,

Managing Aggressive Behaviour in Care Settings: Understanding and applying low arousal approaches
By Andrew A. McDonnell © 2010 John Wiley & Sons, Ltd

environments that have high staff turnover may struggle to maintain training programmes. In the author's experience it is not unusual to find services that initially train large numbers of staff, but the practices learnt are then poorly maintained after the initial enthusiasm begins to ebb.

The content of training is also important when considering evaluation. Training specific skills such as physical interventions may be easier to assess in terms of skill acquisition and use. Similarly, training in behavioural skills may be easier to evaluate, as they can be directly observed after training. Baker (1998) in a multiple-baseline design examined the effects of three video-based training packages (training in basic support, health and safety and values training). Staff observations were conducted with six staff in two residential houses for people with a learning disability. He found positive effects for simple target behaviours (hand washing, glove usage and frequency of positive interaction); the more complex target behaviour (frequency of valued activities in the community) was not easily altered by training.

The evaluation of staff training courses presents significant challenges to researchers. Training course evaluations can have difficulties with the integrity of the independent variable. In reality, most staff training consists of a combination of educational elements rather than one specific entity. Evaluating packages is fraught with difficulties and reflects the theoretical biases of researchers. Paterson and Leadbetter (2002) examined standards for training packages in the management of aggression and recommended that training values are a key component of any programme. Presumably the measurement of these values should be an implicit component of training models. Measuring attitudes and values is a far more complex process than measuring overt behaviours or knowledge.

Methods of teaching training courses are also important. Classroom-based training models appear to predominate. These 'chalk and talk' approaches may not be the most efficient teaching medium. When evaluating training programmes a clear distinction should be made between the acquisition of knowledge and the application and retention of skills. A course participant may be able to pass a paper and pencil test but may not be able to demonstrate the skills learnt.

A practical example of the problems of retaining information is the cardio-pulmonary resuscitation (CPR) training. Hamilton (2005) in a review of the literature reported clear trends where knowledge tends to be retained better than physical skills, but both decline significantly within three to six months after training. Performance and retention were also improved with video self-instruction, peer tuition, computer-based teaching tools and applicable simulations. The evaluation of CPR methods has direct application to staff training in physical interventions.

Training in aggression management that takes place in classrooms may be extremely problematic in terms of skill retention. There is an obvious correlation between quantity of information taught and its retention. With regard to physical interventions, can staff apply the skills they learn in a class-room to real-world settings? Continuation of training outside of the classroom raises real concerns that staff may be expected to be regularly drilled in skills which they rarely have to apply. The cost–benefit analysis of such an approach is arguably open to question. Improving retention by extending training outside of the classroom environment may also be helpful. Recent developments have indicated that training may be more effective if direct coaching in the workplace also takes place (Van Oorsouw, Embregts, Bosman & Jahoda, 2009).

Goodness of fit training is also a clear component of training. Beech and Leather (2006) reviewed the literature and illustrated this problem by maintaining that aggression management training is an established health and safety response in most organizations. In contrast they also acknowledged the limitations of such training: 'Although aggression management training is now widely available it is often inappropriate for the needs of different staff groups' (p. 41).

Training packages may not always meet the needs of a variety of different human services. The range and depth of services are best illustrated by practical example. A member of staff who works in an environment with low-frequency aggression may require only de-escalation training. On the other hand, a staff member who works in a high-risk service where physical aggression may occur on a regular basis may require practice of physical interventions in their training. Staff who work in a single-person service may require a more 'bespoke' training package. The author can think of numerous services which meet this criterion.

Organizational culture and leadership is clearly another important vari-able (Colton, 2004; Deveau & McDonnell, in press). Some evidence has demonstrated that the monitoring by the management of the use of physical interventions can lead to reductions in their use (Sturmey & Palen McGlynn, 2002). Norway has recently implemented legal instruments regulating the use of 'coercive' procedures for people with intellectual disabilities. These have reportedly led to considerable reductions in the use of restrictive interventions for people with learning disabilities (Roed & Syse, 2002). A recent study in the United Kingdom reported that better-service-quality outcomes for people with a learning disability appeared to be more commonplace in services with a more positive organizational culture (Gillett & Stenfert-Kroese, 2003). There is even some limited evidence that certain organizational cultures may actually increase service user vulnerability to abuse (White, Holland, Marsland & Oakes, 2003).

Deveau and McGill (2007) identified gaps in the policy and delivery of organizational responses to physical interventions. The effects of direct staff training per se may well be limited (Deveau & McDonnell, in press). Presumably if training is not placed in context it should not be surprising that staff will use physical interventions as a first rather than as a last resort (Deveau & McDonnell, in press).

Staff training in crisis management strategies has been a primary focus of this book. Reviews of training outcomes have tended to be negative (Allen, 2000; Beech & Leather, 2006; Deb & Roberts, 2005; Stubbs et al., 2009). Large numbers of staff in the United Kingdom receive training in physical interventions. By definition these methods are associated with risk (Leadbetter, 2002). They may also elevate the risk of abuse to high-risk individuals (Baker & Allen, 2001). The next sections will examine the literature relevant to staff training.

Staff Training in Physical Interventions: Best Practice Evidence

Staff training in the use of physical interventions for aggression and other externalizing maladaptive behaviours is widely used in a variety of populations and settings (Deb & Roberts, 2005), including people with psychiatric disorders (Jambunathan & Bellaire, 1996), intellectual disabilities (Allen, 2000, 2002; Harris, 2002; McDonnell, 2005), acquired brain injury (Temple, Zgaljardic, Yancy & Jaffray, 2007) and children and adolescents (Perkins & Leadbetter, 2002.)

The review

The literature search was conducted using the Web of Science search engine, using the following: the Cochrane Database (2001 to October 2008), Medline (1966 to October 2008) and Social Science Citation Index (1956 to October 2008). The following keywords were used: aggression, violence, training, mental retardation, learning disability, mental handicap, elderly, care staff, education, psychiatry, mental health, disruptive behaviour and psychiatric. Staff training was used as the major keyword in all comparisons.

Websites of 12 training organizations approved to deliver training in U.K. services for people with a learning disability (until November 2008) were examined for evidence of published research in staff training in physical interventions. All training papers selected for the review had their reference sections examined in an attempt to discover any papers that may have been missed in the electronic searches. This process produced no new studies.

Papers were included if they were published in a peer-reviewed journal; there was evidence that staff training, rather than service audit, had occurred and that physical interventions were a component of the training. Unpublished papers and studies which only taught defusion skills were excluded.

Main results

53 papers were included in the final review. To screen studies for academic quality, quasi-experimental designs, experimental designs with control groups and time series data were included. This produced 18 studies. Table 9.1 reports the study designs, the measures used and the outcome data reported.

The 18 studies included in this review included 7006 participants, from a variety of backgrounds. Nine studies took place in psychiatric settings (Carmel & Hunter, 1990; Hahn, Needham, Abderhalden, Duxbury & Halfens, 2006; Infantino & Musingo, 1985; Kilick & Allen, 2005; McGowan et al., 1999; Needham et al., 2005a; Phillips & Rudestam, 1995; Rice et al., 1985; Thackrey, 1987) and three in learning disability settings (Allen et al., 1997; Allen & Tynan, 2000; Van den Pol, Reed & Fuqua, 1983). One study each was conducted in an 'acquired brain injury' setting (Temple et al., 2007), an 'older adults' setting (Martin, 1999) and an autism-specific setting (McDonnell et al., 2007). Three of the studies did not appear to specify their setting (Fernandes et al., 2002; Hurlebaus & Link, 1997; Needham et al., 2005b). This review therefore showed a definite imbalance of where training studies were conducted, with a major emphasis on mental health settings.

11 studies appeared to meet a minimum standard of experimental design of having either a control or a contrast group (Allen & Tynan, 2000; Carmel & Hunter, 1990; Hahn et al., 2006; Hurlebaus & Link, 1997; Infantino & Musingo, 1985; McDonnell et al., 2007; McGowan et al., 1999; Needham et al., 2005a, 2005b; Phillips & Rudestam, 1995; Rice et al., 1985; Thackrey, 1987). In addition, multiple-baseline designs were adopted in two studies (Kilick & Allen, 2005; Van den Pol et al., 1983). Time series data without control groups were reported in three cases (Allen et al., 1997; Fernandes et al., 2002; Temple et al., 2007). A further study implied a pre–post design, but the design remained unclear (Martin, 1999).

Outcome measures varied considerably in the above-mentioned studies. Increases in confidence were reported in a number of studies. Allen and Tynan (2000) as well as McGowan and colleagues (1999) reported significant differences in confidence between a trained and an untrained group. McDonnell and co-workers (2007) also reported increases in staff confidence but no increases in other measures such as staff belief, support, coping or perceived control. Needham et al. (2005b) also reported increases in confidence measures after training. Kilick and Allen (2005) as well as Thackrey (1987) reported increases in the confidence of trained participants; however while confidence scores decreased at one-year follow-up for the study by Kilick and Allen (2005), they remained very similar for Thackrey at post-training follow-up. Hurlebaus and Link (1997) on the other hand found no significant changes in measures of confidence and further measures such as safety or knowledge. With regard to other outcome

Table 9.1. A table of the design and settings, course duration and title, description of reliability measures and outcome data for 18 staff training studies on physical interventions

Authors	Design and setting (including control/comparison group and statistics)	Course and its duration	Description and reliability of measures	Outcome data
Allen et al. (1997)	Time series design ($n = 7$ service users). Six-bed unit for adults with learning disabilities and challenging behaviours in the United Kingdom. Combination of descriptive and parametric statistics.	Preventing and responding to aggressive behaviour (the Welsh method). Two- to three-day course (one day theory, one to two days physical interventions).	Aberrant Behaviour Checklist (Aman and Singh, 1986), rates of physical restraint usage, rates of seclusion usage, medication as required usage, staff and service user injuries. No reliability data reported.	Reduction in overall rates of behaviour, reduction in physical restraints and emergency medication. 'Decommissioning' of seclusion, reduction in staff and service user injuries.
Allen & Tynan (2000)	Quasi-experimental design: between-subjects element, trained versus untrained staff; within-subjects element, untrained group, which then received training; $n = 109$, 51 exposed to training, 58 not exposed in United Kingdom, in community services with people with learning disabilities. Non-parametric statistics used.	Preventing and responding to aggressive behaviour (the Welsh method). Two- to three-day course (one day theory, one to two days physical interventions).	A 10-item confidence measure (Thackrey, 1987), Cronbach's alpha = .88). A 20-item reactive strategy questionnaire, Cronbach's alpha = .64.	The trained group was significantly more confident than the untrained group. The trained group scored higher on the reactive strategy questionnaire. Both measures statistically increased when the untrained group received training.

Carmel & Hunter (1990)	Quasi-experimental design comparing staff who had received training in managing assaultive behaviour ($N = 392$) with staff who received no training.	A 16-hour training course in the management of assaultive behaviours by the California Department of Mental Health.	Examined staff injury data and rates of patient aggression. No reliability data provided for either measure.	Staff who received aggression management training reported lower rates of injury. No relationship between CPR training and staff injury.
Fernandes et al. (2002)	Time series pre–post design (baseline and three-month and seven-month follow-ups), 667 completed surveys out of a sample of 798) in a Canadian tertiary-care hospital. Parametric statistics used.	Four-hour training course using the CPI system.	Unclear description of the survey tool. Severity of incidents assessed by using the Overt Aggression Scale (Yudofsky, Silver, Jackson, 1986). No reliability data provided for the survey.	Reported initial decrease of rates of aggression per shift at three-month follow-up. These returned to near-baseline levels at six-month follow-up.
Hahn et al. (2006)	Quasi-experimental pre–post design. Mental health setting ($N = 63$ mental health nurses including control group; $n = 34$ mental health nurses). Acute psychiatric ward setting in Switzerland.	Five-day aggression management training programme developed in the Netherlands (Oud, 1997). The programme consisted of 24 lessons lasting 50 minutes each.	Management of Aggression and Violence Attitude Scale (MAVAS; Duxbury, 2002). Good stability (Pearson's $r = .89$) and construct validity reported. Reported Cronbach's alphas for the four subscales of the MAVAS: 0.54, 0.41, 0.25 and 0.71 (Duxbury, 2002).	No significant attitude change in the intervention group compared with the control group after the test.

(Continued)

Table 9.1. (*Continued*)

Authors	Design and setting (including control/comparison group and statistics)	Course and its duration	Description and reliability of measures	Outcome data
Hurlebaus & Link (1997)	A pre-post design with a control group. Total $N = 32$ nurses based at an inner-city teaching hospital in the United States. A training group ($N = 22$) and a control group that did not receive training ($n = 10$). Parametric statistics used.	A four-hour training course, with one hour devoted to physical skills. The title of the course was unspecified.	A 15-item knowledge test (which consisted of 10 multiple-choice and 5 true/false questions) – no reliability data provided. Two visual analogue scales used to measure safety and confidence (no reliability data).	No significant differences found in the measures of safety, confidence or knowledge in the study. Inappropriate statistical analysis makes this paper difficult to interpret.
Infantino & Musingo (1985)	Quasi-experimental design, examining a group of trained ($N = 31$) versus a group of untrained ($N = 65$) staff in a psychiatric hospital in the United States with a follow-up between 9 and 24 months after training. Non-parametric statistics used.	Three-day training course using aggression control techniques.	Examined rates of staff assaults, injuries and days lost from work. No reliability data reported.	Only one trained staff was assaulted with no injury; 37% of the untrained staff were assaulted, out of which 79% of resulted in injuries. Staff injuries were reported for the untrained staff.

| Kilick & Allen (2005) | Comparison of multiple baselines across the groups (three groups, $N = 27$ staff including a majority of nurses and also comprising psychologists, social workers, psychiatrists, teachers and family therapists). Adult mental health setting. Parametric statistics (ANOVA, t-test) | Positive behaviour management was compared with control and restraint training. Training took place over three consecutive days. All three groups were trained within a six-week time frame. Positive behaviour management training consisted of one day of theoretical teaching and two days focusing on teaching physical intervention skills. | The aggression questionnaire: Cronbach's alpha = .92; (Thackrey, 1987) and .88 (Allen & Tynan, 2000). The reactive strategies questionnaire: Cronbach's alpha = .62 (Allen & Tynan, 2000). Satisfaction questionnaire (Killick & Allen, 2005) devised to assess staff satisfaction with each model of aggression management. | Significant increase in staff confidence which were not maintained at one-year follow-up. Increase in knowledge over time, which, however, the data suggest was not dependent on whether training took place or not. Higher satisfaction rates for staff groups who were trained in positive behaviour manegment compared with those who were trained in control and restraint. |
| Martin (1999) | Implies pre–post design although design of study unclear. Implied a control group but provided no data. Evaluated CPI training in a service, which catered for older adults with dementia in Canada. Staff ($N = 48$). No statistics reported. | Trained in CPI system – time period unclear. | Staff participated in role-play assessments. No reliability data provided. | Reported use of role-play assessment was useful. |

(*Continued*)

Table 9.1. (*Continued*)

Authors	Design and setting (including control/comparison group and statistics)	Course and its duration	Description and reliability of measures	Outcome data
McDonnell et al. (2007)	Quasi-experimental design (between-subjects element trained $N = 43$ comparison group previously received training $N = 47$. Pre–post test, 10-month interval. Services for people with ASDs. Analysis of within-subjects pre-test scores – t-test. Five dependent measures analysed through MANCOVA with experimental group as the between-subjects factor and pre-training as the covariate factor. Each dependent variable analysed using separate ANCOVA.	Studio3 three-day course, half theoretical and half practical.	The 'staff support and satisfaction questionnaire' (3SQ; Harris & Rose 2002) good test–retest reliability ($r = .82$), high-level internal reliability (Cronbach's alpha = .92). The 'shortened ways of coping scale' (Hatton & Emerson, 1995), good reliability and internal consistency (average Cronbach's alpha = .76). The 'thoughts about challenging behaviour questionnaire' (Dagnan, 2007), very high internal consistency (Cronbach's alpha = .85). The 'challenging behaviour confidence scale' (McDonnell, 1997), good internal consistency (Cronbach's alpha = .95). The 'checklist of challenging behaviour' (Harris, Humphreys, & Thompson, 1994). Relationship between measures investigated using Pearson's product moment correlations showed approaching significance for 3SQ and thoughts about behaviour; all other correlations are non-significant and the measures are therefore not inter-correlated.	Staff training showed increases in staff confidence but not in the other measures of staff belief, support, coping or perceived control. No evidence of reduction in the client's challenging behaviour.

Study	Design	Training	Measure	Results
McGowan et al. (1999)	Quasi-experimental design with six-month follow-up, compared trained staff at a psychiatric hospital ($N = 42$) with untrained staff in a secure facility ($N = 15$), who later received training in Australia. Non-parametric statistics used.	A $7\frac{1}{2}$-hour module in 'safe physical restraint'.	A ten-item confidence scale (Thackrey, 1987; no reliability data provided.	Trained group ($N = 42$) had higher confidence scores, than untrained group ($N = 15$) – these significantly increased after training.
Needham et al. (2005b)	Pre–post design with control group. Nursing staff ($N = 117$) received training compared with the control group of staff ($N = 60$) who did not receive training in Switzerland. Non-parametric and parametric statistics used.	Training consisted of four days and 20 lessons of 50 minutes each. Curriculum corresponds approximately to control and restraint training.	A 10-item confidence scale (Thackrey, 1987), Cronbach's alpha = .92). Shortened version the POAS-S (reliability cited in earlier paper), two vision analogue scales (no reliability data).	Significant increases in confidence after training. Experimental group increase in scores in one visual analogue scale (comprehensible/purposeful). No significant difference in POAS-S.
Needham et al. (2005a)	Randomized control trial of 87 acute psychiatric wards in Switzerland. Three wards of staff participated in the trial ($N = 30$) with another three wards acting as a control group ($N = 28$). Non-parametric statistics used.	Consisted of five-day training programme of 20 lessons of 50 minutes each. Management of aggression (Oud, 1997).	POAS-S, 12-item tolerance scale (no reliability data) and the impact of patient aggression on carer scale (IMPACS); Cronbach's alpha = .78.	No effect of measures before and after training.

(Continued)

Table 9.1. (*Continued*)

Authors	Design and setting (including control/comparison group and statistics)	Course and its duration	Description and reliability of measures	Outcome data
Phillips & Rudestam (1995)	Between-subjects pre–post design, two-week follow-up ($N = 14$). Three groups ($N = 24$): didactic training ($n = 8$), didactic plus physical skills training ($n = 8$), no training control group ($n = 8$). Psychiatric staff in two state hospitals in the United States participated. Parametric statistics used.	Untitled training programme of 4 hours 20 minutes.	Hostility inventory (no reliability data), videotapes of physical competence and ratings of behaviour expressed, aggression and fear (high inter-rater reliability, ranging from 0.94 to 0.97).	Judges ratings of fear in role-plays lowest for the didactic and physical intervention group. Physical competency rated as highest for this group. Inverse relationship between judges' ratings of physical competence and observed fear. Follow-up interviews indicated that staff in the trained group of didactic and physical intervention skills reported 23% fewer incidents. Authors claimed that participants with lower levels of physical competence demonstrated significantly lower role-play performances. Participants in the didactic only and control groups appeared unable to maintain a safe distance between themselves and an attacker compared with the didactic training and physical intervention group.

	Design	Training	Measures	Results
Rice et al. (1985)	Between-subjects pre–post design with a 15-month follow-up ($N = 63$). Training provided for mental health staff ($N = 126$) and staff in a maximum-security unit ($N = 89$) and compared with a control group of staff ($N = 37$) in Canada. Parametric statistics used.	Five-day training course in CPI.	Assault rates (inter-rater reliability 69–100%), assault rates leading to days off work (inter-rater reliability 88%), a sensitive situations skills test (inter-rater reliability 81–100%), audio-taped role-play scenarios (inter-rater reliability of 99% and 90%), physical skills test (inter-rater reliability 98%), self-defence and patient restraint written tests (inter-rater reliability 100%), job reaction scale (items unspecified), Cronbach's alpha = .71–.76).	Increases in performance in all pre–post simulations and written tests. Significant reduction in workdays lost owing to patient violence. Assault rates increased after training. Course feedback from course participants remained positive at 15-month follow-up.
Temple et al. (2007)	Time series design ($n = 28$), newly hired rehabilitation comparison group of experienced rehabilitation staff ($n = 10$), comparison between clinical staff ($n = 14$) consisting of	Nonviolent crisis intervention training for 12 hours over two consecutive days. The Rehabilitation	RSI subscales are internally consistent, reliable and differentiated from the other subscales albeit moderately intercor-related (Dunn, 1997).	RSI showed staff discomfort had significantly reduced immediately following training and was maintained a month later. Staff discomfort with sexual situations, aggression and staff–staff interactions were reduced immediately after training and

(Continued)

Table 9.1. (*Continued*)

Authors	Design and setting (including control/comparison group and statistics)	Course and its duration	Description and reliability of measures	Outcome data
	occupational therapists, physical therapists, speech and language pathologists, nurses and supervised students and Therapeutic assistants who provide one-to-one assistance to clients in a post-acute residential rehabilitation facility for moderate to severe acquired brain injury in the United States. Parametric statistics used.	Situations Inventory (RSI) was completed at three time points (just prior to training, immediately following the second day and approximately one month after training).		maintained one month later. The difference between experienced staff and newly hired staff approached significance at baseline but was not significant at both post-test times.
Thackrey (1987)	Between-subjects design comparing a trained ($N = 68$) versus an untrained ($N = 57$) group at three time periods – before, after and 18-month follow-up. Training took place in a community mental health centre, a state psychiatric prison and a state psychiatric hospital in the United States. Parametric statistics used.	An eight-hour programme presented in two sessions of four hours each one week apart, entitled 'Therapeutics for Aggression'.	A 10-item confidence in coping with patient's aggression (Cronbach's alpha = .92).	Trained group showed post-training increases in confidence which did not decrease significantly at post-training follow-up. The untrained group showed no significant changes in the three time periods.

| Van Den Pol et al. (1983) | Multiple-baseline design examining three safety-related skills (fire safety, emergency procedures after a person has had a seizure and physical self-defence). Study took place in an 87-bed residential service for people with a learning disability in the United States; $N = 13$ with 4 trainees, 3 maintenance condition trainees, 4 trainers and 2 control trainees; 23-month follow-up of staff who had received training (telephone interviews). Descriptive statistics reported. | Three workshops of 30 minutes each in emergency procedures. | Role-play assessments of self-defence procedures rated by two independent raters (average inter-rater reliability 90%). Assessments took place on an unannounced basis. Five-item self-report questionnaire (no reliability), telephone follow-up (N = not specified). | Trainers demonstrated competency levels after training in 'self-defence' skills. Control trainees showed no increase in any skill acquisition. None of the trainee staff were still employed at follow-up. One trainee reported using physical intervention in the workplace. |

measures two studies reported reduction in challenging behaviours (Allen et al., 1997; Fernandes et al., 2002), and three studies reported a reduction in injury rates for staff and thus lost workdays (Carmel & Hunter, 1990; Infantino & Musingo, 1985; Rice et al,, 1985). Other outcome measures reported were positive effect of role-plays (Martin, 1999), lower ratings of fear in role-plays (Philips & Rudestam, 1995), increases in performance in pre–post simulations and written tests (Rice et al., 1985), reduced discomfort with difficult situations (Temple et al., 2007) and increased competency levels in 'self-defence' skills (Van den Pol et al., 1983). Two studies found no significant effect of measures before and after the training (Hahn et al., 2006; Needham et al., 2005b).

Table 9.2 reports the course contents, the types of physical interventions used and the descriptions of teaching methods. The course content in all studies varied considerably, both in relation to the material covered and as in relation to the length of the courses. Some courses covered mostly physical interventions (Carmel & Hunter, 1990; Martin, 1999; Temple et al., 2007), while the remaining courses in this review also covered more theoretical elements.

The physical interventions taught also included a variety of techniques. A number of the programmes concentrated mostly on breakaway techniques such as releases from wrist grabs, choke holds, hair pulls and similar as well as blocking skills (Hahn et al., 2006; Hurlebaus & Link, 1997; Philips & Rudestam, 1995; Van den Pol et al., 1983), while others included both breakaway skills and restraint methods (Fernandes et al., 2002; Infantino & Musingo, 1985; Kilick & Allen, 2005; Martin, 1999; McDonnell et al., 2007; Needham et al, 2005a, 2005b; Temple et al., 2007). In many cases breakaway and defence skills are described in detail; descriptions of physical interventions however are often lacking in detail or are non-existent. The interpretation and comparison of these interventions is therefore very difficult. A number of studies in this review failed to describe the interventions which had been taught (Carmel & Hunter, 1990; McGowan et al., 1999; Rice et al., 1985; Thackrey, 1987) or merely referred to specific training manuals (Allen et al., 1997; Allen & Tynan, 2000).

Teaching methods for the above-mentioned training studies also varied between programmes. A high number of studies used lecture-based teaching as well as role-plays (Allen et al., 1997; Allen & Tynan, 2000; Fernandes et al., 2002; Infantino & Musingo, 1985; McDonnell et al., 2007; Needham et al., 2005a, 2005b; Philips & Rudestam, 1995; Rice et al., 1985; Thackrey, 1987; Van den Pol et al., 1983). Role-plays are a very common and effective way of teaching physical interventions. Other studies did not include role-play methods in their teaching but focused on lecture-based formats and practical instructions of physical interventions (Carmel & Hunter, 1990; Hahn et al., 2006; Hurlebaus & Link, 1997). Furthermore, three studies implied the use of theoretical and practical teaching but did not clearly specify their methods, which makes interpretations difficult (Kilick & Allen, 2005; McGowan et al., 1999; Temple et al., 2007). All

Table 9.2. A table of course content, description of physical interventions and description of teaching methods (18 studies)

Author	Course content	Description of physical interventions	Description of teaching methods
Allen et al. (1997)	Understanding aggressive incidents, primary prevention, secondary prevention, reactive strategies including physical interventions and post-incident support for clients and caregivers.	Unclear in the paper, referred to unpublished training manual – Doyle, Dunn, Allen and Hadley (1996, unpublished).	Classroom instruction, role-play and repeated practice of physical interventions.
Allen & Tynan (2000)	Training programme specified in an earlier paper (Allen et al., 1997).	Refer to Allen et al. (1997).	Classroom instruction, role-play and repeated practice of physical interventions.
Carmel & Hunter (1990)	A 16-hour training course which included attention to inter-personal skills and the management of violent patients.	None specified.	Didactic and lecture-based format and practical instruction to the management of violent patients described.
Fernandes et al. (2002)	Identify risk factors, triggers of violence, attitudes to aggressive behaviour, crisis development model, listening skills, non-verbal and para-verbal skills to lower aggression, 'principles and techniques to control oneself, steps to consider after an aggressive incident, 'team control and restraint techniques'.	Two types of aggression – 'strikes' (punching, spitting, kicking) and 'grabs' (pulling hair, choking, biting). Restraint method not clearly specified. Described as 'team control and restraint techniques'.	Role-play techniques, mini lectures, group descriptions of case studies, video tapes of verbal and physical aggression.

(Continued)

Table 9.2. (Continued)

Author	Course content	Description of physical interventions	Description of teaching methods
Hahn et al. (2006)	The programme covered the following areas: definitions of aggression, violence and sexual intimidation; nature and prevalence of aggression; theories of aggression; nursing care plans; nursing interventions (predication, prevention, communication, breakaway techniques, boundary setting and the use of measures to limit patients' freedom); post-incident care; the ethics of aggression management; ward security.	Breakaway techniques.	Problem-based learning, mixture of theoretical elements, exchange of experience and hands-on training.
Hurlebaus & Link (1997)	Aggression, crime, verbal and non-verbal signs of agitation, identification of antecedent signs of aggression, use of body language, tone of voice and eye contact.	Self-defence techniques, breakaway from wrist grabs, chokes (front and rear), hair pulling, blocking kicks, 'how to release from a bite'.	Handouts, group discussions, demonstration of physical techniques.
Infantino & Musingo (1985)	Three training phases over three days: (1) policies and procedures and verbal strategies; (2) physical interventions designed to provide staff with 'release and de-escalation skills'; (3) physical restraint and incident reporting procedures.	Limited description of getting free from hair pulling, choking, headlocks, blocking punches and kicks. Restraint methods not described.	Case vignettes, role-play, video tapes used to demonstrate the physical skills taught.
Kilick & Allen (2005)	Understanding aggressive behaviour, primary prevention, secondary prevention, reactive strategies including pain-free physical skills and breakaway techniques.	Self-protective procedures/breakaway skills, techniques for moving distressed patients, procedure for seated restraint. Details of physical techniques not specified.	Combination of theoretical and skills teaching but not clearly specified.

Martin (1999)	Not specified in the paper, only stated that staff received CPI training.	Partial description. The role-play test evaluated a 'front choke hold release' a 'two-handed wrist grab' and an 'interim hold position'.	Narrative.
McDonnell et al. (2007)	A day and a half of theory including legal issues, causes of aggressive behaviour, staff support and low arousal approaches. A day and a half of high-frequency behaviours including hair pulling, biting, grabbing, airway protection, two-person client chair restraint in upright posture.	High-frequency behaviours including hair pulling, biting, grabbing, airway protection, two-person client chair restraint in upright posture. Course content and format referred to in McDonnell et al. (1991a, 1991b, 1991c, 1993, 1998).	Lectures, modelling of methods, rehearsal using role-play.
McGowan et al. (1999)	An $8\frac{1}{2}$-hour one-day module in 'safe physical restraint.' Including early recognition and management of antecedent behaviours, defusion skills, debriefing, team work and role assignment during the restraint process.	Not specified.	Role-play scenarios and lecture-based methods implied but not clearly specified in paper.
Needham et al. (2005b)	Training programme consisting of 20 lessons each of 50 minutes in caution and genesis of aggression, theories on the various stages of aggressive incidents, behaviours during aggressive situations, reflection on one-zone aggressive components, types of conflict management, communication and interaction, post-aggression procedures, workplace safety, prevention of aggression.	Breakaway techniques, physical restraint not described.	Lecture-based and involving role-play.

(Continued)

Table 9.2. (Continued)

Author	Course content	Description of physical interventions	Description of teaching methods
Needham et al. (2005a)	Training programme consisting of 20 lessons each of 50 minutes in caution and genesis of aggression, theories on the various stages of aggressive incidents, behaviours during aggressive situations, reflection on one-zone aggressive components, types of conflict management, communication and interaction, post-aggression procedures, workplace safety, prevention of aggression, breakaway techniques.	Breakaway techniques, physical restraint not described.	Lecture-based and involving role-play.
Phillips & Rudestam (1995)	Didactic material includes theories of learning, dynamics of violence, warning signs of violence, non-verbal communication, intervention strategies and legal issues.	Specific physical interventions described in a non-visual manner in the paper. Physical skill – 'a repel and push off to invasion skill was taught as a defence to a frontal choking attack'. A posture to block attacks called 'the repel' described. Clear descriptions of both repel and push off techniques.	Role-play and lecture format.
Rice et al. (1985)	Recognition of behavioural cues; verbal techniques to be used with highly upset individuals; 'self-defence techniques'; physical restraints; post-incident responses.	'Self-defence techniques' not clearly specified in paper. No indication of number of techniques taught with regard to patient restraint.	Lecture-based, including live simulation of crisis (role-play); audio-visual materials.

Temple et al. (2007)	Classroom instruction and training in personal safety including blocking kicks and punches, escaping from grabs and chokes and restraint techniques. Participants learnt to identify the nature of verbal outputs from clients and how to implement appropriate verbal intervention.	'[S]afe, non-harmful behaviour management system' (Crisis Prevention Institute, 2004), blocking kicks and punches, escaping grabs and chokes and restraint techniques.	Classroom instruction and training. Rest not specified.
Thackrey (1987)	Legal and ethical issues, psychological intervention and assessment techniques, teamwork, communication skills and physical methods for 'non-abusive self-protection'.	Not specified	Didactic lectures, selected readings, group discussions, experiential exercises, modelling/simulation/role-play and practice of physical manoeuvres.
Van Den Pol et al. (1983)	Three workshops of 30 minutes each. Staff taught how to train new staff. In addition staff taught how to conduct the emergency procedure.	Blocking punches and kicks, releasing clothing grab, using a 'thumb pry', release of a body-part grab and using a chair for protection.	Workshop format used with modelling procedures and role-play.

studies included in this review therefore varied considerably in content, and teaching instructions and comparisons are difficult to make. The review shows a clear need for more detailed and controlled research in this area.

Measuring Outcomes of Studio3 Training Research

Chapters 4–8 have outlined research which evaluates a core training course in the management of challenging behaviours. Some of this research is published in peer-reviewed journals, and other data reflect unpublished work. Based on the evidence presented earlier in this chapter it would be useful to evaluate this information in a systematic manner.

In the United Kingdom the Cochrane library was developed with the main purpose of developing systematic reviews of the strongest evidence available about health care interventions. To give an idea of the levels of evidence they categorize studies ranging from 1 to 5 as follows:

Level 1. For a randomized controlled trial, the lower limit of the confidence interval (expressed as a range) for a measure of effect is still above a meaningful benefit in healthcare terms.
Level 2. For a randomized controlled trial, the lower limit of the confidence interval (expressed as a range) for a measure of effect is less than a meaningful beneficial effect in health care terms; but the point estimate of effect still shows effectiveness of the intervention.
Level 3. Measures of effectiveness are taken from non-randomized studies of groups of people where a control group has run concurrently with the group receiving the intervention being assessed.
Level 4. Measures of effectiveness are taken from non-randomized studies of groups of people where intervention effects are compared with previous or historical information.
Level 5. Evidence is from single-case studies.

The use of low arousal approaches in terms of service impact would appear to be the subject of one single-case design (McDonnell et al., 1998). This would be 'level 5' evidence in the Cochrane system. There are two staff training studies which have been published in peer-reviewed journals (McDonnell, 1997; McDonnell et al., 2008). One study adopted a quasi-experimental design and produced clear effects in the form of confidence increases in care staff and some evidence of reductions of challenging behaviour among service users on the autistic spectrum over a 10-month period. The lack of randomization and behaviourally based observations does make this study relatively weak. The second study reported a 'before and after' design with no control group (McDonnell,

1997). This study reported increases in staff confidence, but no behaviour measures were taken. One of these studies (McDonnell et al., 2008) would achieve 'level 3'. Similarly, the training study reported in children's services in Chapter 6, although containing a relatively small sample size, would possibly meet the criterion for Cochrane rating of 'level 3' or 'level 4'. The series of training 15 training courses using 275 participants described in Chapter 4 would represent a case study (level 5) approach. It is significant that one training course in this study did not produce desirable outcomes.

Studies of the social validity of the physical restraint measures described in Chapters 3 and 4 appear to be more promising. Three studies all used video and other visual materials to rate three methods of physical restraint. McDonnell and colleagues (1993) presented the three restraint methods to a sample of 276 young people. The presentation of materials was counterbalanced to control for order effects. They found that there were consistently higher acceptability ratings for the chair method as opposed to the other methods. In a further study a sample of young people was compared with special-education workers and residential workers (McDonnell & Sturmey, 2000). They found that the chair method was rated as more acceptable than the two other methods.

Finally, a consumer study reported a similar effect (Cunningham et al., 2003). Twenty-four undergraduate students, 21 residential care staff and 18 service users from community settings rated videotapes of the same restraint methods cited in earlier studies (McDonnell et al., 1993; McDonnell & Sturmey, 2000). Participants responded to two open-ended questions to rate the methods of restraint and rated the methods on a five-point scale of satisfaction. Participants also rated the three restraint methods by a forced-choice comparison. Restraint was rated negatively by all participants. However, in both the satisfaction ratings and the ratings for the forced-choice methods the chair method of restraint was rated as most acceptable by all three groups of participants. Consumers rated restraint more negatively than other groups. Restraint was evaluated negatively by all three groups, but the chair method was rated the least intrusive alternative.

These studies would appear to have produced a consistent finding about the preferences of people with regard to the narrow domain of restraint methods. It would be useful to extend the range of this work. The studies would appear to be methodologically competent and have produced a replicable result. Although the Cochrane levels of research are biased towards evaluative research, these methods are taught on the training courses described in this book. In sum they are studies which would meet the criterion of experimental control comparable to at least 'level 3' in the Cochrane classification.

The studies described here represent only limited 'hard evidence' for the approaches described in this book. There are several areas of measurement that would make this research methodologically stronger. First, the inclusion of behaviourally based measures (preferably for both staff and service users) would greatly strengthen the outcome data. Evidence for the reduction of usage of physical interventions would also strengthen findings. More difficult to measure are organizational factors such as staff ethos and service leadership in their role in reducing restrictive practices. There is a growing body of knowledge investigating the influence of organizational factors on the reduction of restrictive practices. Leadership is a mediating variable in training interventions (Colton, 2004), although this construct is poorly understood from an academic perspective (Kaiser, Hogan & Bartholomew Craig, 2008). Staff feedback being a powerful variable, the role of staff feedback systems may also be a critical variable in improving practice (Deveau & McDonnell, 2008). Quilitch (1975) investigated the effects of a staff training workshop, a memorandum to staff and peer performance feedback in increasing the rate of activities in an institutionalized service for people with a learning disability. He found that the effect of performance feedback appeared to be more effective than either training workshops or memorandums. Staff feedback systems have been demonstrated to reduce the use of restrictive practices such as mechanical and physical restraint (Sturmey & Palen-McGlynn, 2002). The effectiveness of organizational policies and guidelines also requires much closer empirical scrutiny (Deveau & McGill, 2007).

Measures such as staff confidence also require a clear theoretical framework for evaluation. The positive impact on the confidence of staff is a reasonably consistent effect of training (Allen & Tynan, 2000; McDonnell et al., 2009; Thackrey, 1987). This construct would appear to have a close relationship with the construct of self-efficacy (Bandura, 1997). Measures should be based on a clear theoretical model. In this case the general aggression model may represent a positive framework (see Chapter 1). The development of a socio-cognitive model in this field would have several clear benefits. First, a clearer model would lead to more emphasis on the development of measures relevant to staff training in aggression management. Second, the theoretical approach of the general aggression model would provide a clearer rationale. Third, the concept of 'hot' and 'cool' memory systems (Metcalfe & Mischel, 1999) described in Chapter 1 has major applications in the training of the front-line staff, especially how carers perceive aggressive behaviour in terms of intent and pre-planning. Fourth, cognitive constructs such as 'scripts' could be examined within organizational group-based frameworks.

Developing Alternative Evaluative Methodologies

The development of research methodologies occurs within a social context. McDonnell (2007) referred to the training industry as the 'fear industry'. It could be argued that there has been no real opportunity to evaluate these programmes before their release into the marketplace. Training in aggression management would appear to be worldwide. This creates a huge problem for researchers who may wish to evaluate existing training programmes. Would training organizations allow their training to be subject to multiple randomized controlled trials? Potentially there would be a relatively large number of systems that would require evaluation. The costs alone of such a programme of research would be very expensive.

An alternative research review to the 'Holy Grail' of the randomized control trial would involve the challenging of the hierarchy of research evidence which represents the randomized controlled trial as the pinnacle of evidence. In medicine there have been challenges to the assumption that this type of evidence may be too narrow by itself and may ignore other useful data (Cohen, Zoë Stavri & Hersh, 2004). Randomized controlled trials are costly and difficult to implement in settings in which there is an urgent need for intervention. In the case of staff training in the management of aggressive behaviours both randomization and the need to deliver training to staff teams that may be experiencing aggressive and violent behaviours rapidly conflict with this approach.

There clearly are tensions between researchers and clinicians, which often reflects a narrow view of the philosophy of science. Kazdin (2008) succinctly described the mismatch between researchers and clinicians, arguing that few researchers would refuse therapies for their own children solely on the basis of absence of efficacy trials. In the field of autism there is a particularly good example of evidence and best practice apparently being ignored. A recent Internet survey of 479 parents of children and adolescents with a diagnosis of autism examined the use of therapies (Goin Kochel, Myers & MacIntosh, 2007). They found in the sample that drug-based intervention appeared to have been more extensively used despite the knowledge base which clearly indicates that the effects of drug-based therapies in the management of challenging behaviours are limited (Matson & Neal, in press). Even applying Cochrane levels of evidence, a recent randomized controlled trial of the drugs Resperidone, Tegretol and a placebo on staff reports of aggressive behaviours in people with intellectual difficulties found that the placebo group had the most positive ratings after a four-week trial (Tyrer et al., 2008).

Any different methodological approach needs to account for the Hawthorne effect (Mayo, 1949). The Hawthorne effect was named after an electrical plant in the United States which was the subject of many productivity studies from 1927 to 1932. It was observed that individual behaviours may be altered because people know that they are being studied. Elton Mayo's experiments showed that an increase in worker productivity was observed by the psychological stimulus of being singled out, involved and made to feel important. Training studies may be particularly susceptible to these effects. This is because it would be difficult to conduct them in completely blind experimental conditions.

If anonymity and randomization are difficulties for researchers, what methodologies are then available to use in non-laboratory-based settings? Quasi-experimental designs are used in settings and environments in which experimental control may be difficult to achieve (including non-equivalent control group design, time series designs). Multiple-baseline designs may reflect a pragmatic approach to this type of data collection. They were originally designed for use in single-case experimental approaches, especially when it is not possible for subjects to return to the original baseline (Hersen & Barlow, 1976). These designs have been adapted for group-based designs.

Killick and Allen (2005) evaluated a three-day training programme in aggression management using such a design in a psychiatric service for adolescents. Staff were trained in small groups with a maximum of 12 people in each group. Training took place over three consecutive days, and all three experimental groups were trained within a six-week time frame. A multiple-baseline design was decided upon to allow the measurement of changes in the attitude and knowledge before and after training in each subgroup and to compare change both within the groups over time and between the groups. Multiple baselines can use random allocation and as such can produce robust findings. Their main advantage is the avoidance of control groups of long duration.

Qualitative research methodologies can involve the systematic collection of data. Grounded theory (Strauss & Corbin, 1994) represents a structured and systematic approach to the collection of data. Furthermore, analytical approaches to qualitative research exist, although they may not be routinely taught in postgraduate syllabi (Kazdin, 2008).

Behaviour management practices can have a considerable impact on the consumers of services. It would be logical to include consumers in the evaluation process, integrating these findings with information gathered from more formal approaches to data collection. Consumer evaluations do provide insights into the experiences of service users (Sequiera & Halstead, 2001). In a follow-up study of 25 people with mild intellectual disabilities and challenging behaviours, 16 reported the experience of being restrained, and all of the subjects reported negative feelings about the procedures (Murphy, Estien & Clare, 1996). Discrepancies can also occur between the views of staff and service users (Fish & Culshaw, 2005). Broadening methodology to include the views of service consumers and staff would represent a significant step forward.

Applied behaviour analyst Montrose Wolf (1978) argued cogently that broadening applied behaviour analysis to include the construct of social validity would help behaviour analysts to 'find their hearts'. He used the phrase to describe a subjective method of measurement in which applied behaviour analysis could in actuality 'find its heart'. In his view applied behaviour analysts had concentrated too much on objective measurement. He argued that three dimensions were important in understanding the concept of social validity. First are goals or objectives that are 'socially significant'. That is to say do they achieve what society wants or requires? Second, are procedures or methods 'socially appropriate'? To put it literally, do the ends of an intervention or approach justify the means? Finally, are the consumers satisfied with the results? These three questions are extremely difficult to evaluate objectively, but there would appear to be a strong case to include social validity in any evaluation process. Wolf (1978) maintains that social validity measures may help to complement existing methodologies:

> It seems to me that by giving the same status to social validity that we now give to objective measurement and its reliability we will bring the consumer, that is society, into our science, soften our image and make sure our pursuit of social relevance. (p. 207)

The training research presented in this book is clearly strong in terms of social validity, but the empirical base is still limited. Future research should focus on using a range of methodologies (including qualitative studies). Measures need to focus on the impact of training on both the consumers and staff. Developing measures that sample organizational influences would appear to be a logical next step.

Conclusions

The evaluation of staff training is a complex process. It would be somewhat naive to view training as a panacea. Staff training is necessary but not sufficient for behavioural change to occur (Cullen, 1987). Training occurs within complex organizational structures and should ideally not be evaluated in isolation. Developing an understanding of the factors which optimize the success of staff training would be a natural next step for researchers. In addition the use of a wider range of experimental methodologies such as qualitative approaches would greatly enrich the data.

The data reported for the training described in this book are to a certain degree limited. Four areas have been described (intellectual disabilities, autism, mental health and services for older adults). Future research needs to focus on establishing independent evaluations of training in these areas.

10

Emerging Themes

In Chapter 9 the limitations of evaluative research were discussed in some detail. The absence of 'hard' evidence for the effectiveness for staff training in physical interventions makes it extremely difficult to make broad claims about the effectiveness of specific training programmes. Within this context of poor-quality research the evidence presented in this book for low arousal approaches would appear to be reasonably robust. In this final chapter an attempt will be made to examine important themes raised by this research.

Low Arousal Approaches: Some Emerging Themes

The low arousal approaches described in this book are not just a collection of strategies for managing crises; they also represent a 'behaviour management' philosophy steeped in humanism. Throughout this book there have been consistent messages, which include the avoidance of punitive consequences and sanctions for behaviour and an emphasis on self-reflection of staff and carers. The importance of person-centred approaches to care has been illustrated to be a clear theme across a variety of service settings. The work of Kitwood (1997) which emphasizes constructs of respect and trust in services for older adults has some themes similar to the Tidal Model in psychiatry (Buchanan-Barker & Barker, 2008) and the person-centred approaches advocated in intellectual disability services that stress the development of positive relationships with individuals who may display aggressive behaviours (see Pitonyak, 2004, for practical examples). Person-centred thinking has also influenced the development

Managing Aggressive Behaviour in Care Settings: Understanding and applying low arousal approaches
By Andrew A. McDonnell   © 2010 John Wiley & Sons, Ltd

of behaviour management approaches such as positive behaviour supports (Carr et al., 1999).

Managing crises in a person-centred way could be construed as a slightly paradoxical stance. It is the author's view that person-centred behaviour management should not be viewed in such a manner. The prevention of aggressive behaviours through mediums such as public health models or developmental organizational cultures which help to eliminate aggressive behaviours should be a primary goal. Although it is a laudable goal, the eradication of crisis management strategies may in some circumstances be unachievable. Even in the most well-resourced services there may be times when behaviours may require physical interventions. In these circumstances aggressive behaviour needs to be managed with strategies that are safe, effective and socially acceptable (McDonnell & Jones, 1999). In residential care environments carers are often expected to maintain a positive relationship with the people in their care. Managing aggressive behaviour in these situations in a manner that maintains a positive relationship between participants should be a major goal. The goal in these circumstances is to manage behaviour before attempting to alter or change it (McDonnell & Anker, 2009).

The development of approaches to managing crises in a person-centred and socially valid manner would have clear benefits in a cost–benefit analysis to both carers and service users. One in 20 workers experiences violence in the workplace, with the highest rates being reported in the Netherlands, France, the United Kingdom and Ireland (Parent-Thirion, Macías, Hurley & Vermeylen, 2007). Reduction in the loss of time because of staff sickness alone could represent a significant saving for human services. Low arousal approaches may represent a small but significant step towards this goal.

There are two elements to the process of demand reduction. First, general demand reduction over a specified time period (such as a day, a week, a month) should reduce the general potential for confrontation. Second, the avoidance of demands and requests in the immediate management of situations should help to prevent the escalation of threatening behaviour to aggression. There is some evidence from a single-case study that even if such strategies are effective there is a possibility that some carers may have strong negative feelings about what they perceive to be 'giving in' (McDonnell, Reeves, Johnson & Lane, 1998). The term 'strategic capitulation' (LaVigna & Willis, 2002) has been used to indicate that to manage crises in the short term, carers may sometimes have to 'give in'. In Chapter 2 a range of antecedent strategies which may help to avoid escalation of crises were described.

The perceptions of carers and service users are clearly an important aspect of the process. The relationship between the carer and the service user is influenced by cognition. In Weiner's attributional model of helping behaviour it is hypothesized that the staff perception of the service user's control of their behaviour may have an impact on their helping behaviour towards those individuals (Dagnan, Trower & Smith, 1998; Weiner, 1986). In essence, the more positively a staff member or carer feels towards a service user, the more likely they are to help that individual. In addition, in times of crisis during which an individual may be experiencing a heightened state of arousal it appears illogical to impose boundaries and rules under the circumstances. In some cases the individual may have limited information processing ability and may be reacting at a physiological rather than at cognitive level, using 'hot' rather than 'cool' cognitive processes (Metcalfe & Mischel, 1999). How 'hot' and 'cool' processes interact may benefit staff in day-to-day practice. It should be stressed that these processes apply to both carers and service users.

Anecdotal evidence strongly indicates that the use of boundaries and sanctions as consequences to threatening behaviour or verbal escalation may potentially escalate aggressive behaviours. The approach has advocated the reduction and not the total eradication of staff demands. In addition the withdrawal of demands may be accompanied by their gradual reintroduction as the crisis situation abates. This may be especially important in educational settings in which there is a clear need to educate individuals. Reducing demands such as structured teaching schedules may sometimes conflict in the short term with educational goals. A rationale for not compelling children in these situations can be provided by understanding arousal mechanisms. Individuals process information less efficiently when they are in a state of 'hyper-arousal' (for a fuller explanation, see Easterbrook, 1959; Yerkes & Dodson, 1908). To continue with an existing high-demand teaching programme in these circumstances could conceivably lead to increasing numbers of aggressive behaviours, which generally does not create the optimal arousal conditions for learning.

Breaking of rules can sometimes be accompanied by sanctions, many of which could be construed as punishment. Strong arguments have been made against the use of consequence-based punishment strategies (Donnellan, LaVigna, Negri-Schoulz & Fassbender, 1988). Punishment strategies may reduce a specific behaviour in the short term, but there are side effects to relationships that also need to be considered. Token economy systems sometimes use the concept of response cost or fines (Kazdin, 1982). The use of response cost and fines can be perceived by practitioners in a negative manner and be too controlling (Corrigan, 1995). The avoidance of sanctions and the reduction of rules and boundaries are key elements of a low arousal approach. Individuals who experience hyper-aroused emotional states in crisis may be experiencing extreme trauma and may therefore perceive sanctions in a threatening manner. There are clear concerns that sanctions can have a negative effect on the development of positive relationships between carers and service users (Pitonyak, 2004). McCord (1997) in discussing the use of sanctions with children argued

Table 10.1. The relationship between control and awareness

	More in control	*Less in control*
More aware	The person appears aggressive with threats and seems to be in control and argumentative.	The person is only partially responsive to conversation and direction and appears to not be focusing on the individual.
Less aware	The person shouts and becomes verbally aggressive but will stop when prompted.	The person is aggressive and distressed and does not respond to external prompts.

that these approaches are not always motivated by altruism on the part of parents:

> If a parent wants to teach a child not to make a mess in the house of a neighbor, the parent can help the child to keep her toys neat or to eat carefully. If the parent couples a request to avoid making a mess with a threat of punishment or promise of reward, the parent has shifted grounds for action from consideration for others to the child's own pains and pleasures (p. 317).

Sanctions also appear to imply that the individuals can control their aggressive behaviours across differing situations. This contrasts with the view that in the case of aggression some people may not always be completely in control of their behaviour at the time (Richetin & Richardson, 2008). The complex interaction of person and situational variables (see Anderson & Bushman, 2002) makes the view that aggression can be controlled by sanction alone an over-simplistic one.

Table 10.1 shows the complex relationship between these two variables. When a person appears more aware and in control, their behaviour may be typified by threats of harm – 'If you do that I will hurt you' – and the individual could appear to be relatively calm. This type of aggression is clearly instrumental in nature. In the second instance the person's arousal level may mean that they are only partially responsive to communication, and an external state of *hyper-arousal* is more obvious. In the third condition the person may be unaware that they are being perceived as aggressive but will stop if politely prompted. In the final situation the person is not responsive to external prompts. Many rage-like states can be reached this point. In sum, it is possible for individuals to fluctuate from one emotional state to another.

The importance of restraint and tolerance from carers is also an implicit component of the approach. The need for more tolerance of aggressive behaviours would appear to be in conflict with the increasing focus on societal and organizational intolerance. Government policies which encourage staff to not tolerate aggressive behaviour would appear to have proponents in the health care sector (Behr, Ruddock, Benn & Crawford, 2005). Intuitively the concept of zero tolerance would appear to have high face validity, although the concept should be distinguished from behavioural outcome data. Whittington and Higgins (2002) speculated that national policies that promote an attitude of zero tolerance may encourage practitioners to assume that any aggressive behaviour by a patient is inappropriate, with the result that any such behaviour will be subject to high-intensity interventions that far outweigh the behaviour per se. Zero-tolerance campaigns often promote a simplistic victim–perpetrator relationship and ignore the possibility that staff may have inadvertently escalated aggressive behaviour in some circumstances (Hastings & Brown, 2000). The area of staff provocation of aggressive behaviour has received relatively limited attention in nursing textbooks (Mohr, 2008).

There is some evidence to suggest that zero-tolerance policies may directly have an impact on carers and their relationships with service users. Middleby-Clements and Grenyer (2007) evaluated the impact of two aggression management training courses, where one course contained information on the policy of zero tolerance. This study found that the training appeared to cause increases in rigid or inflexible attitudes towards the management of aggression in the health workplace while reducing staff tolerance towards aggression. The authors admitted that this result was unexpected, but it does provide many questions for researchers about unintentional effects of training.

Furthermore, reflective practices for staff are critical. The construct of reflective practice describes an individual evaluating their performance in situations and learning from both positive and negative experiences (Schon, 1987). One obvious variable would be altering the carer/staff attribution. Many techniques which could potentially be applied in this context have been developed in cognitive behavioural therapy (Dagnan et al., 1998).

An honest examination of the overt behaviour of carers is clearly an important aspect of the reflective approach. There is the theme in the literature that staff may inadvertently trigger aggression (Hastings & Brown, 2000; Mohr, 2008; Morrison, 1990; Whittington & Wykes, 1996). In therapeutic settings the term 'malignant alienation' has been used to describe negative relationships between service consumers and staff (Watts & Morgan, 1994). Low arousal approaches aim to make staff aware of their own potential contribution to aggression and help them to alter their behaviour. A common theme of the case examples described in this book involves staff viewing themselves as a major potential cause of aggression. This apparently negative statement can be reframed in a positive manner. The author was reminded of a particularly enlightened and reflective carer who worked with a child who initially was very aggressive towards her until she directly altered her own behaviour by not responding to the person's verbal threats: 'If I accidentally make situations worse by my behaviour, then I can also improve things by changing it'.

In this book, training in low arousal approaches has been accompanied by training in physical interventions. The practice of combining both elements in training would appear to be a common practice. Training in physical interventions would appear to be focusing on the 'worst case scenario'; in reality carers are more likely to be confronted by verbal aggression (Nijman, Bowers, Oud & Jansen, 2005). A more rational approach might be to train staff in the principles of low arousal approaches only (including verbal de-escalation). The training course described in Chapter 3 could easily be adapted to contain more practice of low arousal approaches and no physical interventions. There are obviously clear ethical considerations in adopting such an approach. In reality there are many assumptions about training in physical interventions which do not seem to be reflected by the data. In Chapter 9 the paucity of data from good, methodologically sound studies would indicate that the assumption that training in physical interventions reduces staff injuries or assaults is a dubious one.

Physical Interventions

The use of physical interventions (described in Chapter 3) to manage aggressive behaviours should be viewed as a last resort (Deveau & McDonnell, 2009). There are many questions raised when considering the teaching and application of these methods in care environments. Physical interventions such as physical restraint are not a therapeutic intervention but methods of containment (Mohr, 2008). The debate about whether or not to teach these methods is important. There are many practical considerations for any trainer who embarks on the teaching of physical interventions.

Are physical interventions socially valid?

Do the ends justify the means? This is a question which may sometimes be confusing. Care staff can become extremely frightened when confronted with a situation that requires physical intervention. Anecdotal evidence suggests that people in these situations often attempt to justify physical interventions during post-incident debriefing by saying that it was the last resort. It is not uncommon to hear statements such as 'We had to do it' or 'What else could we have done?'

What are the views of people who are not professionals about physical interventions? A cynic might suggest that physical interventions that are carried out in care settings are not particularly a vote-winning issue. A more optimistic view would suggest that the public needs to be informed of the issues to decide on their relevance.

Critics of the 'social validity' arguments have argued that social validity judgements may be overly weighted in terms of the views of service users. Such judgements can though in certain instances result in scenarios wherein the judge is implicitly required to place greater or lesser emphasis on the safety of staff versus that of the service user (Paterson & Duxbury, 2006). The author would claim that social validity data should not be assessed in isolation. In care environments there can be an imbalance of power; in other words, where individuals do not have clear mechanisms to advocate for them, there may be an argument that there should be a positively skewed balance that slightly favours the views of the service consumers.

Teach the minimum number of physical techniques

In Chapter 3 the development of a training course in the management of aggressive behaviours was outlined. The quantity of physical interventions taught was significantly reduced over time. McDonnell and Gallon (2006) have described as the 'kitchen sink' approach the more traditional control and restraint training that teaches a vast range of physical interventions that the participants are unlikely to be able to recall. Recent evidence calls into question the ability of staff to recall and demonstrate physical interventions in simulated conditions (Rogers et al., 2007).

Try to avoid complex techniques and movements

Many physical interventions can be highly complex, involving several sequential movements, which, in team interventions require synchronicity by several individuals. It is clear from the established literature on the acquisition of psychomotor skills that complexity has two dimensions, namely the range of different movements within a single procedure and the need for each aspect to be performed in the prescribed sequence (Stubbs et al., 2009). McDonnell, Dearden and Richens (1991) maintained that teaching fewer physical movements as opposed to specific techniques would help to simplify responses.

Do not teach pain-based techniques

The use of pain compliance continues to be problematic from legal, ethical and value-based perspectives. The wilful infliction of pain on a human being is often justified by arguments that there are no non-pain-related options. A means–end justification has been used to justify the use of electric shock devices for people with autism or intellectual disabilities who self-injure, with claims of no overt signs of distress or pain (Van Oorsouw, Israel, Von Heyn & Duker, 2008). In terms of low arousal strategies the argument against these types of interventions is not one of effectiveness per se (as these methods can certainly be effective) but one of morality. In most therapeutic environments the development of positive relationships between staff and service users is an essential ingredient of the care process. The use of pain-based methods intuitively cannot be conducive to the development of positive relationships.

The work of Smallridge and Williamson (2008), who were commissioned in the wake of restraint deaths in the English Children's Secure Estate, contained an extensive discussion of the role of pain compliance. The authors concluded that there remains a role for pain compliance on operational grounds while recognizing that this potentially contravened the United Nations Convention on the Rights of the Child. Paradoxical statements such as these create 'mixed messages' in organizations. Experimental evidence derived from animal studies has identified aggression elicited by painful stimuli (Ulrich & Azrin, 1962). It appears logical that the use of holds that use pain as a mechanism of control could exacerbate aggressive behaviour. From a carer perspective it is also possible that the increased aggression they would witness during an episode of restraint might not be attributed to the application of such methods per se. The physical interventions described in this book avoid the deliberate use of pain as a method of control. The avoidance of such methods should be the paramount concern of training providers.

Avoid extreme teaching scenarios

The evidence presented in this book clearly shows that training in physical interventions should not be construed as a panacea for aggressive behaviours in care environments. It has been the author's extensive experience that training can only address high-frequency day-to-day situations in which physical interventions may be required. It is not unusual for trainers to be tempted to address extreme scenarios in training courses. Teaching staff who are asking how to defend themselves against a potential edged weapon illustrates this point. In these circumstances it would take considerable time to effectively and safely teach an individual to defend themselves against such an extreme (and relatively rare) form of aggression. Stephen Lawrence, a teacher in the United Kingdom, was stabbed and killed by a youth in 1995 outside his school; this case raised public awareness about knife crime. Are such fatalities good justification for training staff to defend themselves against such weapons? McDonnell (2007) used the example of the killing of 16 pupils and a teacher in a school in Dunblane in Scotland in 1996 by a gunman to illustrate that training responses are not always effective responses to such extreme scenarios.

Research conducted into safety drill produces results that suggest that training in emergency responses may have limitations. For instance, in the case of fire alarms in public buildings there is evidence that people often ignore the signal (Proulx, 1999). Human responses still occur in crisis situations (Reason, 1990). There would appear to be few guarantees that training for extreme scenarios is a simple matter.

The author (along with some of his colleagues) has attended several training courses in the management of aggression where extremely high-risk interventions (usually involving either prone or supine holds) are taught to participants. The main argument used is that these techniques should only be employed as a last resort when 'all other measures have failed'. The real danger of using the 'last resort' argument is that the last resort can become the method of choice, depending on the environmental climate of the organization (Deveau & McDonnell, 2009). In sum, in any training course there is a limited amount of time to train carers; therefore, the avoidance of extreme situations appears to be a logical step to take.

Set limits and boundaries on physical interventions syllabi

The training system described in this book has actively avoided, and in some cases banned, the teaching of some physical methods. Neither prone nor supine holds were taught on the training courses. In addition any method that involved the 'locking' of body joints or the deliberate infliction of pain as a method of control was not included. The author accepts that many training programmes in aggression management do not set limits to what is taught to participants. Training can also be 'menu driven', where individuals are shown a range of methods and asked to choose what they feel would be appropriate.

Of more concern are the so-called graded approaches, where methods are taught in terms of a hierarchy of intrusiveness. This approach does have high face validity but assumes that frightened and scared carers will remember how to do this in a 'real-life situation'. There is a danger that participants will forget the hierarchy in these situations. Setting boundaries to training is a pragmatic approach. The author was asked in an adult psychiatric setting to show a few 'moves' that would help the person fend off a knife. The participant was disappointed with the response that such methods were well beyond the time constraints of a short training course. In essence, not all risk situations have physical intervention solutions.

Make training fit for purpose

Anecdotal evidence appears to indicate that many training seminars occur in classroom environments and that generalization of skills to the work environment will happen using some form of 'psychological osmosis'. Alternative models do exist, where training happens in the environment in which the methods are to be practically taught rather than in a sanitized classroom.

McDonnell and Gallon (2006) argued that teaching physical interventions in 'matted areas' may reduce the risk for course participants, but it limits the generalization of the physical methods taught. Prone and supine holds are nearly always taught in matted environments, but in reality the so-called takedowns occur in environments that often have thin carpets or hard floors. It could be argued that if a method cannot be safely taught in a controlled environment, then it is logical that the application of the method in an uncontrolled environment would create more risks. The training courses described in this book avoided teaching in environments that contained 'matted areas'. In the author's view training environments, wherever possible, should simulate work environments. In ideal circumstances training should take place in the work environments in which physical interventions are to be applied.

Trainer Competency Is an Essential Quality Standard

Training 'trainers' is an area of concern and is relatively poorly evaluated (Paterson & Leadbetter, 2002). Even if a training package is evidence based and well evaluated there is a difference between the programme itself and the competency of trainers to deliver that programme. The training programme described in this book used the 'pass' and 'fail' criteria for trainers and required evidence that trainers could deliver training to staff. More research that investigates the competency of trainers is needed. In the industry it is not unusual for assessors in some programmes to never directly observe and assess trainers actively delivering their training. In vivo assessment of competency would be a good standard. In Chapter 9 only one behavioural study reported evidence for competency of trainers (Van den Pol, Reed & Fuqua, 1983).

Consider the fragility of physical interventions

The construct of technical 'fragility', i.e. where small adjustments (movement or pressure) to the procedure (either intentionally or unintentionally) are likely to result in intentional or unintentional injury or severe pain to an individual, is important to consider when evaluating techniques (Paterson & Duxbury 2006). There are a number of methods which can appear to be of low risk, but simple and sometimes subtle changes in posture can lead to dramatic alterations in the risk posed to the service user (Stubbs et al., 2009). A number of the techniques reviewed were fragile, in that small adjustments potentially foreseeable in practice by either error or wilful adaptation by staff seeking to increase the aversiveness of the technique would have exponentially increased the danger posed by the technique.

Consider service user health factors

There are many factors including gender, age and general health that may have an impact on teaching physical interventions. In Chapter 3 adaptations to physical interventions were briefly discussed. Physical health is an obvious consideration. Older adults can be physically frail, and it would be logical to assume that many restraint techniques are not applicable to this population. In particular, locking movements that involve the manipulation of joints would be difficult to justify, as the risk of harm would be elevated. Other obvious conditions such as osteoporosis are associated with reduced bone mass and increased fracture risk (Kanis, Melton, Christiansen, Johnston & Khaltaev, 1994); this would have specific relevance to older populations. In addition, medical conditions such as anorexia nervosa also have associated complications like osteoporosis (Katzman, 2003).

Finally, obesity rates appear to be increasing in Western society. A recent U.K. survey identified 24% of adults (aged 16 or over) in England as obese, an overall increase from 15% in 1993. It was reported that 17% of boys aged 2 to 15 and 16% of girls in the same age group were classed as obese, an increase from 11% and 12% respectively in 1995 (National Health Service, 2009). With regard to physical interventions (especially increased adipose tissue in the abdominal area), obesity may also have an impact on the risks of specific physical interventions such as prone holds.

Teaching less may be more

In Chapter 9 the evidence for staff training was presented. While staff training in physical interventions is limited in terms of outcomes, there is a reason for teaching some interventions, even if it just makes people 'feel' more confident. Despite this evidence some members of the training industry still make the non-evidence-based claim that training will reduce staff injuries. The evidence for this claim is most definitely 'mixed'. In addition there appears to be an implicit assumption that training in physical interventions will in essence reduce their usage, especially if training also contains methods of de-escalation. The mantra 'We train people not to use these interventions' does appear to be somewhat illogical in the circumstances.

Monitor physical intervention usage

The monitoring of physical interventions is an essential component in their reduction (Deveau & McDonnell, 2009). Staff feedback and monitoring is an important component in this process. Implicit in any monitoring process should be the setting of reduction targets for physical interventions. In the author's experience, services which employ physical interventions on a regular basis can become desensitized to their use. In these circumstances external monitoring can provide a useful 'reality check'.

Risk limitation or risk taking?

A central issue of staff training in physical interventions is the reduction of risk of harm to both staff and service users. The evidence presented in Chapter 9 for risk reduction in terms of staff and service user injury is relatively weak. Managing the risks of aggressive behaviours is a major focus in many organizations.

Prediction is a key aspect of any risk management approach. Grove and Meehl (1996) distinguished between the clinical method that primarily relies on human judgements and mechanical methods which involve a formal, statistical approach to reach decisions. Morcover, there is some evidence that mechanical methods are more reliable. In a meta-analysis of studies on health and behaviour mechanical prediction techniques were on average about 10% more accurate than clinical predictions (Grove, Zald, Lebow, Snitz & Nelson, 2000). Risk models based on statistical approaches may appear to be useful; however, these systems are still interpreted by the same human beings who frequently display many biases in decision making. There are a wide range of reported biases described in the literature.

Analysis of errors in an attempt to avoid them in the future is a major element of organizational approaches to risk reduction (Reason, 1990). Studying situations in which things have gone wrong can identify processes in organizations that may exacerbate risks of aggression. Investigatory models require that the investigator starts by examining the chain of events that led to an accident or adverse outcome and by considering the actions of those involved. The investigator then, crucially, looks further back at the conditions in which staff were working and the organizational context in which the incident occurred (Vincent et al., 2000).

Reason, Carthey and De Laval (2001) examined medical errors from an organizational perspective. They argued that there is a 'vulnerable system syndrome' which may make some systems more vulnerable to risk. They identified negative characteristics of these systems. First, these systems tend to blame the front-line individuals. Second, there is a process of denying the potential existence of systemic error. Organizations can create negative feedback systems which may maintain aggressive behaviours (Braverman, 2002).

Individuals in care environments have to take calculated risks on a routine basis. The limitation of risks to both service users and staff is a clear goal in these circumstances. If an individual has shown aggression in specific public areas, then there may well be a case for avoiding such places in the future. However, it is also possible that individuals will be unable to learn more appropriate behaviours if such a stratagem is adopted on a routine basis.

The main limitation of risk management approaches lies in the fact that exact predictions are not possible and that risk will never be completely eradicated from services (Lamont & Brunero, 2009). Studying specific risk profiles of groups may not be a simple matter of cause and effect. When assessing the potential for aggression, historical information and risk assessment tools may help the predictive processes; however, such mechanisms may be similar to those for the prediction of the weather (Scott & Resnick, 2006). From a practitioner perspective, past history of aggression is still the best predictor of future aggressive behaviour (see MacArthur Foundation, 2001, for a detailed perspective). Judgement calls in situations in which an individual does not commit an act of physical aggression but has been verbally aggressive or threatening are particularly difficult. Research indicates that many individuals show verbal aggression without it necessarily escalating into physical aggression (Nijman et al., 2005). Correspondingly, most physically aggressive behaviour is associated with verbal aggression and threatening behaviour.

In sum, managing the risks of aggression involves a very careful balancing act between statistical evidence and practitioner judgements. In care environments many approaches to managing these situations will require an element of risk taking. It is the author's contention that a positive and constructive approach to risk management requires not only the review of poor practice in terms of critical incident analysis but also careful investigation of situations in which aggressive behaviour did not occur. Similarly, the low arousal approaches described in this book involve diversionary strategies; when successful these may indicate that risks of aggressive behaviour can be reduced. From a cognitive perspective such data could be construed in two completely different views. The first, negative view would be to categorize such a situation as a 'near miss'. A second, more positive approach would classify such as situation as 'successful diversionary tactics'. Calculated risk taking is a major element in the management of aggressive behaviour.

Organizational Responses to Aggression: Creating Cultures That Reduce Restrictive Practices

Throughout this book restrictive and, in some cases, coercive practices have been reported in many different fields. Physical restraint has been reported in Scottish children's services (Bell, 1996), psychiatric services for adults (Wright, Gray, Parkes & Gournay, 2002) and services for people with intellectual disabilities (Emerson et al., 2000). The widespread use of mechanical restraints, such as vest and limb restraints, is reported in the United States (Minnick, Mion, Leipzig, Lamb & Palmer, 1998). Mechanical restraint is reported in Swiss and German psychiatric services (Martin, Bernhardsgrutter, Goebel & Steinert, 2007) and children's services (Fryer, Beech & Byrne, 2004) as well. Seclusion is also used in mental health services in the United Kingdom (Bowers et al., 2004). There are clearly many complex cultural factors that underlie these varying rates of usage. The reduction of such practices in services would represent significant progress.

Training in best practice represents only one element of an organizational response to the reduction of restrictive practices. Aggression management training should be regarded as necessary, but not sufficient, to reduce restrictive practices. Clear statements of intent are a crucial element of the process of change. The reduction of these practices is becoming a major goal of services in the United States, the United Kingdom and the rest of Europe. The recent declaration by the Council of Europe (2004) clearly illustrates the trend:

> Persons with mental disorder should have the right to be cared for in the least restrictive environment available and with the least restrictive treatment available taking into account their health needs and the need to protect the safety of others.

This kind of legislation is difficult to evaluate in terms of direct impact. The positive, the negative and the side effects of such legislation may require long-term evaluation. In adult psychiatry the principle of least restrictiveness has prompted some psychiatrists to state that the service user should be consulted about intrusive interventions such as restraint and seclusion (Jones & Kingdom, 2005).

Organizational cultures have to operate within a legislative framework. Legislation can be used to encourage a process of change often by means of target setting. In contrast, cultures that accept relatively high levels of restrictive practices will probably not radically reduce them. In 1999 the National Association of State Mental Health Program Directors called for the reduction and elimination of restraint and seclusion. A curriculum for organizational approaches was developed in 2004, with six core strategies: leadership and organizational change, the use of data to inform practice, workforce development, the use of seclusion/restraint prevention tools, consumer roles in inpatient settings and debriefing. Colton (2004) developed a comprehensive self-evaluation checklist to assist organizations achieve restraint reduction. This includes guidance on assessing the readiness of organizations to achieve this, by stages starting with 'inaction' through 'espoused action' to 'sustained action and maintenance'.

Deveau and McGill (2007) proposed that organizations seeking to reduce restrictive physical interventions should attend to three core strategies:

- *Leadership and organizational change.* That is to say the top leaders in organizations should expect to receive information on the levels of PI used in services and with individuals and should regard these as key quality indicators (leadership is a relatively poorly understood phenomenon; see Kaiser et al., 2008, for a fuller discussion).
- *Data use to inform practice.* This describes the importance of visual information feedback to staff teams as part of total quality systems.
- *Restraint reduction strategies* at the service and the individual service user level.

A potential moderator variable is the role of leadership in reducing restrictive practices (Colton 2004; Deveau & McDonnell, 2009; Deveau & McGill, 2007). Leadership in organizations may be a significant adjunct to a training programme. In aggression management, leadership has been loosely defined as a solution to the problem of collective effort, the problem of bringing people together and combining their efforts to promote success and survival (Hogan & Kaiser, 2005).

Cultural norms in organizations can also be influenced by some well-known group-based psychological processes. Studies in social psychology have regularly illustrated the power of contextual factors in normalizing practices that would be considered abusive. The most famous study involved ordinary members of the public to participate in an experiment involving learning and electric shock (Milgram, 1974). Similarly, the classic Stanford prison experiment illustrated how simply placing people in specific roles of guards and prisoners led to abusive practices (Haney, Banks & Zimbardo, 1973).

A natural extension of this work involves societal approaches to aggression management such as the public health model initiatives (Butchart, Phinney, Check & Villaveces, 2004). In essence a multi-layered response to aggression management may well be required. This needs to encompass what has been described as primary, secondary and tertiary levels of prevention (see Miller, Paterson & McKenna, 2009). Clearly, responses to aggression reduction need to encompass organizational culture and reflect the dynamic aspects of this phenomenon. Paterson and Leadbetter (2009) illustrated this point by stating that '[o]ccupational violence in human services is an organic interactive phenomenon' (p. 125).

As an aside to organizational approaches, it is interesting to note that the approaches described in this book led to the formation of an organization called Studio3 Training Systems in the early 1990s. Training systems rather than training courses were described as the emphasis at a very early stage of development (McDonnell et al., 1991). The name implies that there should be a systems approach to aggression management. This would appear to be borne out by the more recent research about organizational approaches to the reduction of aggression and violence.

Scientific Inquiry versus Market Forces: The Fear Industry

The evaluation of staff training in physical intervention techniques is a controversial issue. As successive national reports have recognized (e.g. Deveau & McGill, 2007; Hart & Howell, 2004), the present unregulated market economy of training provision and the poor quality of the research literature has come to mean that the commissioners of restraint training are often heavily influenced by the marketing activities of commercial training companies that are promoting proprietary brands of training, which are often unsupported by valid research evidence of effectiveness. McDonnell (2007) has referred to the training industry as the 'fear industry'.

The marketplace for training in aggression is relatively large, although it is difficult to estimate the exact figures spent directly on staff training. Does the perceived fear of aggression of carers fuel the demand for training in physical interventions that will be rarely used by staff? There appears to be the implicit assumption that training in physical interventions will in essence reduce their usage, especially if training also contains methods of de-escalation. Increased regulation in the United Kingdom makes training in physical interventions more widespread.

In Chapter 9 a critical analysis that demonstrates the limitation of training has been provided. Despite the evidence, training would appear to be a popular response of organizations with regard to aggression management. The demand for training in aggression management is not influenced only by the laws of supply and demand. The relatively new field of behavioural economics studies the human components of economics. Decision making is viewed by examining cognitive aspects of judgement and decision making. A consistent theme of the research is that human decision-making processes are not just influenced by rationality but that there are many subjective components in this process:

> A free market based on supply and demand and no friction would be ideal if we were truly rational. Yet, when we are not rational but irrational policies should take this important factor into account. (Ariely, 2008, p. 48)

Consumers' views are a powerful element in any market-led industry. The training industry has many 'blurred boundaries' with regard to who is the consumer of training. There have been several studies which have examined consumer views of physical interventions (Cunningham, McDonnell, Easton & Sturmey, 2002; Fish & Culshaw, 2005; Murphy, Estien & Clare, 1996; Sequiera & Halstead, 2001). Staff are also consumers of services and, presumably, as the recipients of training, their views may at times overshadow those of service users. One study has highlighted the discrepant views between staff and service users (Fish & Culshaw, 2005).

This book has tried to present a strong case for social validity arguments. The views of service users should take paramount importance, but the reality appears to be more confused. Views of the carers, especially about their own safety, should not be disregarded. If there is a balance to be struck between the views of consumers and staff, then this should be positively skewed in favour of the disempowered grouping (in this case consumers).

In sum market forces do appear to dictate the supply and demand curve for training rather than empirical evidence. Allen (2008) has referred to this situation as 'scandalous'. Unfortunately, removing market forces may be akin to placing the genie back in the bottle. Producing evidence-based training in such a climate is fraught with many difficulties. Paradoxically, research that distinguishes between particular systems needs to be independently and systematically evaluated.

Changing Minds about Behaviour Management Approaches

The example of banning prone restraint holds from physical interventions training

There are two fundamental assumptions to this book. First, humanistic strategies such as low arousal approaches need to be adopted by human services to reduce aggression. Second, training in physical interventions should aim to reduce restrictive practices in the workplace. In essence organizations that want to adopt these two stances face a complex process of culture change. For many services this may well involve the altering of their views by individuals, which may be associated with deeply set core beliefs.

Gardner (2006) maintains that the changing of minds is based on a competing number of factors. These include seven key areas: reason and logic (the Socratic method), research and science (empirical approaches), re-descriptions (the appearance of the idea or concept in many forms in different areas), resonance (gut feelings about the subject matter), resources and rewards (reinforcement principles), real-world events and tragedies and finally resistances (rigidity of thinking). The premise of Gardner (2006) is that scientific evidence and logic are only two components in changing minds.

We can apply these principles to one area of the debate about restrictive practices. McDonnell (2007) in a debate paper called for a ban on teaching prone restraint holds on training courses. This has been associated with a protest charter known as the Millfields Charter in the United Kingdom (see www.millfieldscharter.com). Paterson (2007) in response to the call for a ban maintained that this was the wrong question to ask, as the main arguments should focus more on organizational factors. He maintained that the Millfields Charter's proposals were distracting from the most radical changes required to the management of violence. Leadbetter (2007) argued for an approach in which a sector-specific ban might be an achievable outcome. In sum, these papers appear to reflect an impasse in this area. Now, what are the factors which would lead to a change of mind?

A more detailed analysis of the factors listed by Gardner (2006) is illuminating. What does reason and logic say about holding people in the prone position? First, it would be logical to assume that a person's breathing might be restricted, especially if they struggle. Logically the restraint-related deaths may be related to this posture. The scientific evidence is more mixed. Positional asphyxia would appear to be a 'mixed-bag' label applied to many restraint-related deaths. In terms of 're-descriptions' the idea that restraint position may be implicated in deaths appears to be not related to one area alone. In childcare similar concerns have been raised (Nunno, Holden & Tollar, 2006).

Empirical evidence is readily available about prone restraint holds and their risks. Making a clear prima facie case against the use of prone holds is a contentious subject. Leadbetter (2002) referred to 'high-tariff' techniques which may have increased risks. Hard experimental data do not really exist in the field. Paterson and colleagues (2003) argued that laboratory-based studies which examined deaths by 'positional asphyxia' had limited ecological validity. Many of the restraint methods investigated tended to focus on holds such as 'hobble restraints' commonly favoured by the U.S. police. Methods used more commonly in care environments have not really been investigated. Prone restraint is not the only method which has associated risks. There are also issues of misapplication of methods (Nunno et al., 2006) and other risk factors such as the health of the populations, associated use of psychotropic medications and conditions such as 'excited delirium' also need to be considered (Morrison & Saddler, 2001). In the latter cases there have been classic animal studies which have demonstrated that death can occur in excitatory states through what has been described as 'vagal inhibition', where the length of time and the nature of studies required to really answer this question makes what looks very much like a 'straw man' argument. Is there sufficient concern to warrant a change in practice? Allen (2008) reviewed the evidence and stated that

> There is sufficient concern, if not sufficient evidence to suggest that there needs to be a change in the training and practice of prone restraint. (p. 102)

The concept of resonance is perhaps the most subjective and perhaps the most enlightening construct to apply to this argument. Gardner described it as follows: 'A view, idea, or perspective resonates to the extent that it feels right to an individual'. It may seem that such a subjective interpretation is not in keeping with the idea of evidence-based practice. In reality, decisions are sometimes made not using evidence but based on a 'gut feeling'. Clearly, holding an individual in such a posture evokes powerful emotional responses.

In the case of resonance the application of such methods does not 'feel appropriate'. In this book we have outlined social validity studies in which these methods do not receive positive support from consumers (Cunningham et al., 2002) or professional staff (McDonnell & Sturmey, 2000). Staff and service users may have different views about the reasons for the application of these methods. There is certainly a moral case to consider within the context of care environments.

Gardner (2006) has also argued that 'resources and rewards' are important factors in mind-changing events. Are there benefits to the halting of teaching of these methods? It may be possible that training organizations will lose market share if they do not teach these methods. Economic factors may exert a powerful influence in these processes. What are the incentives available to organizations to not actively teach these methods?

There have been many tragedies documented in this area. The report by the *Hartford Courant* in 1998 identified 152 cases of restraint-related deaths in the U.S. care system (Weiss, Altimeri, Blint & Megan, 1998). In California a series of well-publicized restraint-related deaths were investigated in 2002 (Morrison, Duryea, Moore & Nathanson-Shinn, 2002). In the United Kingdom the deaths of David 'Rocky' Bennett in a psychiatric service for adults and Gareth Myatt in a youth offending facility are well publicized and documented cases. Deaths in child services in the United States have also been reported (Nunno et al., 2006). In the United Kingdom the BBC undercover documentary *McIntyre Undercover* showed a reporter who worked in an adult service for people with intellectual disabilities and reported clear abusive practices. After the documentary the service in Kent was eventually closed. In sum, there would appear to be sufficient cases to arouse concern.

Resistances manifest themselves in the form of rigidity of thinking. The types of rigid thinking encountered in the case of banning prone restraint holds can include 'It's not a problem; the number of deaths is relatively small'. According to cognitive therapy rigidly held thoughts may reflect rigid core beliefs. A common core belief involves the idea that there are no alternatives to these methods. A belief this firmly held would be extremely difficult to alter.

In conclusion, Gardner (2006) would maintain that processes that involve changing minds are complex and multi-layered. There is no waiting attached to these principles. Using this viewpoint any process that attempts to change people's minds about teaching and using prone restraint holds in care environments needs to focus on a broad front, using a range of mind-changing tactics. In the case of prone restraint the strongest arguments may well be moral rather than simply empirically based. An understanding of the philosophy of science would indicate that science does not just advance because of bold conjectures and refutations (Popper, 1963). An alternative view is that paradigm shifts occur (Kuhn, 1962). The example of prone restraint represents one issue (and there are of course many) in the field. It could be argued that a paradigm shift is required in the field of physical interventions. This paradigm involves the premise that 'less is more'. Teaching fewer physical interventions and restricting their teaching and proscribing specific methods does require a 'mindset' change. Empirical evidence may be necessary but not sufficient for such a change in practice.

The current reality is that there are also very strong moral arguments for the abolition of specific physical intervention methods. To change the culture of an industry is a mammoth task, especially if the arguments become stuck in an empirical quagmire.

Rediscovering Moral Management

This book has attempted to outline a person-centred approach to the management of aggressive behaviours in care settings. The evidence base outlined in this book represents a small but significant step in the development of best practice. The low arousal approaches and the associated training in behaviour management, including physical interventions, would appear to be based on a humanistic philosophy. Yet the ideas and concepts are not just unique to this book.

For over 700 years in the town of Geel in Belgium, a community-based model of mental health care has been developed, where individuals with a variety of mental health problems are fostered into family environments. The Geel community which fostered an attitude of acceptance of mental illness is still in being (Goldstein & Godemont, 2003). There were many precedents for these approaches. In France, physician Philippe Pinel was influential in the development of humane approaches to care of people with mental illness. In the United Kingdom at the York Retreat, founded by Quaker William Tuke, the carers applied what later became known as moral treatment (Borthwick et al., 2001) to people with mental illness, where respect for individuals and humane approaches to care were a core focus of the approach. Similarly, pioneers such as Robert Gardiner Hill created a non-restraint movement, where mechanical restraints were effectively abolished in some pioneering U.K. institutions (Haw & Yorston, 2004; Hill, 1857). Understanding this historical heritage does have elements of learning for the present day. A recent discussion of the development of the early Victorian pioneers by Yorston and Haw (2009) illustrated this most eruditely:

> We can look back at the long history of restraint in the treatment of the mentally ill and shake our heads at the barbarity of some of the practices. Yet, there remain wide variations in what currently goes on in hospitals even across the developed world (p. 16).[1]

Conclusions

In sum, there are many precedents for the adoption of humane approaches to the management of people in care environments, such as low arousal approaches. This book has demonstrated the application of these approaches in a variety of care environments. Care should be taken in making sweeping claims for the effectiveness of training. The work described in this book is limited by the lack of good-quality comparative research studies. Low arousal approaches are evidenced-based, socially valid approaches to the management of aggressive behaviours in children and adults in a variety of care environments.

Low arousal approaches are based on person-centred approaches and an unashamed humanist philosophy. In conclusion the humanist approach is best illustrated by a historical case example. The case of Victor and his benevolent physician illustrates the humanistic tradition. In 1799, Victor, the so-called wild boy, was discovered in Aveyron in Southern France. Victor was mute and attempts were made by physician Jean Marc Gaspard Itard to restore his speech and socialize the young man. His approach focused on his relationship with Victor, although he viewed his work as a failure, as he did not succeed in teaching Victor to speak. In reality, Victor was reported to be more placid and capable of understanding some verbal communication and showing empathy. Victor lived with Itard and his housekeeper, Madame Guérin, until his death in Paris in 1828. The approach adopted to manage Victor contained strong elements of low arousal approaches which Itard (1802) described very poignantly:

> He was acquainted with four circumstances only; to sleep, to eat, to do nothing, and to run about in the fields. To make him happy, then, after his own manner, it was necessary to put him to bed at the close of the day, to furnish him abundantly with food adapted to his taste, to bear with his indolence, and to accompany him in his walks, or rather in his races in the open air, and this whenever he pleased. (p. 38)

---

[1] Reprinted from *Aggression and Violent Behavior*, Vol. 2, Joan McCord, Discipline and the use of sanctions, p. 7, Copyright (2009), with permission from Elsevier.

References

Chapter 1: Understanding Violence and Aggression in Care Settings

Allen, D. (1999a). Success and failure in community placements for people with learning disabilities and challenging behaviour: An analysis of key variables. *Journal of Mental Health*, **8**, 3, 307–320.

Allen, D. (2000a). Recent research on physical aggression with intellectual disabilities: An overview. *Journal of Intellectual and Developmental Disability*, **25**, 41–57.

Allen, D. (2000b). *Training carers in physical interventions: Research towards evidence based practice*. Kidderminster: BILD.

Allen, D., McDonald, L., Dunn, C., & Doyle, T. (1997). Changing care staff approaches to the preventions and management of aggressive behaviour in a residential treatment unit for persons with mental retardation and challenging behaviour. *Research in Developmental Disabilities*, **18**, 101–112.

Anderson, C. A., & Bushman, B. J. (2002). Human aggression. *Annual Review of Psychology*, **53**, 27–51.

Ayllon, T., & Azrin, N. H. (1968). *The token economy*. New York: Appleton-Century-Crofts.

Azrin, N. H., Hutchinson, R. R., & Hake, D. F. (1966). Extinction-induced aggression. *Journal of the Experimental Analysis of Behavior*, **9**, 191–204.

Bandura, A. (1973). *Aggression: A social learning analysis*. New Jersey: Prentice-Hall.

Bandura, A. (1977). Self-efficacy: Toward a unifying theory of behavioural change. *Psychological Review*, **84**, 191–215.

Bandura, A. (1985). *Self-efficacy in changing societies*. Cambridge University Press: New York.

Managing Aggressive Behaviour in Care Settings: Understanding and applying low arousal approaches
By Andrew A. McDonnell   © 2010 John Wiley & Sons, Ltd

Bandura, A. (1995). *Self-efficacy in changing societies.* New York: Cambridge University Press.

Bandura, A. (1997). *Self-efficacy: the exercise of control.* New York: Freeman.

Beech, B., & Leather, P. (2006). Workplace violence in the health care sector: A review of staff training and integration of training evaluation models. *Aggression and Violent Behaviour,* 11, 27–43.

Berger, T. D., & Trinkaus, E. (1995). Patterns of trauma among Neanderthals. *Journal of Archaeological Science,* 22, 841–852.

Bowie, V. (2002). Defining violence at work: A new typology, In M. Gill, B. Fisher, & V. Bowie (Eds.), *Violence at work.* Cullompton, Devon: Willan Publishing, pp. 1–20.

Braverman, M. (2002). The prevention of violence affecting workers: A systems perspective. In M. Gill, B. Fisher, & V. Bowie (Eds.), *Violence at work: Causes, patterns and prevention.* Cullompton, Devon: Willan Publishing, pp. 114–131.

Bromley, J., & Emerson, E. (1995). Beliefs and emotional reactions of care staff working with people with challenging behaviour. *Journal of Intellectual Disability Research,* 39, 341–352.

Butchart, A., Phinney, A., Check, P., & Villaveces, A. (2004). *Preventing violence: a guide to implementing the recommendations of the world report on violence and health.* Geneva: World Health Organization.

Byrne, J. M., & Stowell, J. (2007). Examining the link between institutional and community violence: Toward a new cultural paradigm. *Aggression and Violent Behavior,* 12, 552–563.

Calhoun, J. B. (1962). Population density and social pathology. *Scientific American,* 206, 139–146.

Carr, E. G., Horner, R. H., Turnbull, A. P., Marquis, J. G., McLaughlin, D. M., McAtee, M. L., Smith, C. E., Ryan, K. A., Ruef, M. B., Doolabh, A., & Baddock, D. (1999). *Positive behavior support for people with developmental disabilities: A research synthesis.* Washington, DC: American Association on Mental Retardation.

Corrigan, P. W. (1995). Use of a token economy with seriously mentally ill patients: Criticisms and misconceptions. *Psychiatric Services,* 46, 1258–1263.

Dagnan, D., Trower, P., & Smith, R. (1998). Care staff responses to people with learning disabilities and challenging behaviour: A cognitive emotional analysis. *British Journal of Clinical Psychology,* 37, 1, 59–68.

Deveau, R., & McDonnell, A. A. (2009). As the last resort: Reducing the use of restrictive physical interventions using an organisational approach. *British Journal of Learning Disabilities,* 37, 172–177.

Di Martino, V. (2005). A cross-national comparison of workplace violence and response strategies. In *Workplace violence: Issues, trends, strategies,* Cullompton, Devon: Willan Publishing, pp. 15–36.

Dollard, J., Doob, L. W., Miller, N. E., Mowrer, O. H., & Seers, R. R. (1939). *Frustration and aggression.* Newhaven, CT: Yale University Press.

Donnellan, A. M., Lavigna, G. W., Negri-Shoultz, N., & Fassbender, L. L. (1988). *Progress without punishment: Effective approaches for learners with behaviour problems.* New York: Teachers College Press.

Emerson, E., Roberston, J., Gregory, N., Hatton, C., Kessissoglou, S., & Hallam, A. (2001). The treatment and management of challenging behaviours in residential settings. *Journal of Applied Research in Intellectual Disabilities,* 13, 197–215.

Feldman, M. A., Atkinson, L., Foti-Gervais, L., & Condillac, R. (2004). Formal versus informal interventions for challenging behavior in persons with intellectual disabilities. *Journal of Intellectual Disabilities Research*, **48**, 60–68.

Freud, S. (1930). *Civilisation and its discontents*. New York: WW Norton.

Fuller, P. R. (1949). Operant conditioning of a vegetative human organism. *American Journal of Psychology*, **62**, 587–590.

Goldiamond, I. (1974). Toward a constructional approach to social problems: Ethical and constitutional issues raised by applied behavior analysis. *Behaviorism*, **2**, 1, 1–84.

Gomes, M. M. (2007). A concept analysis of relational aggression. *Journal of Psychiatric and Mental Health Nursing*, **14**, 5, 510–515.

Hahn, S., Zeller, A., Needham, I., Kok, G., Dassen, T., & Halfens, R. J. G. (2008). Patient and visitor violence in general hospitals: A systematic review of the literature. *Aggression and Violent Behavior*, **13**, 431–441.

Haney, C., Banks, W. C., & Zimbardo, P. G. (1973). Study of prisoners and guards in a simulated prison. *Naval Research Reviews*, **9**, 1–17.

Hastings, R. P., & Remington, B. (1994a). Rules of engagement: Towards an analysis of staff responses to challenging behaviours. *Research in Developmental Disabilities*, **33**, 279–298.

Health and Safety Advisory Committee. (1987). *Violence to Staff. DHSS Advisory Committee on Violence to Staff Report*. London: HMSO.

Hennessy, D. A., & Wiensenthal, D. L. (1999). Traffic congestion, driver stress, and driver aggression. *Aggressive Behavior*, **25**, 409–423.

Huesmann, L. R. (1988). An information-processing model for the development of aggression. *Aggressive Behavior*, **14**, 13–24.

Hyland, M. (1981). *Introduction to theoretical psychology*. London: Macmillan.

Jacobson, J. W. (1982a). Problem behavior and psychatric impairment within a developmentally disabled population. 1: Behavior frequency. *Applied Research in Mental Retardation*, **3**, 121–139.

Jacobson, J. W. (1982b). Problem behavior and psychiatric impairment within a developmentally disabled population. 2: Behavior severity. *Applied Research in Mental Retardation*, **3**, 369–381.

Kahng, S. W., Boscoe, J. H., & Byrne, S. (2003). The use of an escape contingency and a token economy to increase food acceptance. *Journal of Applied Behavior Analysis*, **36**, 349–353.

Kazdin, A. E. (1982). The token economy: A decade later. *Journal of Applied Behavior Analysis*, **15**, 431–445.

King, E. (2004). *Preventing violence: A guide to implementing the recommendations of the world report on violence and health*. Geneva: World Health Organization.

Lavigna, G. W., & Donnellan, A. M. (1986). *Alternatives to punishment: Solving behaviour problems with nonaversive strategies*. New York: Irvington.

Lee, R. B. (1979). *The Kung San: Men, women, and work in a foraging society*. Cambridge, UK: Cambridge University Press.

Lerman, D. C., & Vorndran, C. M. (2002). On the status of knowledge for using punishment: Implications for treating behavior disorders. *Journal of Applied Behavior Analysis*, **35**, 4, 431–464.

Lion, J. R., Snyder, W., & Merrill, G. L. (1981). Under-reporting of assaults on staff in state hospitals. *Hospital and Community Psychiatry*, **32**, 497–498.

Lorenz, K. (1966). *On aggression.* London: Methuen.

MacDonald, G., Zanna, M. P., & Holmes, J. G. (2000). An experimental test of the role of alcohol in a relationship conflict. *Journal of Experimental Social Psychology,* **36,** 182–193.

MacDougall, D. (1947). *The energies of men.* London: Methuen.

Marsh, P., Rosser, E., & Harre, R. (1978). *The rules of disorder.* New York: Routledge.

Martin, J. P. (1984). *Hospitals in trouble.* Oxford: Blackwell.

Matson, J., & Boisjoli, J. A. (2009). The token economy for children with intellectual disability and/or autism: A review. *Research in Developmental Disabilities,* **30,** 240–248.

McCall, G. G., & Shields, N. (2008). Examining the evidence from small scale societies and early prehistory and implications for modern theories of aggression and violence. *Aggression and Violent Behavior,* **13,** 1, 1–9.

McClintock, K., Hall, S., & Oliver, C. (2003). Risk markers associated with challenging behaviours in people with intellectual disabilities: a meta-analytic study. *Journal of Intellectual Disability Research,* **47,** 405–416.

McDonnell, A. A., & Anker, R. (2009). Behaviour management versus behaviour change: A useful distinction? *British Journal of Developmental Disabilities,* **55,** 2, 157–167.

McDonnell, A. A., Gould, A., Adams, T, Sallis, J., & Anker, R. (2009). Staff training in physical interventions: A systematic literature review. Unpublished manuscript.

Metcalfe, J., & Mischel, W. (1999). A hot/cool system analysis of delay of gratification: Dynamics of willpower. *Psychological Review,* **106,** 3–19.

Michael, J. (1993). Establishing operations. *The Behavior Analyst,* **16,** 191–206.

Milgram, S. (1974). *Obedience to authority: An experimental view.* New York: Harper-Collins.

Mischel, W. (1968). *Personality and assessment.* New York: Wiley.

Mischel, W. (2004). Toward an integrative science of the person. *Annual Review of Psychology,* **55,** 1–22.

Moore, J.W., Tingstrom, D. H., Doggett, A., & Carlyon, W. D. (2001). Restructuring an existing token economy in a psychiatric facility for children. *Child & Family Behavior Therapy,* **23,** 3, 53–59.

Morrison, E. F. (1990). Violent psychiatric patients in a public hospital. *Scholarly Inquiry for Nursing Practice: An International Journal,* **4,** 1, 65–82.

Murphy, E. S., McSweeney, F. K., Smith, R. G., & McComas, J. J. (2003). *Journal of Applied Behavior Analysis,* **36,** 4, 421–438.

Nijman, H., Bowers, L., Oud, N., & Jansen, G. (2005). Psychiatric nurses' experiences with inpatient aggression. *Aggressive Behavior,* **31,** 217–227.

Novaco, R. W. (1975). *Anger control: The development and evaluation of an experimental treatment.* Lexington, MA: DC Heath.

Novaco, R. W. (1978). Anger and coping with stress. In J. P. Foreyt, & D. P. Rathzen (Eds.), *Cognitive behaviour therapy.* New York: Plenum Press.

Novaco, R. W., & Welsh, W. N. (1989). Anger disturbances: Cognitive mediation and clinical prescriptions. In K. Howells & C. Hollin (Eds.), *Clinical approaches to violence.* Chichester, UK: Wiley, pp. 39–60.

Parent-Thirion, A., Macías, E. F., Hurley, J., & Vermeylen, G. (2007). *Fourth European working conditions survey.* Luxembourg: Office for Official Publications of the European Communities.

Paterson, B., & Leadbetter, D. (2002). Standards for violence management training. In M. Gill, B. Fisher, & V. Bowie (Eds.), *Violence at work: Causes, patterns and prevention.* Cullompton, Devon: Willan Publishing, pp. 132–150.

Patterson, B., & Leadbetter, D. (1999). De-escalation in the management of aggression and violence: Towards evidence based practice. In B. Patterson & J. Turnball (Eds.), *Aggression and violence.* London: Macmillan, pp. 95–123.

Pulsford, D., & Duxbury, J. (2006). Aggressive behaviour by people with dementia in residential care settings: A review. *Journal of Psychiatric and Mental Health Nursing,* **13**, 611–618.

Ramsden, E., & Adams, J. (2009). Escaping the laboratory: The rodent experiments of John B. Calhoun & their cultural influence. *The Journal of Social History,* **42**, 761–792.

Rao, H., Luty, J., & Trathen, B. (2007). Characteristics of patients who are violent to staff and towards other people from a community mental health service in South East England. *Journal of Psychiatric and Mental Health Nursing,* **14**, 753–757.

Reid, D. H., & Parsons, M. B. (2002). *Working with staff to overcome challenging behaviour among people who have severe learning disabilities: A guide for getting support plans carried out, Habilitative Management Consultants.* North Carolina: Morganton.

Richetin, J., & Richardson, D. S. (2008). Automatic processes and individual differences in aggressive behaviour. *Aggression and Violent Behavior,* **13**, 6, 423–430.

Rusch, R. G., Hall, J. C., & Griffin, H. C. (1986). Abuse-provoking characteristics of institutionalized mentally retarded individuals. *American Journal of Mental Deficiency,* **90**, 6, 618–624.

Sade, R. M. (2004). Evolution, prevention and responses to aggressive behavior and violence. *Journal of Law, Medicine and Ethics,* **32**, 8–17.

Salkovskis, P. M., & Rachman, S. (1997). *Frontiers of cognitive therapy: The state of the art and beyond.* New York: Guilford Press.

Singh, N. N., Lloyd, J. W., & Kendall, K. A. (1990). Non-aversive and aversive interventions: Introduction. In A. Repp & N. N. Singh (Eds.), *Perspectives on the use of non-aversive and aversive interventions for persons with developmental disabilities.* Sycamore, IL: Sycamore Publishing Company.

Skinner, B. F. (1953). *Science and human behavior.* New York: Free Press.

Skinner, B. F. (1957). *Verbal behavior.* New York: Appleton-Century-Crofts.

Skinner, B. F. (1959). An experimental analysis of certain emotions. *Journal of the Experimental Analysis of Behavior,* **2**, 264.

Stott, C. J., & Adang, O. M. J. (2004). 'Disorderly' conduct: Social psychology and the control of football 'hooliganism' at 'Euro2004'. *The Psychologist,* **17**, 318–319.

Stubbs, B., Leadbetter, D., Paterson, B., Yorston, G., Knight, C., & Davis, S. (2009). Physical interventions: A review of the literature on its use, staff and patients' views and the impact of training. *Journal of Psychiatric and Mental Health Nursing,* **16**, 1, 99–105.

Tajfel, H., & Turner, J. C. (1979). An integrative theory of intergroup conflict. In W. G. Austin & S. Worchel (Eds.), *The social psychology of intergroup relations.* Monterey, CA: Brooks/Cole, pp. 33–47.

Turnbull, J. (1999). Theoretical approaches to aggression and violence. In B. Patterson & J. Turnball (Eds.), *Aggression and violence.* London: Macmillan, pp. 31–51.

Wahler, R. G., & Fox, J. J. (1981). Setting events in applied behavior analysis: Towards a conceptual and methodological expansion. *Journal of Applied Behavior Analysis*, **14**, 327–338.

Wanless, L. K., & Jahoda, A. (2002). Responses of staff towards people with mild to moderate intellectual disability who behave aggressively: A cognitive emotional analysis. *Journal of Intellectual Disability Research*, **46**, 507–516.

Weiner, B. (1986). *An attributional theory of motivation and emotion.* Berlin: Springer-Verlag.

Whittington, R., & Wykes, T. (1994). An observational study of associations between nurse behaviour and violence in psychiatric hospitals. *Journal of Psychiatric and Mental Health Nursing*, **1**, 2, 85–92.

Winstanley, S. (2005). Cognitive model of patient aggression towards health care staff: The patient's perspective. *Work & Stress*, **19**, 4, 340–350.

Zuidema, S. U., Derksen, E., Verhey, F. R. J., & Koopmans, R. T. C. M. (2007). Prevalence of neuropsychiatric symptoms in a large sample of Dutch nursing home patients with dementia. *International Journal of Geriatric Psychiatry*, **22**, 7, 632–638.

Chapter 2: The Development of a Low Arousal Approach

Anderson, C. A., & Bushman, B. J. (2002). Human aggression. *Annual Review of Psychology*, **53**, 27–51.

Argyle, M. (1986). *Social interaction.* London: Methuen.

Bandura, A. (1997). *Self-efficacy: The exercise of control.* New York: Freeman.

Barker, P. (2005). *The Tidal Model: A guide for mental health professionals.* Brunner-Routledge: London and New York.

Beck, A. T. (1975). *Cognitive therapy and the emotional disorders.* New York: International Universities Press.

Braverman, M. (2002). Prevention of violence affecting workers: A systems perspective, In M. Gill, B. Fisher, & V. Bowie (Eds.), *Violence at work.* Cullompton, Devon: Willan Publishing, pp. 114–131.

Breakwell, G. M. (1997). *Coping with aggressive behaviour.* London: BPS.

Brookes N (2006). Phil Barker: Tidal Model of mental health recovery. In A. M. Tomey & M. R. Alligood (Eds.), *Nursing theorists and their work* (6th edition). St. Louis, MI: Mosby Elsevier, Chapter 32.

Buchanan-Barker, P., & Barker, P. J. (2008). The Tidal Commitments: extending the value base of mental health recovery. *Journal of Psychiatric and Mental Health Nursing*, **15**, 93–100.

Calhoun, J. B. (1962). Population density and social pathology. *Scientific American*, **206**, 139–146.

Carr, J. E., Austin, J. L., Britton, L. N., Kellum, K. K., & Bailey, J. S. (1999). An assessment of social validity trends in applied behavior analysis. *Behavioral Interventions*, **14**, 223–231.

Chen, P., & Spector, P. (1991). Relationship of work stressors with aggression, withdrawal, theft and substance abuse. *Journal of Occupational and Organisational Psychology*, **65**, 4, 177–185.

Dagnan, D., Trower, P., & Smith, R. (1998). Care staff responses to people with learning disabilities and challenging behaviour: A cognitive emotional analysis. *British Journal of Clinical Psychology*, **37**, 1, 59–68.

Easterbrook, J. A. (1959). The effect of emotion on cue utilisation and the organisation of behaviour. *Psychological Review*, **66**, 183–201.

Flannery, R. B., Jr. (1998). *The Assaulted Staff Action Program (ASAP): Coping with the psychological aftermath of violence.* Ellicott City, MD: Chevron Publishing Corporation.

Flannery, R. B., Jr. (2002). The Assaulted Staff Action Program (ASAP): Ten year analysis of empirical findings. In M. Gill, B. Fisher, & V. Bowie (Eds.), *Violence at work.* Cullompton, Devon: Willan Publishing, pp. 180–191.

Flannery, R. B., Jr., Penk, W. E., & Corrigan, M. (1999). The Assaulted Staff Action Program (ASAP) and declines in the prevalence of assaults: Community-based replication. *International Journal of Emergency Mental Health*, **1**, 1, 19–21.

Foa, E., Keane, T., & Friedman, M. (2000). *Effective treatment for PTSD: Practice guidelines from the International Society for Traumatic Stress Studies.* New York, NY: Guilford Press.

Goodwin, M. S., Groden, J., Velicer, W. F., Lipsitt, L. P., Grace Baron, M., Hofmann, S. G., & Groden, G. (2006). Cardiovascular arousal in individuals with autism. *Focus on Autism and Other Developmental Disabilities*, **21**, 100–123.

Groden, J., Cautela, J., Prince, S., & Berryman, J. (1994). The impact of stress and anxiety on individuals with autism and other developmental disabilities. In E. Schopler & G. Mesibov (Eds.), *Behaviour issues and autism.* New York: Plenum Press.

Hanoch, Y., & Vitouch, O. (2004). When less is more: Information, emotional arousal and the ecological reframing of the Yerkes Dodson law. *Theory and Psychology*, **14**, 427–452.

Harris, M., & Fallot, R. D. (2001). Envisioning a trauma-informed service system: A vital paradigm shift. *New Dir Mental Health Service*, Spring, **89**, 3–22.

Hayduk, L. A. (1983). Personal space: Where we stand now? *Psychological Bulletin*, **94**, 293–335.

Hirstein, W., Iversen, P & Ramachandran, V. S. (2001). Autonomic responses of autistic children to people and objects. *Proceedings of the Royal Society B: Biological Sciences*, **268**, 1883–1888.

Howlin, P. (1998). *Children with autism and Aspergers syndrome: A guide for practitioners and carers.* Chichester, UK: Wiley.

Huesmann, L. R. (1998). The role of social information processing and cognitive schema in the acquisition and maintenance of habitual aggressive behaviour. In R. G. Geen & E. Donnerstein (Eds.), *Human aggression: Theories, research, and implications for policy.* New York: Academic Press, pp. 73–109.

Jennings, A (2004). Models for developing trauma informed behavioral health systems and trauma specific care. Report produced for the National Association of State Mental Health Program Directors (NASMHPD).

Kaplan, S. G., & Wheeler, E. G. (1983). Survival skills for working with potentially violent service users. *Social Casework*, **64**, 339–345.

Kiely, J., & Pankhurst, H. (1998). Violence faced by staff in a learning disability service. *Disability and Rehabilitation*, **20**, 81–89.

Kinzel, A. F. (1970). Body buffer zones in violent persons. *American Journal of Psychiatry*, **127**, 59–64.

Kitwood, T. (1997). *Dementia reconsidered: The person comes first*. Buckingham: Open University Press.

Lazarus, R. S., & Folkman, S. (1984). *Stress, appraisal, and coping*. New York: Springer.

Linsley, P. (2006). *Violence and aggression in the workplace: A practical guide for all healthcare staff*. Oxford: Radcliffe Publishing.

Martin, J. P. (1984). *Hospitals in trouble*. Oxford: Blackwell.

McDonnell, A. A., Dearden, R., & Richens, A. (1991b) Staff training in the management of violence and aggression. 2: Avoidance and escape principles. *Mental Handicap*, **19**, 109–112.

McDonnell, A. A., McEvoy, J., & Dearden, R. L. (1994). Coping with violent situations in the caring environment. In T. Wykes (Ed.), *Violence and health care professionals*. London: Chapman & Hall, pp. 189–206.

McDonnell, A. A., Reeves, S., Johnson, A., & Lane, A. (1998). Management of challenging behaviours in an adult with learning disabilities: The use of low arousal. *Behavioural and Cognitive Psychotherapy*, **26**, 163–171.

McDonnell, A., & Sturmey, P. (1993a) Managing aggressive behaviours of people with learning difficulties. In R. S. P. Jones & C. Eayrs (Eds.), *Challenging behaviours and mental handicap: A psychological perspective*. Kidderminster: BILD.

McDonnell, A. A. Waters, T., & Jones D. (2002). Low arousal approaches in the management of challenging behaviours. In D. Allen (Ed.), *Ethical approaches to physical interventions: Responding to challenging behaviours in people with intellectual disabilities*. Plymouth: BILD, pp. 104–113.

Mehrabian, A. (1972). *Nonverbal communications*. Chicago: Aldune, Atherton.

Milgram, S. (1974). *Obedience to authority: An experimental view*. New York: Harper-Collins.

Moran, T., & Mason, T. (1996). Revisiting the nursing management of the psychopath. *Journal of Psychiatric and Mental Health Nursing*, **3**, 189–194.

NICE. (2007). Anxiety: Management of anxiety (panic disorder, with or without agoraphobia and generalised anxiety disorder) in adults in primary, secondary and tertiary care. Clinical Guideline 22. Available at www.nice.org.uk.

Novaco, R. W., & Welsh, W. N. (1989). Anger disturbances: Cognitive mediation and clinical prescriptions. In K. Howells & C. Hollin (Eds.), *Clinical approaches to violence*, Chichester, UK: Wiley, pp. 39–60.

O'Neill, M., & Jones R. S. P. (1997). Sensory perceptual abnormalities in autism: A case for more research. *Journal of Autism and Developmental Disorders*, **27**, 283–293.

Patterson, B., & Leadbetter, D. (1999). De-escalation in the management of aggression and violence: Towards evidence based practice. In B. Patterson & J. Turnbull (Eds.), *Aggression and violence*. London: Macmillan, pp. 95–123.

Peplau, H. E. (1952). *Interpersonal relations in nursing*. New York: G.P. Putnam's Sons.

Pfaff, D. (2005). *Brain, arousal and information theory: neural and genetic mechanisms*. Boston: Harvard University Press.

Pitonyak, D. (2004). 10 things you can do to support a person with difficult behaviors. Available at www.dimagine.com.

Read, J., Perry, B., Moskowitz, A., & Connolly, J. (2001). The contribution of early traumatic events to schizophrenia in some patients: A traumagenic neurodevelopmental model. *Psychiatry*, **64**, 4, 319–345.

Reich, J. W., & Zautra, A. (2002). Arousal and the relationship between positive and negative affect: An analysis of the data of Ito Cacioppo and Lang (1998). *Motivation and Emotion*, **26**, 209–222.

Richetin, J., & Richardson, D. S. (2008). Automatic processes and individual differences in aggressive behaviour. *Aggression and Violent Behavior*, **13**, 6, 423–430.

Rick, J., Perryman, S., Young, K., Guppy, A., & Hillage, J. (1998). *Workplace trauma and its management: A review of the literature.* Contract Research Report 170/98, Health and Safety Executive.

Rogers, D. M. (1992c). *Motor disorder in psychiatry: Towards a neurological psychiatry.* Chichester, UK: Wiley.

Schon, D. (1987), *Educating the reflective practitioner.* San Francisco: Jossey-Bass.

Tehrani, N. (2002). Violence at work: Supporting the employee. In M. Gill, B. Fisher, & V. Bowie (Eds.), *Violence at work.* Cullompton, Devon: Willan Publishing, pp. 192–208.

Watts, D., & Morgan, G. (1994). Malignant alienation: Dangers for patients who are hard to like. *The British Journal of Psychiatry*, **164**, 11–15.

Weiner, B. (1986). *An attributional theory of motivation and emotion.* Berlin: Springer-Verlag.

Whittington, R., & Wykes, T. (1994). An observational study of associations between nurse behaviour and violence in psychiatric hospitals. *Journal of Psychiatric and Mental Health Nursing*, **1**, 2, 85–92.

Yerkes, R. M., & Dodson, J. D. (1908). The relation of strength of stimulus to rapidity of habit-formation. *Journal of Comparative Neurology and Psychology*, **18**, 459–482.

Zajonc, R. B. (1980). Feeling and thinking: Preferences need no inferences. *American Psychologist*, **35**, 117–123.

Zimbardo, P. G. (1969). The human choice: Individuation, reason, and order versus deindividuation, impulse, and chaos. In W. T. Arnold & D. Levine (Eds.), *Nebraska symposium on motivation*, **17**, 237–307.

Chapter 3: Developing a Core Training Course

Allen, D. (1999a). Success and failure in community placements for people with learning disabilities and challenging behaviour: An analysis of key variables. *Journal of Mental Health*, **8**, 3, 307–320.

Allen, D. (2000b). *Training carers in physical interventions: Research towards evidence based practice.* Kidderminster: BILD.

Allen, D. (2001). *Training carers in physical interventions.* Kidderminster: BILD.

Allen, D. (2002). Behaviour change and behaviour management. In D. Allen (Ed.), *Ethical approaches to physical interventions.* Plymouth: BILD, pp. 3–14.

Althaus, M., van Roon, A. M., Mulder, L. J. M., Mulder, G., Aarnoudse, C. C., & Minderaa, R. B. (2000). Autonomic response patterns observed during the performance of an attention demanding task in two groups of children with autistic-type difficulties in social adjustment. *Psychophysiology*, **41**, 893–904.

Attwood, T. (2007). *The complete guide to Aspergers syndrome*. London: Jessica Kingsley.

BILD (2001). *BILD code of practice for trainers in the use of physical interventions: Learning disability, autism and pupils with special needs*. Plymouth: BILD.

Cullen, C. (1992). Staff training and management for intellectual disability services. *International Review of Research in Mental Retardation*, **18**, 225–245.

Cunningham, J., McDonnell, A. A., Easton, S., & Sturmey, P. (2002). Social validation data on three methods of physical restraint: Views of consumers, staff and students. *Research in Developmental Disabilities*, **21**, 85–92.

Donnellan, A. M., Lavigna, G. W., Negri-Shoultz, N., & Fassbender, L. L. (1988). *Progress without punishment: Effective approaches for learners with behaviour problems*. New York: Teachers College Press.

Fein, B. A., Gareri, E., & Hansen, P. (1981). Teaching styles to cope with patient violence. *Journal of Continuing Education in Nursing*, **12**, 7–11.

Gardner, W. I., & Moffatt, C. W. (1990). Aggressive behavior: definition, assessment, treatment. *International Review of Psychiatry*, **2**, 1, 91–100.

George, M. J., & Baumeister, A. A. (1981). Employee withdrawal and job satisfaction in community residential facilities for mentally retarded persons. *American Journal of Mental Deficiency*, **85**, 639–647.

Gertz, B. (1980). Training for prevention of assaultive behavior in a psychiatric setting. *Hospital and Community Psychiatry*, **31**, 9, 628–630.

Gilbert, P. (1988). Exercising some restraint. *Social Work Today*, **30**, 16–18.

Hanson, R. H., & Weiseler, N. A. (2002). The challenges of providing behavioural support and crisis response services in the community. In R. H. Hanson, N. A. Weiseler, C. K. Lakin, & D. L. Braddock (Eds.), *Crisis prevention and response in the community*. Washington, DC: AAMR.

Harris, J. (2002). Training on physical interventions: Making sense of the market. In D. Allen (Ed.), *Ethical approaches to physical interventions: Responding to challenging behaviour in people with intellectual disabilities*. Plymstock: BILD, pp. 134–152.

Harvey, E. R., & Schepers, J. (1977). Physical control techniques and defensive holds for use with aggressive retarded adults. *Mental Retardation*, **15**, 29–31.

Hastings, R. P., & Remington, B. (1994a). Rules of engagement: Towards an analysis of staff responses to violence and aggression. *Research in Developmental Disabilities*, **33**, 279–298.

Hill, B. K., & Bruininks, R. H. (1984). Maladaptive behavior of mentally retarded individuals in residential facilities. *American Journal of Mental Deficiency*, **88**, 380–387.

Hill, J., & Spreat, S. (1987). Staff injury rates associated with the implementation of contingent restraint. *Mental Retardation*, **25**, 3, 141–145.

Hirstein, W., Iversen, P., & Ramachandran, V. S. (2001). Autonomic responses of autistic children to people and objects. *Proceedings of the Royal Society B: Biological Sciences*, **268**, 1883–1888.

Hutt, C., Hutt, S. J., Lee, D., & Ounsted, C. (1964). Arousal and childhood autism. *Nature*, **204**, 908–909.

Infantino, J. A., & Musingo, S. (1985). Assaults and injuries among staff with and without training in aggression control techniques. *Hospital and Community Psychiatry*, **36**, 1312–1314.

Kaplan, S. G., & Wheeler, E. G. (1983). Survival skills for working with potentially violent service users. *Social Casework*, **64**, 339–345.

Kitwood, T. (1997). *Dementia reconsidered: The person comes first*. Buckingham: Oxford Univeristy Press.

Lakin, K. C., Hill, B. K., Hauber, F. A., Bruininks, R. H., & Heal, L. W. (1983). New admissions and readmissions to a national sample of public residential facilities. *American Journal of Mental Deficiency*, **88**, 13–20.

Lakin, K. C., & Larson, S. A. (2002). The social and policy context of community centred behavioural supports and crisis response. In R. H. Hanson, N. A. Weiseler, C. K. Lakin, & D. L. Braddock (Eds.), *Crisis prevention and response in the community*. Washington, DC: AAMR.

Leadbetter, D. (2002). Good practice in physical interventions. In D. Allen (Ed.), *Ethical approaches to physical interventions*. Plymouth: BILD, pp. 114–133.

Lefensky, B., De Palma, B. T., & Lociercero, D. (1978). Management of violent behaviors. *Perspectives in Psychiatric Care*, **16**, 212–217.

Lehmann, L. S., Padilla, M., Clark, S., & Loukes, S. (1983). Training personnel in the training of aggression of management behaviour. *Hospital and Community Psychiatry*, **34**, 40–43.

McClintock, K., Hall, S., & Oliver, C. (2003). Risk markers associated with violence and aggression in people with intellectual disabilities: a meta-analytic study. *Journal of Intellectual Disability Research*, **47**, 405–416.

McDonnell, A. A. (1988). The evaluation of a two day training course in the management of aggressive behaviour. Unpublished MSc Thesis, University of Birmingham.

McDonnell, A. A.,(1998). The physical restraint minefield: A professional's guide. *The British Journal of Therapy and Rehabilitation*, **3**, 45–48.

McDonnell, A. A. (2007). Why I am in favour of the Millfields Charter. *Learning Disability Practice*, **10**, 26–29.

McDonnell, A. A., Dearden, R., & Richens, A. (1991a) Staff training in the management of violence and aggression. 1: Setting up a training system. *Mental Handicap*, **19**, 73–76.

McDonnell, A. A., Dearden, R., & Richens, A. (1991b) Staff training in the management of violence and aggression. 2: Avoidance and escape principles. *Mental Handicap*, **19**, 109–112.

McDonnell, A. A., Dearden, R., & Richens, A. (1991c) Staff training in the management of violence and aggression. 3: Physical restraint. *Mental Handicap*, **19**, 151–154.

McDonnell, A. A., & Gallon, I. G. (2006). Issues and concerns about control and restraint training: Moving the debate forward. In M. Ward & J. Cutcliffe (Eds.), *Key Debates in Psychiatric Nursing*. London: Wiley.

McDonnell, A. A., Gould, A., & Adams, T. (2009). Staff training in physical interventions: A systematic literature review. Unpublished manuscript.

McDonnell, A. A., Hardman, J., Knight, L., Manning, P., & Semple, C. (2004a) An investigation into the topography of referrals to a community challenging behaviour service: Implications for research and training. Unpublished manuscript.

McDonnell, A. A., & Jones, P. (1999). The role of clinical psychology in the physical management of challenging behaviour. *Clinical Psychology Forum*, **12**, 20–23.

McDonnell, A. A., Mills, R., & Jones, N (2008). The role of physiological arousal in the management of violence and aggression in individuals with autistic spectrum disorders. Unpublished manuscript.

McDonnell, A. A., Reeves, S., Johnson, A., & Lane, A. (1998). Management of violence and aggression in an adult with intellectual disabilities: The use of low arousal. *Behavioural and Cognitive Psychotherapy*, **26**, 163–171.

McDonnell, A., & Sturmey, P. (1993a) Managing violent and aggressive behaviours of people with learning difficulties. In R. S. P. Jones & C. Eayrs (Eds.), *Violence and aggression and mental handicap: A psychological perspective*. Kidderminster: BILD.

McDonnell, A. A., & Sturmey, P. (1993b).The acceptability of physical restraint procedures for people with a learning difficulty. *Behavioural and Cognitive Psychotherapy*, **21**, 225–264.

McDonnell, A. A., & Sturmey, P. (2000). The social validation of three physical restraint procedures: A comparison of young people and professional groups. *Research in Developmental Disabilities*, **21**, 85–92.

McDonnell, A. A., Sturmey, P., & Dearden, B. (1993). The acceptability of physical restraint procedures for people with a learning difficulty. *Behavioural and Cognitive Psychotherapy*, **21**, 255–264.

McDonnell, A. A., Waters, T., & Jones D. (2002). Low arousal approaches in the management of violence and aggression. In D. Allen (Ed.), *Ethical approaches to physical interventions: Responding to violence and aggression in people with intellectual disabilities*. Plymouth: BILD, pp. 104–113.

Morrison, L., Duryea, P. B., Moore, C., & Nathanson-Shinn, A. (2002). *The lethal hazard of prone restraint: Positional asphyxiation*. Oakland, CA: Protection & Advocacy Inc.

Nunno, M., Holden, M., & Tollar, A. (2006). Learning from tragedy: A survey of child and adolescent restraint facilities. *Child Abuse & Neglect: The International Journal*, **30**, 1333–1342.

Paterson, B. (2007). Millfields Charter: Drawing the wrong conclusions. *Learning Disability Practice*, **10**, 30–33.

Paterson, B., Bradely, P., Stark, C., Saddler, D., Leadbetter, D., & Allen, D. (2003). Deaths associated with restraint use in health and social care in the UK: The results of a preliminary survey. *Journal of Psychiatric and Mental Health Nursing*, **10**, 3–15.

Paterson, B., & Leadbetter, D. (2002). Standards for violence management training. In M. Gill, B. Fisher, & V. Bowie (Eds.), *Violence at work*. Cullompton, Devon: Willan Publishing, pp. 132–150.

Paterson, B., Turnbull, J., & Aitken,(1992). An evaluation of a training course in the short term management of violence. *Nurse Education Today*, **12**, 368–375.

Razza, N. J. (1993). Determinants of direct care staff turnover in group homes for individuals with mental retardation. *Mental Retardation*, **31**, 284–291.

Rousey, A. B., Blacher, J. B., & Hauneman, R. A. (1990). Predictors of out of home placement of children with severe handicaps: A cross-sectional analysis. *American Journal on Mental Retardation*, **94**, 522–531.

St Thomas' Psychiatric Hospital Ontario, Canada. (1976). A program for the prevention and management of disturbed behaviour. *Hospital & Community Psychiatry, 27,* 724–727.

Tarbuck, P. (1992). Use and abuse of control and restraint. *Nursing Standard, 6,* 30–32.

Van Den Pol, R. A., Reed, D. H., & Fuqua, R. W. (1983). Peer training of safety related skills to institutional staff: Benefits for trainers and trainees. *Journal of Applied Behavior Analysis, 16,* 139–156.

Van Engeland, H., Roelofs, J. W., Verbaten, M. N., & Slangen, J. L. (1991). Abnormal electrodermal reactivity to novel visual stimuli in autistic children. *Psychiatry Research, 38,* 27–38.

VanVonderen, A. (2004). Effectiveness of feedback on trainer behaviour. *Journal of Intellectual Disability Research, 48,* 245–251.

Weiner, B. (1986). *An attributional theory of motivation and emotion.* Berlin: Springer-Verlag.

Weiss, E. M. (1998, October 11–15). Deadly restraint: A nationwide pattern of death. *Hartford Courant.*

Wolf, M. M. (1978). Social validity: The case for subjective measurement or how applied behavior analysis if finding its heart. *Journal of Applied Behavior Analysis, 11,* 203–214.

Wright, S., Gray, R., Parkes, J., & Gournay, K. (2002). *The recognition, prevention and therapeutic management of violence in acute in-patient psychiatry: A literature review and evidence based recommendations for good practice.* United Kingdom Central Council for Nursing, Midwifery and Health Visiting.

Chapter 4: Managing Aggressive Behaviour in Services for People with an Intellectual Disability

Allen, D. (1999a). Success and failure in community placements for people with learning disabilities and challenging behaviour: An analysis of key variables. *Journal of Mental Health, 8,* 3, 307–320.

Allen, D. (1999b). Mediator analysis: an overview of recent research on carers supporting people with intellectual disability and challenging behaviour. *Journal of Intellectual Disability Research, 43,* 325–339.

Allen, D. (2001). *Training carers in physical interventions: Research towards evidence based practice.* Kidderminster: BILD.

Allen, D. (2008). Risk and prone restraint – reviewing the evidence. In M. Nunno, D. Day, & L. Bullard (Eds.), *Ensuring the safety of high-risk intervention.* New York: Child Welfare League of America, 87–106.

Allen, D., Doyle, T., & Kaye, N. (2002). Plenty of gain, but no pain: A systems wide initiative. In D. Allen (Ed.), *Ethical approaches to physical interventions.* Plymouth: BILD, pp. 219–232.

Allen, D., McDonald, L., Dunn, C., & Doyle, T. (1997). Changing care staff approaches to the preventions and management of aggressive behaviour in a residential treatment unit for persons with mental retardation and challenging behaviour. *Research in Developmental Disabilities*, **18**, 101–112.

Allen, D., & Tynan, H (2000). Responding to aggressive behaviour: Impact of training on staff members' knowledge and confidence. *Mental Retardation*, **38**, 97–104.

Baker, P. (2002). Best interest? Seeking the views of service users. In D. Allen (Ed.), *Ethical approaches to physical interventions*. Plymouth: BILD, pp. 153–163.

Baker, P., & Bissmire, D. (2000). A pilot study of the use of physical intervention in the crisis management of people with intellectual disabilities who present challenging behaviour. *Journal of Applied Research in Intellectual Disabilities*, **13**, 38–45.

Baker, D. J., & Feil, E. G. (2000). A self evaluation by agencies providing residential support regarding capacity to support persons with disabilities and challenging behaviours. *International Journal of Disability, Development and Education*, **47**, 171–181.

Baker, P., & Allen, D. (2001). Physical abuse and physical interventions in learning disabilities: An element of risk? *Journal of Adult Protection*, **3**, 25–32.

Bihm, E. M., Sigelman, C. K., & Westbrook, J. P. (1997). Social implications of behavioural interventions for persons with mental retardation. *American Journal on Mental Retardation*, **101**, 567–578.

BILD (2006). *BILD code of practice for trainers in the use of physical interventions: Learning disability, autism and pupils with special needs* (2nd edition). Plymouth: BILD.

Bromley, J., & Emerson, E. (1995). Beliefs and emotional reactions of care staff working with people with challenging behaviour. *Journal of Intellectual Disability Research*, **39**, 341–352.

Campbell, M. (2007). Staff training and challenging behaviour. *Journal of Intellectual Disabilities*, **11**, 143–156.

Carr, E. G., Horner, R. H., Turnbull, A. P., Marquis, J. G., McLaughlin, D. M., McAtee, M. L., Smith, C. E., Ryan, K. A., Ruef, M. B., Doolabh, A., & Braddock, D. (1999). *Positive behaviour support for people with developmental disabilities: A research synthesis*. Washington, DC: AAMR.

Carr, E. G., Levin, L., McConnachie, G., Carlson, J. I., Kemp, D. C., & Smith, C. E. (1994). *Communication based intervention for problem behaviour: A users guide for producing positive change*. London: Paul Brookes.

Cullen, C. (1992). Staff training and management for intellectual disability services. *International Review of Research in Mental Retardation*, **18**, 225–245.

Cunningham, J., McDonnell, A. A., Easton, S., & Sturmey, P. (2003). Social validation data on three methods of physical restraint: Views of consumers, staff and students. *Research in Developmental Disabilities*, **24**, 307–316.

Dagnan, D., & Weston, S. (2006). Physical intervention with people with intellectual disabilities: The influence of cognitive and emotional variables. *Journal of Applied Research in Intellectual Disabilities*, **19**, 219–222.

Deaveau, R., & McDonnell, A. A. (2009). As the last resort: Reducing the use of restrictive physical interventions using an organisational approach. Manuscript submitted for publication to the *British Journal of Learning Disabilities*, **37**, 172–177.

Donnellan, A. M., LaVigna, G. W., Negri-Schoulz, N., & Fassbender, L. L. (1988). *Progress without punishment: Effective approaches for learners with behaviour problems*. New York: Teachers College Press.

Duker, P. C., & Seys, D. M. (1996). Long-term use of electrical aversion treatment with self-injurious behaviours. *Research in Developmental Disabilities*, 17, 293–301.

Emerson, E. (1992). Self injurious behaviour: An overview of recent trends in epidemiological and behavioural research. *Mental Handicap Research*, 5, 49–81.

Emerson, E., & Hatton, C. (1996). De-institutionalization in the U.K. and Ireland: Outcomes for service users. *Journal of Intellectual and Developmental Disability*, 21, 17–37.

Emerson, E., Robertson, J., Gregory, N., Hatton, C., Kessissoglou, S., Hallam, A., & Hillery, J. (2000). The treatment and management of challenging behaviours in residential settings. *Journal of Applied Research in Intellectual Disabilities*, 13, 197–215.

Favell, J. E., McGimsey, J. F., & Jones, M. L. (1978). The use of physical restraint in the treatment of self injury and as positive reinforcement. *Journal of Applied Behavior Analysis*, 11, 225–241.

Feldman, M. A., Atkinson, L., Foti-Gervais, L., & Condillac, R. (2004.) Formal versus informal interventions for challenging behaviour in persons with intellectual disabilities. *Journal of Intellectual Disabilities Research*, 48, 60–68.

Fish, R., & Culshaw, E. (2005). The last resort: Staff and client perspectives on physical interventions. *Journal of Intellectual Disability Research*, 9, 93–107.

Fisher, W. W., Piazza, C. C., Bowman, L. G., Hanley, G. P, & Adelinis, J. D. (1997). Direct and collateral effects of restraint and restraint fading. *Journal of Applied Behavior Analysis*, 30, 105–120.

Flynn, M. C. (1986). Adults who are mentally handicapped as consumers: Issues and guidelines. *Journal of Mental Deficiency Research*, 30, 369–377.

George, M. J., & Baumeister, A. A. (1981). Employee withdrawal and job satisfaction in community residential facilities for mentally retarded persons. *American Journal of Mental Deficiency*, 85, 639–647.

Gillett, E., & Stenfert Kroese, B. (2003). Investigating organizational cultures: A comparison of a 'high' and a 'low' performing residential unit for people with intellectual disabilities. *Journal of Applied Research in Intellectual Disabilities*, 16, 279–284.

Griffin, J. C., Williams, D. E., Stark, M. T., Altmeyer, B. K., & Mason, M. (1986). Self injurious behavior: A state wide prevalence survey of the extent and circumstances. *Applied Research in Mental Retardation*, 7, 105–116.

Hanley, G. P., Piazza, P. C., Keeney, K. M., Bakely-Smith, A. B., & Worsdell, A. F. (1998). Effects of wrist weights on self injurious and adaptive behaviors. *Journal of Applied Behavior Analysis*, 31, 307–310.

Hanson, R. H., & Weiseler, N. A. (2002). The challenges of providing behavioral support and crisis response services in the community. In R. H. Hanson, N. A. Weiseler, C. K. Lakin, & D. L. Braddock (Eds.), *Crisis prevention and response in the community*. Washington, DC: AAMR.

Harris, J. (1996). Physical restraint procedures for managing challenging behaviors presented by mentally retarded adults and children. *Research in Developmental Disabilities*, 17, 2, 99–134.

Harris, J. (2002a). From good intentions to improved practice – developing effective policies. In D. Allen (Ed.), *Ethical approaches to physical interventions*. Plymouth: BILD, pp. 31–50.

Harris, J. (2002b). Training on physical interventions: Making sense of the market.

In D. Allen (Ed.), *Ethical approaches to physical interventions*. Plymouth: BILD, pp. 134–139.

Harris, P., & Russell, O. (1989). *The prevalence of aggressive behaviour among people with learning difficulties (mental handicap) in a single health district*. Interim report. Bristol: University of Bristol, Norah Fry Research Centre.

Hastings, R. (2002). Do challenging behaviors affect staff psychological well-being? Issues of causality and mechanism. *American Journal on Mental Retardation, 107*, 455–467.

Hastings, R., & Brown, T. (2000). Functional assessment and challenging behaviors. *Journal of the Association for Persons with Severe Handicaps. 25*, 229–240.

Hastings, R. P., & Remington, B. (1994a). Rules of engagement: Towards an analysis of staff responses to challenging behaviours. *Research in Developmental Disabilities, 33*, 279–298.

Hawkins, S., Allen, D., & Jenkins, R. (2005). The use of physical interventions with people with intellectual disabilities and challenging behaviour: The experience of service users and staff members. *Journal of Applied Research in Intellectual Disabilities, 18*, 19–34.

Hill, B. K., & Bruininks, R. H. (1984). Maladaptive behavior of mentally retarded individuals in residential facilities. *American Journal of Mental Deficiency, 88*, 380–387.

Hill, J., & Spreat, S. (1987). Staff injury rates associated with the implementation of contingent restraint. *Mental Retardation, 25*, 3, 141–145.

Iwata, B. A., Dorsey, M. F., Slifer, K. J., Bauman, K. E., & Richman, G. S. (1982). Toward a functional analysis of self injury. *Analysis and Intervention in Developmental Disabilities, 2*, 1–20.

Jacobson, J. W. (1982a) Problem behavior and psychatric impairment within a developmentally disabled population. 1: Behavior frequency. *Applied Research in Mental Retardation, 3*, 121–139.

Jacobson, J. W. (1982b) Problem behavior and psychiatric impairment within a developmentally disabled population. 2: Behavior severity. *Applied Research in Mental Retardation, 3*, 369–381.

Jones, E.M., Allen, D., Moore, K., Phillips, B., & Lowe, K. (2007). Restraint and self injury in people with intellectual disabilities. *Journal of Intellectual Disabilities, 11*, 105–118.

Khang, S. W., Iwata, B. A., & Wilder, D. A. (2001). Behavioral treatment of self injury 1964–2000. *American Journal on Mental Retardation, 107*, 212–221.

Kiernan, C., & Alborz, A. (1996). Persistence in challenging and problem behaviors of young adults with intellectual disability living in the family home. *Journal of Applied Research in Intellectual Disabilities, 9*, 3, 181–193.

Kroese, B. S., Gillott, A., & Atkinson, V. (1998). Consumers with intellectual disabilities as service evaluators. *Journal of Applied Research in Intellectual Disabilities, 11*, 116–128.

Lakin, K. C., Hill, B. K., Hauber, F. A., Bruininks, R. H., & Heal, L. W. (1983). New admissions and readmissions to a national sample of public residential facilities. *American Journal of Mental Deficiency, 88*, 13–20.

Lakin, K. C., & Larson, S. A. (2002). The social and policy context of community centred behavioral supports and crisis response. In R. H. Hanson, N. A. Weiseler, C. K. Lakin, & D. L. Braddock (Eds.), *Crisis prevention and response in the community*. Washington, DC: AAMR.

LaVigna, G. W., & Donnellan, A. M. (1986). *Alternatives to punishment: Solving behavior problems with nonaversive strategies.* New York: Irvington.

LaVigna, G. W., & Willis, T. J. (2002). Counter-intuititive strategies for crisis management within a non-aversive framework. In D. Allen (Ed.), *Ethical approaches to physical interventions: Responding to challenging behavior in people with intellectual disabilities.* Kidderminster: BILD, pp. 89–103.

Leadbetter, D. (2002). Good practice in physical interventions. In D. Allen (Ed.), *Ethical approaches to physical interventions.* Plymouth: BILD, pp. 114–133.

Lerman, D. C., & Vorndran, C. M. (2002). On the status of knowledge for using punishment: Implications for treating behavior disorders. *Journal of Applied behavior Analysis,* **35,** 4, 431–464.

Lion, J. R., Snyder, W., & Merrill, G. L. (1981). Under-reporting of assaults on staff in state hospitals. *Hospital and Community Psychiatry,* **32,** 497–498.

Lowe, K., & Felce, D. (1995). How do carers assess the severity of challenging behavior? A total population study. *Journal of Intellectual Disability Research,* **39,** 2, 117–127.

Lowe, K., Allen, D., Jones, E., Brophy, K., Moore, K., & James, W. (2007). Challenging behaviours: Prevelance and topographies. *Journal of Intellectual Disability Research,* **51,** 625–636.

McClintock, K., Hall, S., & Oliver, C. (2003). Risk markers associated with challenging behaviors in people with intellectual disabilities: A meta-analytic study. *Journal of Intellectual Disability Research,* **47,** 405–416.

McDonnell, A. (1997). Training care staff to manage challenging behavior: An evaluation of a three-day course. *British Journal of Developmental Disabilities,* **43,** 2, 156–161.

McDonnell, A. A., Dearden, R., & Richens, A. (1991a) Staff training in the management of violence and aggression. 1: Setting up a training system. *Mental Handicap,* **19,** 73–76.

McDonnell, A. A., Dearden, R., & Richens, A. (1991b) Staff training in the management of violence and aggression. 2: Avoidance and escape principles. *Mental Handicap,* **19,** 109–112.

McDonnell, A. A., Dearden, R., & Richens, A. (1991c) Staff training in the management of violence and aggression. 3: Physical restraint. *Mental Handicap,* **19,** 151–154.

McDonnell, A. A., Reeves, S., Johnson, A., and Lane, A. (1998). Management of challenging behaviours in an adult with learning disabilities: The use of low arousal. *Behavioural and Cognitive Psychotherapy,* **26,** 163–171.

McDonnell, A. A., Sturmey, P., & Dearden, B. (1993). The acceptability of physical restraint procedures for people with a learning difficulty. *Behavioural and Cognitive Psychotherapy,* **21,** 255–264.

McDonnell, A., & Sturmey, P. (1993a) Managing violent and aggressive behaviors of people with learning difficulties. In R. S. P. Jones & C. Eayrs (Eds.), *Challenging behaviors and mental handicap: A psychological perspective.* Kidderminster: BILD, p. 4.

McDonnell, A. A., & Sturmey, P. (1993b) The acceptability of physical restraint procedures for people with a learning difficulty. *Behavioral and Cognitive Psychotherapy,* **21,** 225–264.

McDonnell, A. A., & Sturmey, P. (2000). The social validation of three physical restraint procedures: A comparison of young people and professional groups. *Research in Developmental Disabilities*, **21**, 85–92.

McDonnell, A. A., Sturmey, P., Gould, A., & Butt, S. (2007). Staff training in physical interventions: A review of the literature (Unpublished manuscript).

Moores, B., & Grant, G. W. B. (1976). On the nature and incidence of staff patient interactions in hospitals for the mentally handicapped. *International Journal of Nursing Studies*, **13**, 69–81.

Morrison, L., Duryea, P. B., Moore, C., & Nathanson-Shinn, A. (2002). *The lethal hazard of prone restraint: Positional asphyxiation*. Oakland, CA: Protection & Advocacy Inc.

Murphy, G. H., Estien, D., & Clare, I. C. H. (1996). Services for people with mild intellectual disabilities and challenging behaviour: Service users' views. *Journal of Applied Research in Intellectual Disabilities*, **9**, 256–283.

Nord, G., Wieseler, N. A., & Hanson, R. H. (1991). Aversive procedures: The Minnesota experience. *Behavioral and Residential Treatment*, **6**, 197–205.

O'Dell, S. (1974). Training parents in behaviour modification: A review. *Psychological Bulletin*, **81**, 418–433.

Oliver, C. (1993). Self injurious behaviour: From response to strategy. In C. Kiernan (Ed.), *Challenging behaviour and learning disabilities: Research to practice? Implications of research on the challenging behaviour of people with learning disabilities*. Clevedon: BILD, pp. 77–99.

Oliver, C., Hall, S., Hales, J., Murphy, G, & Watts, D. (1998). The treatment of severe self injurious behavior by the systematic fading of restraints: Effects on self injury, self restraint, adaptive behavior and behavioral correlates. *Research in Intellectual Disabilities*, **19**, 143–165.

Paniagua, F. A., Bravermen, C., & Capriotti, R. M. (1986). Use of a treatment package in the management of a profoundly mentally retarded girl's pica and self stimulation. *American Journal of Mental Deficiency*, **90**, 550–557.

Parkes, J. (1996). Control and restraint training: A study of its effectiveness in a medium secure unit. *Journal of Forensic Psychiatry*, **7**, 525–534.

Patterson, B., Leadbetter, D., & McComish, A. (1998). Restraint and sudden death from asphyxia. *Nursing Times*, **94**, 34–36.

Patterson, B. A., Miller, G., & Leadbetter, D. (2005). Beyond zero tolerance: A varied approach to workplace violence. *British Journal of Nursing*, **14**, 810–815.

Patterson, B., Turnbull, J., & Aitken, I. (1992). An evaluation of a training course in the short term management of violence. *Nurse Education Today*, **12**, 368–375.

Perkins, J., & Leadbetter, D. (2002). An evaluation of an aggression management training in a special educational setting. *Emotional and Behavioral Difficulties*, **6**, 1, 19–34.

Razza, N. J. (1993). Determinants of direct care staff turnover in group homes for individuals with mental retardation. *Mental Retardation*, **31**, 284–291.

Rousey, A. B., Blacher, J. B., & Hauneman, R. A. (1990). Predictors of out of home placement of children with severe handicaps: A cross-sectional analysis. *American Journal on Mental Retardation*, **94**, 522–531.

Rusch, R. G., Hall, J. C., & Griffin, H. C. (1986). Abuse-provoking characteristics of institutionalized mentally retarded individuals. *American Journal of Mental Deficiency*, **90**, 6, 618–624.

Sailas, E., & Fenton, M. (1999). Seclusion and restraint as a treatment for people with severe mental illness. *The Cochrane Library*, Issue 3, Art. No. CD001163.

Sequeira, H., & Halstead, S. (2001). Is it meant to hurt, is it? *Violence against Women*, 4, 462–476.

Sigafoos, J., Elkins, J., Kerr, M., & Atwood, T. (1994). A survey of aggressive behavior among a population of persons with intellectual disability in Queensland. *Journal of Intellectual Disability Research*, 38, 369–381.

Singh, N. N., & Baker, L. (1984). Suppression of pica by over-correction and physical restraint: A comprehensive analysis. *Journal of Autism and Developmental Disorders*, 14, 331–341.

Singh, N. N., Dawson, M. J., & Manning, P. J. (1981). The effects of physical restraint on self injurious behavior. *Journal of Mental Deficiency Research*, 25, 207–216.

Singh, N. N., Lloyd, J. W., & Kendall, K. A. (1990). Non-aversive and aversive interventions: Introduction. In A. Repp & N. N. Singh (Eds.), *Perspectives on the use of non-aversive and aversive interventions for persons with developmental disabilities.* Sycamore, IL: Sycamore Publishing Company.

Singh, N. N., Winton, S. W., & Ball, P. M. (1984). Effects of physical restraint on the behavior of hyperactive mentally retarded persons. *American Journal of Mental Deficiency*, 89, 16–22.

Spain, B., Hart, S. A., & Corbett, J. (1984). The use of appliances in the treatment of severe self injurious behaviour. In G. Murphy & B. Wilson (Eds.), *Self Injurious behaviour: A collection of published papers on prevelance, causes and treatment in people who are mentally handicapped or autistic.* Kidderminster, BIMH, pp. 59–77.

Spengler, P., Gilman, B., & La Borde, R. (1990). Frequency and types of incidents occurring in urban based group homes. *Journal of Mental Deficiency Research*, 34, 371–378.

Storey, K., & Horner, R. H. (1991). An evaluative review of social validation research involving persons with handicaps. *The Journal of Special Education*, 25, 352–401.

Sturmey, P. (2009). It is time to safely reduce and eliminate restrictive behavioural practices. *Journal of Applied Research in Intellectual Disabilities*, 22, 105–110.

Sturmey, P., & Palen-McGlynn, A. P. (2002). Restraint reduction. In D. Allen (Ed.), *Ethical approaches to physical interventions.* Plymouth: BILD, pp. 203–218.

Tarbuck, P. (1992). Use and abuse of control and restraint. *Nursing Standard*, 6, 30–32.

Taylor, J. C., & Carr, E.G. (1992). Severe problem behaviors related to social interaction. 2: A systems analysis. *Behavior Modification*, 16, 336–371.

Thompson, R. H., & Iwata, B. A. (2000). Response acquisition under direct and indirect contingencies of reinforcement. *Journal of Applied Behavior Analysis*, 33, 1–11.

Topping-Morris, B. (1995). Break the lock. *Nursing Standard*, 9, 55.

Tutton, C., Wynne-Wilson, S., & Piachaud, J. (1990). Rating management difficulty: A study into the prevalence and severity of difficult behavior displayed by residents in a large residential hospital for the mentally handicapped. *Journal of Mental Deficiency Research*, 34, 325–329.

Weiss, E. M. (1998, October 11–15). *Deadly restraint:* A nationwide pattern of death. *Hartford Courant.*

White, C., Holland, E., Marsland, D., & Oakes, P. (2003). The identification of environments and cultures that promote abuse of people with intellectual disabilities:

A review of the literature. *Journal of Applied Research in Intellectual Disabilities*, **16**, 1–9.

Williams, D. E. (2009). Restraint safety: An analysis of injuries related to restraint of people with intellectual disabilities. *Journal of Applied Research in Intellectual Disabilities*, **22**, 135–139.

Willis, T. J., & La Vigna, G. W. (1985). *Emergency management guidelines*. Los Angeles: Institute for Applied Behaviour Analysis.

Wolf, M. M. (1978). Social validity: The case for subjective measurement or how applied behavior analysis is finding its heart. *Journal of Applied Behavior Analysis*, **11**, 203–214.

Woods, P., & Cullen, C. (1983). Determinants of staff behavior in long-term care. *Behavioral Psychotherapy*, **11**, 4–18.

Chapter 5: Managing Aggressive Behaviour in Individuals with Autistic Spectrum Disorders

Allison, D. B., Basile, V. C., & Mcdonald, R. B. (1991). Brief report: Comparative effects of antecedent exercise and lorazepam on the aggressive behaviour of an autistic man. *Journal of Autism and Developmental Disorders*, **21**, 89–94.

Althaus, M., van Roon, A. M., Mulder, L. J. M., Mulder, G., Aarnoudse, C. C., & Minderaa, R. B. (2000). Autonomic response patterns observed during the performance of an attention demanding task in two groups of children with autistic-type difficulties in social adjustment. *Psychophysiology*, **41**, 893–904.

Asperger, H. (1944). Die autischen psychopathen im kindersalter. *Archive fur Psychiatrie und Nervenkrankheiten*, **177**, 76–137.

Attwood, T. (2004). *Exploring feelings: Cognitive behavior therapy to manage anger*. Arlington, TX: New Horizons.

Attwood, T. (2007). *The complete guide to Aspergers syndrome*. London: Jessica Kingsley.

Baker, P. (2002). Best interest? Seeking the views of service users. In D. Allen (Ed.), *Ethical approaches to physical interventions*. Plymouth: BILD, pp. 153–163.

Baranek, G. T., David, F. J., Poe, M. D., Stone, W. L., & Watson, L. R. (2006). Sensory experiences questionnaire: Discriminating sensory features in young children with autism, developmental delays, and typical development. *Journal of Child Psychology and Psychiatry, and Allied Disciplines*, **47**, 6, 591–601.

Baron-Cohen, S. (1995). *Mindblindness: An essay on autism and theory of mind*. Cambridge, MA: The MIT Press.

Bird, F., Dores, P. A., Moniz, D., & Robinson, J. (1989). Reducing severe aggressive and self injurious behaviours with functional communication training. *American Journal on Mental Retardation*, **94**, 37–48.

Blackburn, R. (2006). Physical interventions and autism: a service user's perspective. In S. Paley & J. Brooke (Eds.), *Good practice in physical interventions: A guide for staff and managers*. Kidderminster: BILD, pp. 37–49.

Bogadashina, O. (2003). *Sensory perceptual issues in autism and Aspergers syndrome – different sensory experiences, different sensory worlds*. London: Jessica Kingsley.

Bromley, J., Hare, D. J., Davison, K., & Emerson, E. (2004). Mothers supporting a child with autistic spectrum disorders: Social support, mental health status and satisfaction with services. *Autism*, **8**, 419–433.

Brown, C., Tollefson, N., Dunn, W., Cromwell, R., & Filion, D. (2001). The adult sensory profile: Measuring patterns of sensory processing. *The American Journal of Occupational Therapy*, **55**, 75–82.

Campenni, C. E., Crawley, E. J., & Meier, M. E. (2004). Role of suggestion in odor-induced mood change. *Psychological Reports*, **94**, 3, 1127–1136.

Chan, S., Yeun Fung, M., Wai Tong, C., & Thompson, D. (2005). The clinical effectiveness of multisensory therapy on service users with developmental disability. *Research in Developmental Disabilities*, **26**, 131–142.

Charlop-Christy, M. H., Carpenter, H., Le, L., LeBlanc, L. A., & Kellet, K. (2002). Using the picture exchange communication system (PECS) with children with autism: Assessment of PECS acquisition, speech, social-communicative behavior and problem behavior. *Journal of Applied Behavior Analysis*, **35**, 213–231.

Dagnan, D., & Jahoda, A. (2006). Cognitive behavioural intervention for people with intellectual disability and anxiety disorders. *Journal of Applied Research in Intellectual Disabilities*, **19**, 91–97.

Damasio, A. R., & Maurer, R. G. (1978). A neurological model for childhood autism. *Archives of Neurology*, **35**, 777–786.

Dunn, W. (1997). The impact of sensory processing abilities on the daily lives of young children and their families. *Infants and Young Children*, **9**, 23–35.

Dunn, W. (1999). *The sensory profile.* San Antonio, TX: Psychological Corporation.

Dunn, W. (2001). The sensations of everyday life: Empirical, theoretical and pragmatic considerations. *American Journal of Occupational Therapy*, **55**, 608–620.

Dunn, W., Smyth Myles, B., & Orr, S. (2002). Sensory processing issues associated with Aspergers syndrome: A preliminary investigation. *The American Journal of Occupational Therapy*, **56**, 97–102.

Favell, J. E., McGimsey, J. F., & Jones, M. L. (1978). The use of physical restraint in the treatment of self injury and as positive reinforcement. *Journal of Applied Analysis*, **11**, 225–241.

Frith, U. (1989). *Autism: Explaining the enigma.* Oxford: Blackwell.

Frith, U. (2003). *Autism: Explaining the enigma* (2nd Edition). Oxford: Blackwell.

Gomez, P., & Danuser, B. (2004). Affective and physiological responses to environmental noises and music. *International Journal of Psychophysiology*, **53**, 2, 91–103.

Goodwin, M. S., Groden, J., Velicer, W. F., Lipsitt, L. P., Grace Baron, M., & Hofmann, S. G. (2006). Cardiovascular arousal in individuals with autism. *Focus on Autism and Other Developmental Disabilities*, **21**, 100–123.

Grandin, T. (1992a). An inside view of autism. In E. Schopler & G. B. Mesibov (Eds.), *High functioning individuals with autism.* New York: Plenum Press, pp. 105–126.

Grandin, T. (1992b). Calming effects of deep pressure in patients with autistic disorder, college students and animals. *Journal of Child and Adolescent Psychopharmacology*, **2**, 1, 63–70.

Grandin, T. (1996, February). My experiences with visual thinking, sensory problems and communication difficulties. Available: http://www.autism.org/

Groden, J., Cautela, J., Prince, S., & Berryman, J. (1994). The Impact of stress and anxiety on individuals with autism and other developmental disabilities. In E. Schopler & G. Mesibov (Eds.), *Behaviour issues and autism*. New York: Plenum Press.

Happe, F. (1996). Studying weak central coherence at low levels: Children with autism do not succumb to visual illusions. A research note. *Journal of Psychology and Psychiatry*, **37**, 873–877.

Hirstein, W., Iversen, P., & Ramachandran, V. S. (2001). Autonomic responses of autistic children to people and objects. *Proceedings of the Royal Society B: Biological Sciences*, **268**, 1883–1888.

Horner, R. H., Carr, E. G., Strain, P. S., Todd, A. W., & Reed, H. K. (2002). Problem behavior interventions for young children with autism: A research synthesis. *Journal of Autism and Developmental Disorders*, **32**, 5, 423–446.

Hutt, C., Hutt, S. J., Lee, D., & Ounsted, C. (1964). Arousal and childhood autism. *Nature*, **204**, 908–909.

Iwata, B. A., Dorsey, M. F., Slifer, K. J., Bauman, K. E., & Richman, G. S. (1982). Toward a functional analysis of self injury. *Analysis and Intervention in Developmental Disabilities*, **2**, 1–20.

Jansen, L. M. C., Gispen-de Wied, C. C., Wiegant, V. M., Westenberg, H. G. M., Lahuis, B. E., & van Engeland, H. (2006). Autonomic and neuroendocrine responses to a psychosocial stressor in adults with autistic spectrum disorder. *Journal of Autism and Developmental Disorders*, **36**, 7, 891–899.

Kanner, L. (1943). Autistic disturbances of affective contact. *Nervous Child*, **2**, 217–250.

Kaplan, H., Clopton, M., Kaplan, M., Messbauer, A., & McPherson, K. (2006). Snoezelen multisensory environments: Task engagement and generalization. *Research in Developmental Disabilities*, **27**, 443–445.

Kern, J. K., Garver, C. R., Grannemann, B. D., Trivedi, M. H., Carmody, T., Andrews, A. A., & Mehta, J. A. (2007). Response to vestibular sensory events in autism. *Research in Autistic Spectrum Disorders*, **1**, 67–74.

Kern, J. K., Trivedi, M. H., Garver, C. R., Grannemann, B. D., Andrews, A. A., Savla, J. S., Johnson, D. G., Mehta, J. A., & Schroeder, J. L. (2006). The pattern of sensory processing abnormalities in autism. *Autism*, **10**, 480–494.

Kern, L., Koegel, R. L., & Dunlap, G. (1984). The influence of vigorous versus mild exercise on autistic stereotyped behaviours. *Journal of Autism and Developmental Disorders*, **14**, 57–67.

Kinsbourne, M. (1980). Do repetitive movement patterns in children and animals serve a dearousing function? *Developmental and Behavioural Paediatrics*, **1**, 39–42.

Lathe, R. (2006). *Autism, brain and environment*. London: Jessica Kingsley.

Lazarus, R. S., & Folkman, S. (1984). *Stress, appraisal, and coping*. New York: Springer.

Leadbetter, D. (2002). Good practice in physical intervention. In D. Allen (Ed.), *Ethical approaches to physical intervention: Responding to challenging behaviour in people with intellectual disabilities*. Kidderminster: BILD, pp. 114–133.

Leary, M., & Hill, D. (1996). Moving on: Autism and movement disturbance. *Mental Retardation*, **34**, 1, 39–53.

Leekam, S. R., Nieto, C., Libby, S. J., Wing, L., & Gould, J. (2006). Describing the sensory abnormalities of children and adults with autism. *Journal of Autism and Developmental Disorders*, **37**, 894–910.

Lindsay, W. R., Picaithly, D., Geelen, N., Buntin, S., Broxholme, S., & Ashby, M. (1997).

A comparison of the effects of four therapy procedures on concentration and responsiveness in people with profound learning disabilities. *Journal of Intellectual Disability Research*, **41**, 201–207.

Lipsky, D., & Richards, W. (2009). *Managing meltdowns: Using the SCARED calming technique with children and adults with autism*. London: Jessica Kingsley.

Liss, S. M., Saulnier, C., Fein, D., & Kinsbourne, M. (2006). Sensory and attention abnormalities in autistic spectrum disorders. *Autism*, **10**, 155–172.

Matson, J. L., & Dempsey, T. (2009). The nature and treatment of compulsions, obsessions and rituals in people with developmental disabilities. *Research in Developmental Disabilities*, **30**, 603–611.

McClintock, K., Hall, S., & Oliver, C. (2003). Risk markers associated with challenging behaviours in people with intellectual disabilities: A meta-analytic study. *Journal of Intellectual Disability Research*, **47**, 405–416.

McDonnell, A. (1997). Training care staff to manage challenging behaviour: An evaluation of a three-day course. *British Journal of Developmental Disabilities*, **43**, 2, 156–161.

McDonnell A. A. (2007). Why I am in favour of the Millfields Charter. *Learning Disability Practice*, **10**, 26–29.

McDonnell, A. A., & Jones, P. (1999). The role of clinical psychology in the physical management of challenging behaviour. *Clinical Psychology Forum*, May, 20–23.

McDonnell, A. A., Mills, R., & Sallis, J. (2009). The role of physiological arousal in the management of challenging behaviours in individuals with autistic spectrum disorders. Unpublished manuscript.

McDonnell, A. A., Peter Sturmey, Oliver, C., Cunningham, J., Hayes, S., Galvin, M., Walshe, C., & Cunningham, C. (2008) The effects of staff training on staff confidence and challenging behavior in services for people with autism spectrum disorders. *Research in Autism Spectrum Disorders*, **2**, 2, 311–319.

McDonnell, A. A., Reeves, S., Johnson, A., & Lane, A. (1998). Management of violence and aggression in an adult with intellectual disabilities: The use of low arousal. *Behavioural and Cognitive Psychotherapy*, **26**, 163–171.

McGimsey, J. F., & Favell, J. E. (1988). The effects of increased physical activity on disruptive behaviour in retarded persons. *Journal of Autism and Developmental Disorders*, **18**, 167–179.

Merrett, B., McDonnell, A. A., & Jones, D. (2009). Reducing physical intervention usage in service for adults with intellectual disabilities and challenging behaviour: A four year study. Unpublished manuscript.

Morgan, K. (2006). Is autism a stress disorder? In M. G. Baron, J. Groden, G. Groden, & L. P. Lipsitt (Eds.), *Stress and coping in autism*. New York: Oxford University Press.

Mukhopadhyay, T. R. (2003). *The mind tree: A miraculous child breaks the silence of autism*. New York: Arcade Publishing.

Murphy, O., Healy, O., & Leader, G. (2009). Risk factors for challenging behaviors among 157 children with autism spectrum disorder in Ireland. *Research in Autism Spectrum Disorders*, **3**, 474–482.

Nunno, M. A., Holden, M. J., & Tollar, A. (2006). Learning from tragedy: A survey of child and adolescent restraint fatalities. *Child Abuse & Neglect*, **30**, 1333–1342.

O'Neill, M. O., & Jones, R. S. P. (1997). Sensory–perceptual abnormalities in autism:

A case for more research. *Journal of Autism and Developmental Disorders*, **27**, 283–293.

Oliver, C. (1993). Self injurious behaviour: From response to strategy. In C. Kiernan (Ed.), *Challenging behaviour and learning disabilities: Research to practice? Implications of research on the challenging behaviour of people with learning disabilites*. Clevedon: BILD.

Ornitz, E. (1988). Autism a disorder of directed attention. *Brain Dysfunction*, **1**, 309–322.

Ozonoff, S., Strayer, D., McMahon, W., & Fillouz, F. (1994). Executive function abilities in autism. *Journal of Child Psychology and Psychiatry*, **35**, 1015–1031.

Paterson, B. (2007). Millfields Charter: Drawing the wrong conclusions. *Learning Disability Practice*, **10**, 30–33.

Rajendran, G., & Mitchel, P. (2007). Cognitive theories of autism. *Developmental Review*, **27**, 224–260.

Rogers, S. J., Hepburn, S., & Wehner, E. (2003). Parent reports of sensory symptoms in toddlers with autism and those with other developmental disorders. *Journal of Autism and Developmental Disorders*, **33**, 6, 631–642.

Rojahn, J., Schroeder, S. R., & Hoch, T. A. (2008). *Self-injurious behavior in intellectual disabilities*. New York: Elsevier.

Romanczyk, R., Kistner, J. A., & Plienis, A. (1982). Self stimulatory and self injurious behaviour: Etiology and treatment. In J. Steffan & P. Karoly (Eds.), *Advances in child behavioural analysis and therapy*. Lexington, KY: Lexington Books, pp. 189–254.

Rosenthal-Malek, A., & Mitchell, S. (1997). Brief report: The effects of exercise on the self stimulatory behaviours and positive responding of adolescents with autism. *Journal of Autism and Developmental Disorders*, **27**, 193–202.

Shapiro, M., Parush, S., Green, M., & Roth, D. (1997). The efficacy of the 'Snoezelen' in management of children who exhibit maladaptive behaviors. *British Journal of Developmental Disabilities*, **43**, 140–155.

Shore, S. (2003). *Beyond the wall: Personal experiences with autism and Asperger syndrome*. Shawnee Mission, KS: Autism Asperger Publishing Company.

Sinclair, J. (1992). What does being different mean? *Our Voice: The Newsletter of Autism Network International*, Issue 1, pp. 1–12.

Singh, N. N., Lancioni, G. E., Winton, A. S. W., Molina, E. J., Sage, M., Brown, S., & Groenweg, J. (2004). Effects of snoezelen room, activities of daily living skills, training and vocational skills training on aggression and self injury by adults with mental retardation and mental illness. *Research in Developmental Disabilities*, **25**, 285–293.

Smith, S. A., Press, B., Koenig, K. P., & Kinnealey, M. (2005). Effects of sensory integration intervention on self-stimulating and self-injurious behaviors. *American Journal of Occupational Therapy*, **59**, 418–425.

Sofronoff, K., & Attwood, T. (2003). A cognitive behaviour therapy intervention for anxiety in children with Aspergers syndrome. *Good Autism Practice*, **4**, 228–237.

Sofronoff, K., Attwood, T., & Hinton, S. (2005). A randomised control trial of a CBT intervention for anxiety in children with Aspergers syndrome. *Journal of Child Psychology and Psychiatry*, **46**, 1152–1160.

Stephenson, J. (2002). Characterization of multisensory environments: Why do teachers use them? *Journal of Applied Research in Intellectual Disabilities*, **15**, 73–90.

Symons, F. J., Harper, V. N., McGrath, P. J., Breau, L. M., & Bodfish, J. W. (in press). Evidence of increased non-verbal behavioral signs of pain in adults with neurodevelopmental disorders and chronic self-injury, *Research in Developmental Disabilities.*

Van Engeland, H., Roelofs, J. W., Verbaten, M. N., & Slangen, J. L. (1991). Abnormal electrodermal reactivity to novel visual stimuli in autistic children. *Psychiatry Research,* **38**, 27–38.

Wing, L. (1981). Aspergers syndrome: A clinical account. *Psychological Medicine,* **11**, 115–130.

Wing, L., & Gould, J. (1979). Severe impairments of social interaction and associated abnormalities in children: Epidemiology and classification. *Journal of Autism and Developmental Disorders,* **9**, 11–29.

Chapter 6: Applying Low Arousal Approaches in Children and Adolescents in Residential Care Services

Bell, L. (1996). The physical restraint of young people. *Child and Family Social Work,* **1**, 37–47.

Bloom, R. B. (1992). When staff members sexually abuse children in residential care. *Child Welfare,* **71**, 131–145.

Butt, S. S., McDonnell, A. A., Sturmey, P., Brewerton, E., & Semple, C. (2004). *The development of a staff fear of physical aggression scale.* Unpublished Master's dissertation, University of Birmingham, Birmingham.

Cathcart Shabat J., Lyons, J. S., & Martinovich, Z. (2008). Exploring the relationship between conduct disorder and residential treatment outcomes. *Journal of Child and Family Studies,* **17**, 353–371.

Child Welfare League of America. (2004). *Achieving better outcomes for children and families – Reducing restraint and seclusion.* Washington, DC: Child Welfare League of America.

Dagnan, D., McDonnell, A. A., & Grant, F. (2005). Understanding challenging behaviour in older people: The development of the controllability beliefs scale. *Behavioural and Cognitive Psychotherapy,* **32**, 501–506.

Day, D. M. (2002). Examining the therapeutic utility of restraints and seclusion with children and youth: The role of theory and research in practice. *American Journal of Orthopsychiatry,* **72**, 266–278.

Fiering, C., Simon, V. A., & Cleland, C. M. (2009). Childhood sexual abuse, stigmatization, internalizing symptoms and the development of sexual difficulties and dating aggression. *Journal of Consulting and Clinical Psychology,* **77**, 1, 127–137.

Fryer, M. A., Beech, M., & Byrne, G. J. A. (2004). Seclusion use with children and adolescents: An Australian experience. *Australian and New Zealand Journal of Psychiatry,* **38**, 26–33.

Handwerk, M. L., Clopton, K., Huefner, J. C., Smith, G. L., Hoff, K. E., & Lucas, C. P. (2006). Gender differences in adolescents in residential treatment. *American Journal of Orthopsychiatry,* **76**, 312–324.

Kendrick, A. (1998) 'Who do we trust?' The abuse of children living away from home in the United Kingdom. Paper presented to the *12th International Congress on Child Abuse and Neglect; Protecting Children: Innovation and Inspiration*. West Chicago, IL: International Society for Prevention of Child Abuse and Neglect.

Knorth, E. J., Klomp, M., Van den Bergh, P. M., & Noom, M. J. (2003). Aggressive adolescents in residential care: A selective review of treatment requirements and models. *Adolescence*, **42**, 167, 461–485.

Larson, T. C., Sheitman, B. B., Kraus, J. E., Mayo, J., & Leidy, L. (2008). Managing treatment resistant violent adolescents: A step forward by substituting seclusion for mechanical restraint? *Administration Policy and Mental Health*, **35**, 198–203.

Leadbetter, D. (2002). Good practice in physical intervention. In D. Allen (Ed.), *Ethical approaches to physical intervention: Responding to challenging behaviour in people with intellectual disabilities*. Kidderminster: BILD, pp. 114–133.

Leidy, B. D., Haugaard, J. J., Nunno, M. M., & Kwartner, J. K. (*2006*). Review of restraint data in a residential treatment center for adolescent females. *Child Youth Care Forum*, **35**, 339–352.

Levy, A., & Kahan, B. (1991). *The pindown experience and the protection of children: The report of the Staffordshire Child Care Inquiry 1990*. Staffordshire, England: Staffordshire County Council.

Lyons, J. S., & Schaefer, K. (2000). Mental health and dangerousness: Characteristics and outcomes of children and adolescents in residential placements. *Journal of Child and Family Studies*, **9**, 67–73.

Lyons, J. S., Terry, P., Martinovich, Z., Peterson, J., & Bouska, B. (2001). Outcome trajectories for adolescents in residential treatment: A statewide evaluation. *Journal of Child and Family Studies*, **10**, 333–345.

Madge, N., Hewitt, A., Hawton, K., Jan de Wilde, E., Corcoran, P., Fekete, S., Van Heeringen, K., De Leo, D., & Ystgaard, M. (2008). Deliberate self-harm within an international community sample of young people: Comparative findings from the Child & Adolescent Self-harm in Europe (CASE) Study. *Journal of Child Psychology and Psychiatry*, **49**, 6, 667–677.

McDonnell, A. (1997). Training care staff to manage challenging behaviour: An evaluation of a three-day course. *British Journal of Developmental Disabilities*, **43**, 2, 156–161.

McDonnell, A. A. (2005). *The development and evaluation of a three day training course in aggressive behaviour*. Unpublished doctoral dissertation, School of Psychology, University of Birmingham, Birmingham.

McDonnell, A. A., McEvoy, J., & Dearden, R. L. (1994). Coping with violent situations in the caring environment. In T. Wykes (Ed.), *Violence and health care professionals*. London: Chapman & Hall, pp. 189–206.

Mercer, J. (2001). 'Attachment therapy' using deliberate restraint: An object lesson on the identification of unvalidated treatments. *Journal of Child and Adolescent Psychiatric Nursing*, **14**, 3, 105–114.

Mercer, J. (2002). Child psychotherapy involving physical restraint: Techniques used in four approaches. *Child and Adolescent Social Work Journal*, **19**, 4, 303–314.

Miller-Perrin, C. L., Perrin, R. D., & Kocurb, J. L. (2009). Parental physical and psychological aggression: Psychological symptoms in young adults. *Child Abuse & Neglect*, **33**, 2009, 1–11.

Mohr, W. K., Mahon, M. M., & Noone, M. J. (1998). A restraint on restraints: The need to reconsider the use of restrictive interventions. *Archives of Psychiatric Nursing*, **12**, 2, 112–129.

Mohr, W. K., Petti, T. A., & Mohr, B. D. (2003). Adverse effects associated with physical restraint. *Canadian Journal of Psychiatry*, **48**, 5, 330–337.

Noll, J. G. (2008). Sexual abuse of children: Unique in its effects on development? *Child Abuse & Neglect*, **32**, 603–605.

Nunno, M. A., Holden, M. J., & Leidy, B. (2003) Evaluating and monitoring the impact of a crisis intervention system on a residential child care facility. *Children & Youth Services Review*, **24**, 4, 295–315.

Nunno, M., Holden, M., & Tollar, A. (2006). Learning from tragedy: A survey of child and adolescent restraint facilities. *Child Abuse & Neglect: The International Journal*, **30**, 12, 1333–1342.

O'Malley, F. (1993). Short-term residential treatment of disturbed adolescents in a continuum of care. *Children and Youth Services Review*, **15**, 245–260.

Perkins, J., & Leadbetter, D. (2002). An evaluation of an aggression management training in a special educational setting. *Emotional and Behavioural Difficulties*, **6**, 1, 19–34.

Priebea, G., & Svedinb, C. G. (2008). Child sexual abuse is largely hidden from the adult society: An epidemiological study of adolescents' disclosures. *Child Abuse & Neglect*, **32**, 1095–1108.

Sinclair, R., & Bullock, R. (2002). *Learning from past experience – A review of serious case reviews*. Lund, Sweden: Department of Child and Adolescent Psychiatry, IKVL, Lund University.

Smallridge, P. & Williamson, A. (2008). *Independent Review of Restraint in Juvenile Secure Settings*. London: Ministry of Justice, Department for Children, Schools and Families, Ministry of Justice.

Titus, R. (1989). Therapeutic crisis intervention training. *Journal of Child and Youth Care*, **4**, 61–71.

Whittington, R., & Wykes, T. (1996). An evaluation of staff training in psychological techniques for the management of patient aggression. *Journal of Clinical Nursing*, **5**, 257–261.

Wolf, M. M. (1978). Social validity: The case for subjective measurement or how applied behavior analysis is finding its heart. *Journal of Applied Behavior Analysis*, **11**, 203–214.

Chapter 7: Developing Alternatives to Coercive Behaviour Management Approaches in Psychiatric Settings

Allen, D. (2001). *Physical interventions: theory and research*. Avon, England: BILD.

Arnetz, J. E., & Arnetz, B. B. (2000). Implementation and evaluation of a practical intervention programme for dealing with violence towards health care workers. *Journal of Advanced Nursing*, **31**, 3, 668–680.

Batty, D. (2005, February 2). Call for restraint to tackle violent mental health patients. Available at SocietyGuardian.co.uk.

Beech, B., & Leather, P. (2006). Workplace violence in the healthcare sector: A review of staff training and an integration of training evaluation models. *Aggression and Violent Behaviour*, **11**, 27–43.

Bisconer, S. W., Green, M.,Mallon-Czaijka, J., & Johnson, J. S. (2006). Managing aggression in a psychiatric hospital using a behaviour plan. *Journal of Psychiatric and Mental Health Nursing*, **13**, 515–521.

Bowers, L. (2005, February 2). Less is more. Available at SocietyGuardian.co.uk.

Bowers, L., Douzenis, A., Galeazzi, G. M., Forghieri, M., Tsopelas, C., Simpson, A., & Allan, T. (2005). Disruptive and dangerous behaviour by patients on acute on psychiatric wards in three European countries. *Social Psychiatry and Psychiatric Epidemiology*, **40**, 822–828.

Bowers, L., Van Der Werf, B., Vokkolainen, A., Muir-Cochrane, E., Allan, T., & Alexander, J. (2006). International variation in containment measures for disturbed psychiatric inpatients: A comparative questionnaire survey. *International Journal of Nursing Studies*, **44**, 357–364.

Carmel, H., & Hunter, M. (1990). Compliance with training in managing assaultive and injuries from in-patient violence. *Hospital and Community Psychiatry*, **41**, 5, 558–560.

Collins, J. (1994). Nurses' attitudes towards aggressive behaviour, following attendance at 'The Prevention and Management of Aggressive Behaviour Programme'. *Journal of Advanced Nursing*, **20**, 117–131.

Corrigan, P., Holmes, E. P., Luchins, D., Basit, A., Delaney, E., Gleason, W., Buican, B., & McCracken, S. (1995). The effects of interactive staff training on staff programming and patient aggression in a psychiatric inpatient ward. *Behavioral Interventions*, **10**, 17–32.

Corrigan, P. W., & Liberman, R. P. (1999). *Behavior therapy in psychiatric hospitals.* New York: Springer.

Currie, C. G. (2005). SAMHSA's commitment to eliminating the use of seclusion and restraint. *Psychiatric Services*, **56**, 1139–1140.

D'Orio, B. M., Purselle, D., Stevens, D., & Garlow, S. J. (2004). Reduction of episodes of seclusion and restraint in a psychiatric emergency service. *Psychiatric Services*, **55**, 581–583.

Daffern, M., Mayer, M., & Martin, T. (2003). A preliminary investigation into patterns of aggression in an Australian forensic psychiatric hospital. *The Journal of Forensic Psychiatry and Psychology*, **14**, 67–84.

Davison, S. E. (2005). The management of violence in general psychiatry. *Advances in Psychiatric Treatment*, **11**, 362–370.

Delaney, K. R. (2006). Evidence base for practice: Reduction of restraint and seclusion use during child and adolescent psychiatric inpatient treatment. *Worldview on Evidenced Based Nursing*, **3**, 19–30.

Donat, D. C. (2003). An analysis of successful efforts to reduce the use of seclusion and restraint at a public psychiatric hospital. *Psychiatric Services*, **54**, 1119–1123.

Donat, D. C. (2005). Encouraging alternatives to seclusion, restraint and reliance PRN drugs in a public psychiatric hospital. *Psychiatric Services*, 56, 1105–1108.

Donavan, A., Plant, R., Peller, A., Siegel, L., & Martin, A. (2003). Two year trends in the use of seclusion and restraint among psychiatrically hospitalised youths. *Psychiatric Services*, 54, 987–993.

Donavan, A., Siegel, L., Zera, G., Plant, R., & Martin, A. (2003). Seclusion and restraint reform: An initiative by a child and adolescent psychiatric hospital. *Psychiatric Services*, 54, 958–959.

Duxbury, J. (2002). An evaluation of staff and patient views of strategies employed to manage inpatient aggression and violence on one mental health unit: A pluralistic design. *Journal of Psychiatric and Mental Health Nursing*, 9, 325–337.

Duxbury, J. (2003). National directives on managing 'violent' patients: a critique. *Nursing Times*, 99, 6, 30–32.

Duxbury, J. (2005, February 2). We cannot avoid this debate. SocietyGuardian.co.uk.

Duxbury, J., & Whittington, R. (2005). Causes and management of patient aggression and violence: Staff and patient perspectives. *Journal of Advanced Nursing*, 50, 469–478.

Flannery, R. B., Hanson, M. A., Penk, W. E., Goldfinger, S., Pastva, G. J., & Navon, M. A. (1998). Replicated declines in assault rates after implementation of the assault Staff Action Program. *Psychiatric Services*, 49, 241–243.

Gournay, K. (2001). *The recognition, prevention and therapeutic management of violence in mental health care: A consultation document*. United Kingdom Central Council for Nursing, Midwifery and Health Visiting.

Hahn, S., Needham, I., Abderhalden, C., Duxbury, J. A. D., & Halfens, R. J. G. (2006). The effect of a training course on mental health nurses' attitudes on the reasons of patient aggression and its management. *Journal of Psychiatric and Mental Health Nursing*, 13, 197–204.

Haw, C., & Yorston, G. (2004). Thomas Prichard and the non restraint movement at the Northampton Asylum. *Psychiatric Bulletin*, 28, 140–142.

Huckshorn, K. (2004). Reducing seclusion restraint in mental health use settings: Core strategies for prevention. *Journal of Psychosocial and Mental Health Nursing*, 42, 22–33.

Hurlebaus, A. (1994). Aggressive behaviour management for nurses: An international issue? *Journal of Healthcare Protection Management*, 10, 2, 97–106.

Hurlebaus, A., & Link, S. (1997). The effect of aggressive behavior management programme on nurses' levels of knowledge, confidence and safety. *Journal of Nursing Staff Development*, 13, 5, 260–265.

Ilkiw-Lavelle, O., & Grenyer, B. F. S. (2003). Differences between patient and staff perceptions of aggression in mental health units. *Psychiatric Services*, 54, 389–393.

Infantino, J. A., & Musingo, M. S. (1985). Assaults and injuries among staff with and without training in aggression control techniques. *Hospital and Community Psychiatry*, 36, 12, 1312–1314.

Jansen, G. J., Dassen, W. N., & Groot Jebbink, G. (2005). Staff attitudes towards aggression in health care: A review of the literature. *Journal of Psychiatric and Mental Health Nursing*, 12, 3–13.

Jonikas, J. A., Cook, J. A., Rosen, C., Laris, A., & Kym, J. B. (2005). A program to reduce use of physical restraint in a psychiatric inpatient facilities. *Psychiatric Services*, **55**, 818–820.

Laurance, J. (2002). *Pure madness: How fear drives the mental health system*. London: Kings Fund Lectures.

Leadbetter, D. (2002). Good practice in physical interventions. In D. Allen (Ed.), *Ethical approaches to physical interventions*. Plymouth: BILD, pp. 114–133.

Leadbetter, D. (2007). Millfields Charter: Finding the middle ground. *Learning Disability Practice*, **10**, 34–37.

LeBel, J., Stromberg, N., Duckworth, K., Kerzner, J., Goldstein, R., Weeks, N., Harper, G., Laflair, L., & Sudders, M. (2004). Child and adolescent inpatient restraint reduction: A state initiative to promote strength based care. *Journal of the American Academy of Child and Adolescent Psychiatry*, **43**, 1–20.

Lee, S., Wright, S., Sayer, J., Parr, A. M., Gray, R., & Gournay, K. (2001). Physical restraint training in English and Welsh psychiatric intensive care and regional secure units. *Journal of Mental Health*, **10**, 151–162.

Leggett, J., & Silvester, J. (2003). Care staff attributions for violent incidents involving male and female patients. *British Journal of Clinical Psychology*, **42**, 393–406.

Martin, V., Bernhardsgrutter, R., Goebel, R., & Steinert, T. (2007). The use of mechanical restraint and seclusion in patients with schizophrenia: A comparison of the practice in Germany and Switzerland. *Clinical Practice and Epidemiology in Mental Health*, **3**, 1–6.

McDonnell, A., Sturmey, P., & Dearden, R. (1993b). The acceptability of physical restraint procedures for people with a learning difficulty. *Behavioural and Cognitive Psychotherapy*, **21**, 225–264.

McDonnell, A. A. (1997). Training care staff to manage challenging behaviour: An evaluation of a three day course. *British Journal of Developmental Disabilities*, **43**, 2, 156–161.

McDonnell, A. A. (2007). Why I am in favour of the Millfields Charter. *Learning Disability Practice*, **10**, 26–29.

McDonnell, A. A., & Gallon, I. G. (2006). Issues and concerns about control and restraint training: Moving the debate forward. In M. Ward & J. Cutcliffe (Eds.), *Key debates in psychiatric nursing*. London: Wiley, pp. 77–99.

McDonnell, A. A., Gould, A., Adams, T., Sallis, J., & Anker, R. (2009). Staff training in physical interventions. Unpublished manuscript.

McDonnell, A. A., McEvoy, J., & Dearden, R. L. (1994). Coping with violent situations in the caring environment. In T. Wykes (Ed.), *Violence and health care professionals*. London: Chapman & Hall, pp. 189–206.

McDonnell, A. A., Reeves, S., Johnson, A., & Lane, A. (1998). Management of challenging behaviours in an adult with learning disabilities: The use of low arousal. *Behavioural and Cognitive Psychotherapy*, **26**, 163–171.

McNeil, D. E., Eisner, J. P., & Binder, R. L. (2000). The relationship between command hallucinations and violence. *Psychiatric Services*, **51**, 1299–1292.

McGowan, S., Wynaden, D., Harding, N., Yassine, A., & Parker, J. (1999). Staff confidence in dealing with aggressive patients: A benchmarking exercise. *Australian and New Zealand Journal of Mental Health Nursing*, **8**, 104–108.

McGuire, J., & Ryan, D. (2007). Aggression and violence in mental health services:

Categorizing the experiences of Irish nurses. *Journal of Psychiatric and Mental Health Nursing*, **14**, 120–127.

Meehan, T., Bergen, H., & Fjeldsoe, K. (2004). Staff and patient perceptions of seclusion: Has anything changed? *Journal of Advanced Nursing*, **47**, 33–38.

Middleby-Clements, J. L., & Grenyer, B. F. L. (2007). Zero tolerance approach to aggression and its impact on mental health staff attitudes. *Australian and New Zealand Journal of Psychiatry*, **41**, 187–191.

Morrison, E. F. (1998). The culture of caregiving and aggression in psychiatric settings. *Archives of Psychiatric Nursing*, **12**, 21–31.

Morrison, E. F., & Carney Love, C. (2003). An evaluation of four programs for the management of aggression in psychiatric settings. *Archives of Psychiatric Nursing*, **57**, 146–155.

Needham, I., Abderhalden, C., Halfens, R. J. G., Dassen, T., Haug, H. J., & Fischer, J. E. (2005a) The effect of a training course in aggression management on mental health nurses' perception of aggression: A randomised controlled trial. *International Journal of Nursing Studies*, **42**, 649–655.

Needham, I., Abderhalden, C., Zeller, A., Dassen, T., Haug, H. J., Fischer, J. E., & Halfens, R. J. (2005b). The effect of a training course on nursing students' attitudes towards, perception of and confidence in managing patient aggression. *Journal of Nursing Education*, **44**, 415–420.

Nijman, H., & Rector, G. (1999). Crowding and aggression on inpatient psychiatric wards. *Psychiatric Services*, **50**, 830–831.

Nijman, H., A'Campo, J. M. L. G., Ravelli, D. P., & Merkelbach, H. L. G. J. (1999). A tentative model of aggression on inpatient psychiatric wards. *Psychiatric Bulletin*, **50**, 832–834.

Nijman, H., Bowers, L., & Oud, N. (2005). Psychiatric nurses' experiences with in patient aggression. *Aggressive Behaviour*, **31**, 217–227.

Nolan, P., Dallender, J., Soares, J., Thomsen, S., & Arnetz, B. (1999). Violence in mental health care: The experiences of mental health nurses and psychiatrists. *Journal of Advanced Nursing*, **30**, 934–941.

Parkes, J. (1996). Control and restraint training: A study of its effectiveness in a medium secure psychiatric unit. *Journal of Forensic Psychiatry*, **7**, 525–534.

Paterson, B. (2006). Developing a perspective on restraint and the least intrusive intervention. *British Journal of Nursing*, **15**, 1235–1241.

Paterson, B. (2007). Millfields Charter: Drawing the wrong conclusions. *Learning Disability Practice*, **10**, 30–33.

Paterson, B., & Leadbetter, D. (1999). De escalation in the management of aggression and violence, towards evidence based practice. In J. Turnbull & B. Paterson (Eds.), *Aggression and violence: Approaches to effective management*. London: Macmillan, pp. 99–119.

Paton, N. (2004). In the line of fire. *Nursing Times*, **100**, 36, 26–27.

Pescisolido, B., Monahan, J., Link, B. G., Stueve, A., & Kikuzawa, S. (1999). The public's view of the competence, dangerousness and need for legal coercion among person with mental illness. *American Journal of Public Health*, **89**, 1339–1345.

Phillips, D., & Rudestam, K. E. (1995). The effect of non-violent self defence training on male psychiatric staff members: Aggression and fear. *Psychiatric Services*, **43**, 164–168.

Reay, D. T., Fligner, C. L., Stilwell, A. D., & Arnold, J. (1992). Positional asphyxia during law enforcement transport. *The American Journal of Forensic Medicine & Pathology*, **13**, 90–97.

Rice, M. E., Helzel, M. F., Varney, D. W., & Quinsey, V. L. (1985). Crisis prevention and intervention training for psychiatric hospital staff. *American Journal of Community Psychology*, **13**, 289–304.

Riley, D., Meehan, C., Whittington, R., Lancaster, G. A., & Lane, S. (2006). Patient restraint positions in a psychiatric inpatient service. *Nursing Times*, **102**, 42–45.

Ryan, C. J., & Bowers, L. (2006). An analysis of nurses post incident manual restraint reports. *Journal of Psychiatric and Mental Health Nursing*, **13**, 527–532.

Sailas, E., & Fenton, M. (1999). Seclusion and restraint as a treatment for people with severe mental illness. *The Cochrane Library*, Issue 3, Art. No. CD001163.

Sailas, E., & Wahlbeck, K. (2005). Restraint and seclusion in psychiatric inpatient wards. *Current Opinion in Psychiatry*, **18**, 555–559.

Sallah, D., Sashidharan, S., Stone, R., Struthers, J., & Blofeld, J. (2003). *Independent inquiry into the death of David Bennett.* Norfolk, Suffolk and Cambridgeshire Strategic Health Authority.

Spokes, K., Bond, K., Lowe, T., Jones, J., Illingworth, P., Brimblecombe, N., & Wellmam, N. (2002). HOVIS The Hertfordshire/Oxfordshire violent incident study. *Journal of Psychiatric and Mental Health Nursing*, **9**, 199–209.

Taylor, P. J., & Gunn, J. (1999). Homicides by people with mental illness: Myth and reality. *British Journal of Psychiatry*, **174**, 9–14.

Turgut, T., Lagace, D., Izmir M., & Dursen, S. (2006). Assessment of violence and aggression in psychiatric settings: Descriptive approaches. *Bulletin of Clinical Psychopharmacology*, **16**, 179–194.

Walsh, E., Buchanan, A., & Fahy, T. (2002). Violence and schizophrenia: Examining the evidence. *British Journal of Psychiatry*, **180**, 490–495.

Wells, J., & Bowers, L. (2002). How prevalent is violence towards nurses working in general hospitals in the UK? *Journal of Advanced Nursing*, **39**, 230–240.

Whitington, R., Baskind, E., & Paterson, B. (2007). Observation, restraint and seclusion in the management of imminent violence. In D. Richter & R. Whittington (Eds.), *Violence in mental health settings.* London: Springer, pp. 54–87.

Whittington, R., & Wykes, T. (1996a) Aversive stimulation by staff and violence by psychiatric patients. *British Journal of Clinical Psychology*, **35**, 11–20.

Whittington, R., & Wykes, T. (1996b) An evaluation of staff training in psychological techniques for the management of patient aggression. *Journal of Clinical Nursing*, **5**, 257–261.

Willetts, L., & Leff, J. (2003). Improving the knowledge and skills of psychiatric nurses: Efficacy of a staff training programme. *Issues and Innovations in Nursing Education*, **42**, 237–243.

Wondrak, R. F., & Dolan, B. (1992). Dealing with verbal abuse: Evaluation of the efficacy of a workshop for student nurses. *Nurse Education Today*, **12**, 108–115.

Wright, S. (2003). Control and restraint techniques in the management of violence in inpatient psychiatry. *Medicine Science and the Law*, **43**, 31–38.

Wright, S., Gray, R., Parkes, J., & Gournay, K. (2002). *The recognition, prevention and therapeutic management of violence in acute in-patient psychiatry: A literature review and evidence based recommendations for good practice.* United Kingdom Central Council for Nursing, Midwifery and Health Visiting.

Chapter 8: Low Arousal Approaches in Care Environments for Older Adults

Almvik, R., Rasmusssen, K., & Woods, P. (2006). Challenging behaviour in the elderly – Monitoring violent incidents. *International Journal of Geriatric Psychiatry*, **21**, 368–374.

Battar, S., & Nichols, C. (2004). Successful creation of a restraint free environment with decreased falls and fall related injuries in a large rural federal medical centre. *The Gerontologist*, **44**, 358.

Beck, C., Frank, L., Chumbler, N. R., O'Sullivan, P., Vogelpohl, T. S., Rasin, J., Walls, R., & Baldwin, B. (1998). Correlates of disruptive behaviour in severely cognitively impaired nursing home residents. *The Gerontologist*, **38**, 189–198.

Bredthauer, D., Becker, C., Eichner, B., Koczy, P., & Nikolaus, T. (2005). Factors relating to the use of physical restraints in psychogeriatric care: A paradigm for elder abuse. *Zeitschrift für Gerontologie und Geriatrie: Organ der Deutschen Gesellschaft für Gerontologie und Geriatrie*, **38**, 1, 10–18.

Conlin Shaw, M. M. (2004). Aggression towards staff by nursing home residents: Findings from a grounded theory study. *Journal of Gerontological Nursing*, **30**, 43–54.

Dunbar, J. M., Neufeld, R. R., White, H. C., & Libow, L. S. (1996). Retrain, don't restrain: The educational intervention of the national nursing home restraint removal project. *The Gerontologist*, **36**, 539–542.

Ejaz, F. K., Folmar, S. J., Kaufmann, M., Rose, M. S., & Goldman, B. (1994). Restraint reduction: Can it be achieved? *The Gerontologist*, **34**, 694.

Gallinagh, R., Nevin, R., McIlroy, D., Mitchell, F., Campbell, L., McKenna, H., & Ludwick, R.,(2002). The use of physical restraints as a safety measure in the care of older people in four rehabilitation wards: Finding from an exploratory study. *International Journal of Nursing Studies*, **39**, 147–156.

Hill-Westmoreland, E. E., & Gruber-Baldini, A. L. (2005). Falls documentation in nursing homes: Agreement of the minimum data set with chart abstractions of medical and nursing documentation. *Journal of the American Geriatrics Society*, **53**, 2, 268–273.

Holden, U. P., & Woods, R. P. (1982). *Realty orientation: Psychological approaches to the confused elderly.* Edinburgh: Churchill Livingstone.

Karlsson, S., Bucht, G., Eriksonn, S., & Olof Sandman, P. (2001). Factors relating to the use of physical restraints in geriatric care settings. *Journal of the American Geriatrics Society*, **49**, 1722–1728.

Killick, J., & Allen. K. (2001). *Communication and the care of people with dementia.* Buckingham: Open University Press.

Kirkevold, O., Sandevik, L., & Engedal, K. (2004). Use of constraints and their correlates in Norwegian nursing homes. *International Journal of Geriatric Psychiatry*, **19**, 980–988.

Kitwood, T. (1997). *Dementia reconsidered: The person comes first*. Buckingham: Open University Press.

Kovach, C. R., Kelber, S. T., Simpson, M., & Wells, T. (2006). Behaviors of nursing home residents with dementia: Examining nurse responses. *Journal of Gerontological Nursing*, **32**, 13–21.

Kovach, C. R., Noonan, P. E., Matovina Schildt, A., Reynolds, S., & Wells, T. (2006). The serial trial intervention: An innovative approach to meeting the needs of individuals with dementia. *Journal of Gerontological Nursing*, **32**, 18–25.

Ljunggren, G., Philips, C. D., & Sgadari, A. (1997). Comparisons of restraint use in nursing homes in eight countries. *Age and Aging*, **26**, 43–47.

Martin, L. S. (1999). Nursing home uses skills lab to determine impact of non-violent crisis intervention. *Journal of Safe Management of Disruptive and Assaultive Behavior*, **7**, 4, 12–13.

Maxfield, M. C., Lewis, R. E., & Cannon, S. (1996). Training staff to prevent aggressive behaviour of cognitively impaired elderly patients during bathing and grooming. *Journal of Gerontological Nursing*, **22**, 37–43.

McDonnell, A. A. (1997). Training care staff to manage challenging behaviour: An evaluation of a three day course. *British Journal of Developmental Disabilities*, **43**, 2, 156–161.

McDonnell, A. A., Sturmey, P., Oliver, C., Cunningham, J., Hayes, S., Galvin, M., Walshe, C.. & Cunningham, C. (2008). The effects of staff training on staff confidence and challenging behavior in services for people with autism spectrum disorders. *Research in Autism Spectrum Disorders*, **58**, 1–9.

Mentes, J. C., & Ferrario, J. (1989). Calming aggressive reactions: A preventative programme. *Journal of Gerontological Nursing*, **15**, 22–27.

Mildner, A., Snell, A., Arora, A., Sims D., & Wales, E. (2003). The prevalence of bedrail use in British hospitals. *Age and Aging*, **32**, 555.

Miles, S. H., & Irvine, P. (1992). Deaths caused by physical restraints. *The Gerontologist*, **32**, 762–766.

Minnick, A., Mion, L., Lamb, K., Leipzig, R., & Palmer, R. (1998). Prevalence and patterns of physical restraint use in the acute care setting. *Journal of Nursing Administration*, **28**, 11, 19–24.

Molassiotis, A., & Newell, R. (1996). Nurses' awareness of restraint use with elderly people in Greece and the UK: A cross cultural pilot study. *International Journal of Nursing Studies*, **33**, 201–211.

Moniz-Cook, E. D., Agar, S., Silver, M., Woods, R. T., Wang, M., Elston, C., Win, T. (1998). Can staff training reduce behavioural problems in residential care for the elderly mentally ill. *International Journal of Geriatric Psychiatry*, **13**, 149–158.

O'Connor, D., Horgan, L., Cheung, A., Fisher, D., George, K., & Stafrace, S. (2004). An audit of physical restraint and seclusion in five psychogeriatric admission wards in Victoria, Australia. *International Journal of Geriatric Psychiatry*, **19**, 797–799.

Pulsford, D., & Duxbury, J. (2006). Aggressive behaviour by people with dementia in residential care settings: A review. *Journal of Psychiatric and Mental Health Nursing*, **13**, 611–618.

Rateau, M. R. (2000). Confusion and aggression in restrained elderly persons undergoing hip repair surgery. *Applied Nursing Research,* **13,** 50–54.

Retsas, A. P., & Crabbe, H. (1998). Use of physical restraints in nursing homes in New South Wales, Australia. *International Journal of Nursing Studies,* **35,** 177–183.

Ryden, M. B., Feldt, K. S., Oh, H. L., Brand, K., Warne, M., Weber, E., Nelson, J., & Gross, C. (1999). Relationships between aggressive behavior in cognitively impaired nursing home residents and use of restraints, psychoactive drugs and secured units. *Archives of Psychiatric Nursing,* **13, 4,** 170–178.

Schnelle, J. F., Bates-Jensen, B. M., Levy-Storms, L., Grbic, V., Yoshii, J., Cadogan, M., & Simmons, S. F. (2004). The minimum data set prevalence of restraint quality indicator: Does it reflect differences in care? *The Gerontologist,* **44,** 2, 245–255.

Shah, A., Chiu, E., Ames, D., Harrigan, S., & McKenzie, D. (2000). Characteristics of aggressive subjects in Australian (Melbourne) nursing homes. *International Psychogeriatrics,* **12,** 145–161.

Shah, A., & De, T. (1998). The effect of an educational intervention package about aggressive behaviour directed at the nursing staff on a continuing care psychogeriatric ward. *International Journal of Geriatric Psychiatry,* **35,** 35–40.

Shore, R. I., Guillen, M. K., Rosenblatt, L. C., Walker, K., Caudle, C. E., & Kritchevsky, S. B. (2002). Restraint use, restraint orders, and the risks of falls in hospitalised patients. *Journal of the American Geriatric Society,* **50,** 526–529.

Spector, A., Davies, S., Woods, B., & Orrell, M. (2000). Reality orientation for dementia: A systematic review of the evidence of effectiveness from randomised controlled trials. *The Gerontologist,* **40,** 206–212.

Spira, A. P., & Edelstein, B. A. (2006). Behavioural interventions for agitation in older adults: An evaluative review. *International Psychogeriatrics,* **18,** 195–125.

Stevens, J. A., Hasbrouck, L., Durant, T. M., Dellinger, A. M., Batabyal, P. K., Crosby, A. E., Valluru, B. R., Kresnow, M., & Guerrero, J. L. (1999). Surveillance for injuries and violence among older adults. *CDC Surveillance Summaries,* **48,** 27–50.

Stokes, G. (2001). *Challenging behaviour in dementia: A person centred approach.* Milton Keynes, UK: Speechmark.

Strumpf, N. F., Evans, L. K., Wagner, J., & Patterson, J. (1992). Reducing physical restraints: Developing an educational program. *Journal of Gerontological Nursing,* **18,** 11, 21–27.

Testad, I., Aarsland, A. M., & Aarsland, D. (2005). The effect of staff training on the use of restraint in dementia: A single-blind randomised controlled trial. *International Journal of Geriatric Psychiatry,* **20,** 587–590.

Testad, I., Aarsland, A. M., & Aarsland, D. (2007). Prevalence and correlates of disruptive behaviour in patients in Norwegian nursing homes. *International Journal of Geriatric Psychiatry,* **33,** 24–30.

Turner, S. (2005). Behavioural symptoms of dementia in residential settings: A selective review of non pharmacological interventions. *Aging and Mental Health,* **9,** 93–104.

Twining, T. C. (1988). *Helping older people: A psychological approach.* Chichester: Wiley.

Woods, B. (2002). Reality orientation a welcome return? *Age and Aging,* **31,** 155–156.

Zuidema, S. U., Derksen, E., Verhey, F. R. J., & Koopmans, R. T. C. M. (2007). Prevalence of neuropsychiatric symptoms in a large sample of Dutch nursing home patients with dementia. *International Journal of Geriatric Psychiatry*, **22**, 7, 632–638.

Chapter 9: Evaluating the Outcomes of Crisis Management Training

Allen, D. (2000). Recent research on physical aggression in persons with intellectual disability: An overview. *Journal of Intellectual and Developmental Disability*, **25**, 41–57.

Allen, D. (2002). Behaviour change and behaviour management. In D. Allen (Ed.), *Ethical Approaches to Physical Interventions*. Plymouth: BILD, pp. 3–14.

Allen, D., McDonald, L., Dunn, C., & Doyle, T. (1997). Changing care staff approaches to the preventions and management of aggressive behaviour in a residential treatment unit for persons with mental retardation and challenging behaviour. *Research in Developmental Disabilities*, **18**, 101–112.

Allen, D., & Tynan, H. (2000). Responding to aggressive behavior: Impact of training on staff members' knowledge and confidence. *Mental Retardation*, **38**, 2, 97–104.

Baker, D. J. (1998). Effects of video based staff training with manager led exercises in residential support. *Mental Retardation*, **36**, 198–204.

Baker, P., & Allen, D. (2001). Physical abuse and physical interventions in learning disabilities: An element of risk? *Journal of Adult Protection*, **3**, 2, 25–31.

Bandura, A. (1997). *Self-efficacy: The exercise of control.* New York: Freeman.

Beech, B., & Leather, P. (2006). Workplace violence in the health care sector: A review of staff training and integration of training evaluation models. *Aggression and Violent Behavior*, **11**, 27–43.

Campbell, M. (2007). Staff training and challenging behaviour – Who needs it? *Journal of intellectual Disabilities*, **11**, 2, 143–156.

Carmel, H., & Hunter, M. (1990). Compliance with training in managing assaultive and injuries from in-patient violence. *Hospital and Community Psychiatry*, **41**, 5, 558–560.

Cohen, A. M., Zoe Stavri, P., & Hirsch, W. (2004). A categorization and analysis of the criticisms of evidence-based medicine. *International Journal of Medical Informatics*, **73**, 35–43.

Colton, D. (2004). *Checklist for assessing your organization's readiness for reducing seclusion and restraint.* Staunton, VA: Commonwealth Center for Children and Adolescence.

Cullen, C. (1992). Staff training and management for intellectual disability services. *International Review of Research in Mental Retardation*, **18**, 225–245.

Cunningham, J., McDonnell, A. A., Easton, S., & Sturmey, P. (2003). Social validation data on three methods of physical restraint: Views of consumers, staff and students. *Research in Developmental Disabilities*, **24**, 307–316.

Deb, S., & Roberts, K. (2005). *The evidence base for the management of imminent violence in learning disability settings.* Occasional Paper OP57. London: Royal College of Psychiatrists.

Deveau, R., & McDonnell, A. A. (2009). As the last resort: Reducing the use of restrictive physical interventions using organisational approaches. *British Journal of Learning Disabilities*, **37**, 172–177.

Deveau, R., & McGill, P. (2007). *As the last resort: Reducing the use of restrictive physical interventions*. Canterbury, Kent: Tizard Centre, University of Kent.

Fernandes, C. M., Raboud, J. M., & Bouthillette, et al. (2002). The effect of an education program on violence in the emergency department. *Annals of Emergency Medicine*, **39**, 47–55.

Fish, R., & Culshaw, E. (2005). The last resort: Staff and client perspectives on physical interventions. *Journal of Intellectual Disability Research*, **9**, 93–107.

Gillett, E., & Stenfert-Kroese, B. (2003). Investigating organizational cultures: A comparison of a 'high' and a 'low' performing residential unit for people with intellectual disabilities. *Journal of Applied Research in Intellectual Disabilities*, **16**, 279–284.

Goin-Kochel, R. P., Myers, B., & Macintosh, V. (2007). Parental reports on the use of treatment and therapies for children with autism spectrum disorders. *Research in Autistic Spectrum Disorders*, **1**, 195–209.

Hahn, S., Needham, I., Abderhalden, C., Duxbury, J. A. D., & Halfens, R. J. G. (2006). The effect of a training course on mental health nurses' attitudes on the reasons of patient aggression and its management. *Journal of Psychiatric and Mental Health Nursing*, **13**, 197–204.

Hamilton, R. (2005). Nurses' knowledge and skill retention following cardiopulmonary resuscitation training: A review of the literature. *Journal of Advancing Nursing Research*, **51**, 288–297.

Harris, J. (2002). Training in physical interventions: Making sense of the market. In D. Allen (Ed.), *Ethical approaches to physical interventions*. Plymouth: BILD, pp. 134–152.

Hersen, M., & Barlow, D. H. (1976). *Single-case experimental designs strategies for studying behavior change*. Elmsford, NY: Pergamon Press Ltd.

Hurlebaus, A., & Link, S. (1997). The effect of aggressive behavior management programme on nurses' levels of knowledge, confidence and safety. *Journal of Nursing Staff Development*, **13**, 5, 360–365.

Infantino, J. A, & Musingo, M. S. (1985). Assaults and injuries among staff with and without training in aggression control techniques. *Hospital and Community Psychiatry*, **36**, 12, 1312–1314.

Jambunathan, J., & Bellaire, K. (1996). Evaluating staff use of crisis prevention intervention techniques. *Issues in Mental Health Nursing*, **17**, 6, 541–548.

Kaiser, B. K., Hogan, R., & Bartholomew Craig, S. (2008). Leadership and the fate of organizations. *American Psychologist*, **63**, 96–110.

Kazdin, A. (2008). Evidence-based treatment and practice new opportunities to bridge clinical research and practice, enhance the knowledge base, and improve patient care. *American Psychologist*, **63**, 156–159.

Killick, S., & Allen, D. (2005). Training staff in an adolescent inpatient psychiatric unit in positive approaches to managing aggressive and harmful behaviour: Does it improve confidence and knowledge? *Child Care in Practice*, **11**, 3, 323–339.

Leadbetter, D. (2002). Good practice in physical interventions. In D. Allen (Ed.), *Ethical approaches to physical interventions*. Plymouth: BILD, pp. 114–133.

Martin, L. S. (1999). Nursing home uses skills lab to determine impact of non-violent crisis intervention. *Journal of Safe Management of Disruptive and Assaultive Behavior*, **7**, 4, 12–13.

Matson, J., & Neal, D. (2009). Psychotropic medication use for challenging behaviors in persons with intellectual disabilities: An overview. *Research in Developmental Disabilities*, **30**, 572–586.

Mayo, E. (1949). *Hawthorne and the Western Electric Company, The social problems of an industrial civilisation*. London: Routledge.

McDonnell, A. (1997). Training care staff to manage challenging behaviour: An evaluation of a three-day course. *British Journal of Developmental Disabilities*, **43**, 2, 156–161.

McDonnell, A. (2005). *Developmental and evaluation of a three day training course in the management of aggressive behaviours for staff who work with people with learning disabilities*. Doctoral Thesis, University of Birmingham.

McDonnell, A. A. (2007). Why I am in favour of the Millfields Charter. *Learning Disability Practice*, **10**, 26–29.

McDonnell, A. A., Gould, A., Adams, T., Sallis, J., & Anker, R. (2009). Staff training in physical interventions. Unpublished manuscript.

McDonnell, A. A., Reeves, S., Johnson, A., & Lane, A. (1998). Management of challenging behaviours in an adult with learning disabilities: The use of low arousal. *Behavioural and Cognitive Psychotherapy*, **26**, 163–171.

McDonnell, A. A., & Sturmey, P. (1993). The acceptability of physical restraint procedures for people with a learning difficulty. *Behavioural and Cognitive Psychotherapy*, **21**, 225–264.

McDonnell, A. A., & Sturmey, P. (2000). The social validation of three physical restraint procedures: A comparison of young people and professional groups. *Research in Developmental Disabilities*, **21**, 85–92.

McDonnell, A. A., Sturmey, P., Oliver, C., et al. (2008). The effects of staff training on staff confidence and challenging behaviour in services for people with autism spectrum disorders. *Research in Autism Spectrum Disorders*, in press.

McGowan, S., Wynaden, D., Harding, N., Yassine, A., & Parker, J. (1999). Staff confidence in dealing with aggressive patients: A benchmarking exercise. *Australian and New Zealand Journal of Mental Health Nursing*, **8**, 104–108.

Murphy, G. H., Estien, D., & Clare, I. C. H. (1996). Services for people with mild intellectual disabilities and challenging behaviour: Service users' views. *Journal of Applied Research in Intellectual Disabilities*, **9**, 256–283.

Needham, I., Abderhalden, C., Zeller, A., Dassen, T., Haug, H. J., Fischer, J. E., & Halfens, R. J. G. (2005a). The effect of a training course on nursing students' attitudes towards, perception of and confidence in managing patient aggression. *Journal of Nursing Education*, **44**, 415–420.

Needham, I., Abderhalden, C., Zeller, A., Dassen, T., Haug, H. J., Fischer, J. E., & Halfens, R. J. G. (2005b). The effect of a training course in aggression management on mental health nurses' perception of aggression: A randomised controlled trial. *International Journal of Nursing Studies*, **42**, 649–655.

Paterson, B., & Leadbetter, D. (2002). Standards for violence management training.

In Gill, M., Fisher, B., & Bowie, V. (Eds.), *Violence at work: Causes, patterns and prevention*. Collompton, Devon: Willan Publishing, pp. 132–150.

Paterson, B., Turnbull, J., & Aitken, A. (1992). An evaluation of a training course in the short term management of violence. *Nurse Education Today*, **12**, 368–375.

Perkins, J., & Leadbetter, D. (2002). An evaluation of aggression management training in a special educational setting. *Emotional and Behavioral Difficulties*, **6**, 1, 19–34.

Peterson, L., Homer, A. L., & Wonderlich, S. A. (1982). The integrity of independent variables in behaviour analysis. *Journal of Applied Behavior Analysis*, **15**, 477–492.

Phillips, D., & Rudestam, K. E. (1995). The effect of non-violent self defence training on male psychiatric staff members: Aggression and fear. *Psychiatric Services*, **43**, 164–168.

Quilitch, H. R. (1975). A comparison of three staff management procedures. *Journal of Applied Behavior Analysis*, **8**, 59–66.

Reid, D. H., & Parsons, M. B. (2002). *Working with staff to overcome challenging behaviour among people who have severe learning disabilities: A guide for getting support plans carried out, Habilitative Management Consultants*. North Carolina: Morganton.

Rice, M. E., Helzel, M. F., Varney, D. W., et al. (1985). Crisis prevention and intervention training for psychiatric hospital staff. *American Journal of Community Psychology*, **13**, 289–304.

Roed, O. L., & Syse, A. (2002). Physical interventions and aversive techniques in relation to people with learning disabilities in Norway. *The Journal of Adult Protection*, **4**, 1, 25–32.

Sequeira, H., & Halstead, S. (2001). Is it meant to hurt, is it? *Violence against Women*, **4**, 462–476.

Smith, B., & Cumella, S. (1996). Training for staff caring for people with learning disability. *British Journal of Learning Disabilities*, **24**, 20–25.

Strauss, A., & Corbin, J. (1994). Grounded theory methodology: An overview. In N. K. Denzin & Y. S. Lincoln (Eds.), *Handbook of qualitative research*. London: Sage Publications, pp. 1–18.

Stubbs, B., Leadbetter, D., Paterson, B., Yorston, G., Knights, C., & Davis, S. (2009). Physical interventions: A review of the literature on its use, staff and patients' views and the impact of training. *Journal of Psychiatric and Mental Health Nursing*, **16**, 1, 99–105.

Sturmey, P., & Palen-McGlynn, A. P. (2002). Restraint reduction. In D. Allen (Ed.), *Ethical approaches to physical interventions*. Plymouth: BILD, pp. 203–218.

Temple, R. O., Zgaljardic, D. J., Yancy, S., & Jaffray, S. (2007). Crisis intervention training program: Influence on staff attitudes in a post acute residential brain injury rehabilitation setting. *Rehabilitation Psychology*, **4**, 429–434.

Thackrey, M. (1987). Clinician confidence in coping with patient aggression: Assessment and enhancement. *Professional Psychiatry: Research and Practice*, **18**, 57–60.

Tyrer, P., Oliver-Africano, P. C., Ahmed, Z., Bouras, N., Cooray, S., Deb, S., Murphy, D., Monica Hare, D., Meade, M., Reece, B., Kramo, K., Bhaumik, S., Harley, D., Regan, R., Bharti Rao, T., North, B., Eliahoo, J., Karatela, S., Soni, A., & Crawford, M. (2008). Risperidone, haloperidol, and placebo in the treatment of aggressive challenging behaviour in patients with intellectual disability: A randomised controlled trial. *The Lancet*, **371**, 57–63.

Van Den Pol, R. A., Reed, D. H., & Fuqua, R. W. (1983). Peer training of safety related skills to institutional staff: Benefits for trainers and trainees. *Journal of Applied Behavior Analysis,* **16**, 139–156.

Van Oorsouw, W. M. W. J., Embregts, P. J. C. M., Bosman, A. M. T., & Jahoda, A. (2009). Training staff serving clients with intellectual disabilities: A meta-analysis of aspects determining effectiveness. *Research in Developmental Disabilities,* **30**, 3, 503–511.

White, C., Holland, E., Marsland, D., & Oakes, P. (2003). The identification of environments and cultures that promote abuse of people with intellectual disabilities: A review of the literature. *Journal of Applied Research in Intellectual Disabilities,* **16**, 1–9.

Wolf, M. M. (1978). Social validity: The case for subjective measurement or how applied behavior analysis is finding its heart. *Journal of Applied Behavior Analysis,* **11**, 203–214.

Chapter 10: Emerging Themes

Allen, D. (2008). Risk and prone restraint-reviewing the evidence. In M. Nunno, D. Day, & L. Bullard (Eds.), *Examining the safety of high-risk interventions for children and young people.* New York: Child Welfare League of America, pp. 87–106.

Anderson, C. A., & Bushman, B. J. (2002). Human aggression. *Annual Review of Psychology,* **53**, 27–51.

Ariely, D. (2008). *Predictably irrational: The hidden forces that shape our decisions.* New York: HarperCollins.

Behr, G. M., Ruddock, J. P., Benn, P., & Crawford, M. J. (2005). Zero tolerance of violence by users of mental health services: The need for an ethical framework *The British Journal of Psychiatry,* **187**, 7–8.

Bell, L. (1996). The physical restraint of young people. *Child and Family Social Work,* **1**, 37–47.

Borthwick, A., Holman, C., Kennard, D., McFetridge, M., Messruther, K., & Wilkes, J. (2001). The relevance of moral treatment to contemporary mental health care. *Journal of Mental Health,* **10**, 427–439.

Bowers, L., Douzenis, A., Galeazzi, G. M., Forghieri, M., Tsopelas, C., Simpson, A., & Allan, T. (2005). Disruptive and dangerous behaviour by patients on acute on psychiatric wards in three European countries. *Social Psychiatry and Psychiatric Epidemiology,* **40**, 822–828.

Braverman, M. (2002). The prevention of violence affecting workers: A systems perspective. In M. Gill, B. Fisher, & V. Bowie (Eds.), *Violence at work: Causes, patterns and prevention.* Cullompton, Devon: Willan Publishing, pp. 114–131.

Buchanan-Barker, P., & Barker, P. J. (2008). The Tidal Commitments: Extending the value base of mental health recovery. *Journal of Psychiatric and Mental Health Nursing,* **15**, 93–100.

Butchart, A., Phinney, A., Check, P., & Villaveces, A. (2004). *Preventing violence: A guide to implementing the recommendations of the world report on violence and health.* Geneva: World Health Organization.

Carr, E. G., Horner, R. H., Turnbull, A. P., Marquis, J. G., McLaughlin, D. M., McAtee, M. L., Smith, C. E., Ryan, K. A., Ruef, M. B., Doolabh, A., & Baddock, D. (1999). *Positive behavior support for people with developmental disabilities: A research synthesis.* Washington, DC: American Association on Mental Retardation.

Colton, D. (2004). *Checklist for reducing your organisation's readiness for reducing seclusion and restraint.* Staunton, VA: Commonwealth Center for Children and Adolescence.

Corrigan, P. W. (1995). Use of a token economy with seriously mentally ill patients: Criticisms and misconceptions. *Psychiatric Services, 46,* 1258–1263.

Council of Europe. (2004). *Recommendation 10 of the Committee of Ministers to Member States concerning the protection of the human rights and dignity of persons with mental disorder and its explanatory memorandum.* Strasbourg, France: Council of Europe.

Cunningham, J., McDonnell, A. A., Easton, S., & Sturmey, P. (2002). Social validation data on three methods of physical restraint: Views of consumers, staff and students. *Research in Developmental Disabilities, 21,* 85–92.

Dagnan, D., Trower, P., & Smith, R. (1998). Care staff responses to people with learning disabilities and challenging behaviour: A cognitive emotional analysis. *British Journal of Clinical Psychology, 37,* 1, 59–68.

Deveau, R., & McDonnell, A. A. (2009). As the last resort: Reducing the use of restrictive physical interventions using an organisational approach. Manuscript submitted for publication to the *British Journal of Learning Disabilities, 37,* 172–177.

Deveau, R., & McGill, P. (2007). *As the last resort: Reducing the use of restrictive physical interventions.* Canterbury, Kent: Tizard Centre, University of Kent.

Donnellan, A. M., LaVigna, G. W., Negri-Schoulz, N., & Fassbender, L. L. (1988). *Progress without punishment: Effective approaches for learners with behaviour problems.* New York: Teachers College Press.

Easterbrook, J. A. (1959). The effect of emotion on cue utilisation and the organisation of behaviour. *Psychological Review, 66,* 183–201.

Emerson, E., Robertson, J., Gregory, N., Hatton, C., Kessissoglou, S., Hallam, A., & Hillery, J. (2000). The treatment and management of challenging behaviours in residential settings. *Journal of Applied Research in Intellectual Disabilities, 13,* 197–215.

Fish, R., & Culshaw, E. (2005). The last resort: Staff and client perspectives on physical interventions. *Journal of Intellectual Disability Research, 9,* 93–107.

Fryer, M. A., Beech, M., & Byrne, G. J. A. (2004). Seclusion use with children and adolescents: An Australian experience. *Australian and New Zealand Journal of Psychiatry, 38,* 26–33.

Gardner, H. (2006). *Changing minds.* Boston: Harvard Business School Press.

Goldstein, J. L., & Godemont, M. L. (2003). The legend and lessons of Geel, Belgium: A 1500-year-old legend, a 21st-century model. *Community Mental Health Journal, 39,* 5, 441–458.

Grove, W. M., & Meehl, P. E. (1996). Comparative efficiency of informal (subjective and impressionistic) and formal (mechanical and algorithmic) prediction procedures: The clinical-statistical controversy. *Psychology Public Policy and the Law, 2,* 293–323.

Grove, W. M., Zald, D. H., Lebow, B. S., Snitz, B. E., & Nelson, C. (2000). Clinical versus mechanical prediction: A meta-analysis. *Psychological Assessment, 12,* 1, 19–30.

Haney, C., Banks, W. C., & Zimbardo, P. G. (1973). Study of prisoners and guards in a simulated prison. *Naval Research Reviews, 9,* 1–17.

Hart, D., & Howell, S. (2004). *Report on the use of physical intervention across children's services*. London: National Children's Bureau.

Hastings, R., & Brown, T. (2000). Functional assessment and challenging behaviors. *Journal of the Association for Persons with Severe Handicaps*, **25**, 229–240.

Haw, C., & Yorston, G. (2004). Thomas Prichard and the non restraint movement at the Northampton Asylum. *Psychiatric Bulletin*, **28**, 140–142.

Hill, R. G. (1857). *A concise history of the entire abolition of mechanical restraint in the treatment of the insane*. London: Longmans.

Hogan, R., & Kaiser, R. B. (2005). What we know about leadership. *Review of General Psychology*, **9**, 169–180.

Itard, E. M. (1802). *An historical account of the discovery and education of a savage man: Or the first developments, physical and moral of the young savage caught in the woods near Aveyron in the year 1798*. London: Richard Phillips.

Jones, R., & Kingdon, D. (2005). Council of Europe recommendation on human rights and psychiatry: A major opportunity for mental health services. *European Journal of Psychiatry*, **20**, 461–464.

Kaiser, R. B., Hogan, R., & Bartholomew Craig, S. (2008). Leadership and the fate of organizations. *American Psychologist*, **63**, 96–110.

Kanis, J. A., Melton, L. J., Christiansen, C., Johnston, C. C., & Khaltaev, N. (1994). The diagnosis of osteoporosis. *Journal of Bone Mineral Research*, **9**, 1137–1141.

Katzman, D. K. (2003). Osteoporosis in anorexia: A brittle future? *Current Drug Targets – CNS and Neurological Disorders*, **2**, 11–15.

Kazdin, A. E. (1982). The token economy: A decade later. *Journal of Applied Behavior Analysis*, **15**, 431–445.

Kitwood, T. (1997). *Dementia reconsidered: The person comes first*. Buckingham: Open University Press.

Kuhn, T. (1962). *The structure of scientific revolutions*. Chicago: Chicago University Press.

Lamont, S., & Brunero, S. (2009). Risk analysis: An integrated approach to the assessment and management of aggression/violence in mental health. *Journal of Psychiatric Nursing Care*, **1**, 25–32.

LaVigna, G. W., & Willis, T. J. (2002). Counter-intuititive strategies for crisis management within a non-aversive framework. In D. Allen (Ed.), *Ethical approaches to physical interventions: Responding to challenging behavior in people with intellectual disabilities*. Kidderminster: BILD, pp. 89–103.

Leadbetter, D. (2002). Good practice in physical interventions. In D. Allen (Ed.), *Ethical approaches to physical interventions*. Plymouth: BILD, pp. 114–133.

Leadbetter, D. (2007). Millfields Charter: Finding the middle ground. *Learning Disability Practice*, **10**, 34–37.

MacArthur Foundation. (2001). The MacArthur violence risk assessment study executive summary. http://macarthur.virginia.edu/risk.html

Martin, V., Bernhardsgrutter, R., Goebel, R., & Steinert, T. (2007). The use of mechanical restraint and seclusion in patients with schizophrenia: A comparison of the practice in Germany and Switzerland. *Clinical Practice and Epidemioloy in Mental Health*, **3**, 1–6.

McCord, J. (1997). Discipline and the use of childhood sanctions. *Aggression and Violent Behavior*, **2**, 313–319.

McDonnell, A. A. (2007). Why I am in favour of the Millfields Charter. *Learning Disability Practice*, **10**, 26–29.

McDonnell, A. A., & Anker, R. (2009). Behaviour management versus behaviour change: A useful distinction? *British Journal of Developmental Disabilities*, **55**, 2, 157–167.

McDonnell, A. A., Dearden, R., & Richens, A. (1991). Staff training in the management of violence and aggression. 2: Avoidance and escape principles. *Mental Handicap*, **19**, 109–112.

McDonnell, A. A., & Gallon, I. G. (2006). Issues and concerns about control and restraint training: Moving the debate forward. In M. Ward & J. Cutcliffe (Eds.), *Key debates in psychiatric nursing*. London: Wiley.

McDonnell, A. A., & Jones, P. (1999). The role of clinical psychology in the physical management of challenging behaviour. *Clinical Psychology Forum*, 20–23.

McDonnell, A. A., Reeves, S., Johnson, A., & Lane, A. (1998). Management of challenging behaviours in an adult with learning disabilities: The use of low arousal. *Behavioural and Cognitive Psychotherapy*, **26**, 163–171.

McDonnell, A. A., & Sturmey, P. (2000). The social validation of three physical restraint procedures: A comparison of young people and professional groups. *Research in Developmental Disabilities*, **21**, 85–92.

Metcalfe, J., & Mischel, W. (1999). A hot/cool system analysis of delay of gratification: Dynamics of willpower. *Psychological Review*, **106**, 3–19.

Middleby-Clements, J. L., & Grenyer, B. F. S. (2007). Zero tolerance approach to aggression and its impact upon mental health staff attitudes. *Australian and New Zealand Journal of Psychiatry*, **41**, 187–191.

Milgram, S. (1974). *Obedience to authority: An experimental view*. New York: Harper & Row.

Miller, G., Paterson, B., & McKenna, K. (2009). Changing the culture of care. In R. Hughes (Ed.), *Reducing restraints in health and social care: Practice and policy perspectives*. London: Quay Books, pp. 97–114.

Minnick, A., Mion, L., Lamb, K., Leipzig, R., & Palmer, R. (1998). Prevalence and patterns of physical restraint use in the acute care setting. *Journal of Nursing Administration*, **28**, 11, 19–24.

Mohr, W. (2008). Perilous omissions and misinformation. *Archives of Psychiatric Nursing*, **22**, 315–317.

Morrison, A., & Saddler, D. (2001). Death of a psychiatric patient during physical restraint: Excited delirium a case report. *Medicine, Science and the Law*. **41**, 46–50.

Morrison, E. F. (1990). Violent psychiatric patients in a public hospital. *Scholarly Inquiry for Nursing Practice: An International Journal*, **4**, 1, 65–82.

Morrison, L., Duryea, P. B., Moore, C., & Nathanson-Shinn, A. (2002). *The lethal hazard of prone restraint: Positional asphyxiation*. Oakland, CA: Protection & Advocacy Inc.

Murphy, G. H., Estien, D., & Clare, I. C. H. (1996). Services for people with mild intellectual disabilities and challenging behaviour: Service users' views. *Journal of Applied Research in Intellectual Disabilities*, **9**, 256–283.

NHS. (2009). *Statistics on obesity, physical activity and diet*. England: The Information Centre for Health and Social Care. www.ic.nhs.uk.

Nijman, H., Bowers, L., Oud, N., & Jansen, G. (2005). Psychiatric nurses' experiences with inpatient aggression. *Aggressive Behavior*, **31**, 217–227.

Nunno, M., Holden, M., & Tollar, A. (2006). Learning from tragedy: A survey of child and adolescent restraint facilities. *Child Abuse & Neglect: The International Journal,* **30**, 12, 1333–1342.

Parent-Thirion, A., Macías, E. F., Hurley, J., & Vermeylen, G. (2007). *Fourth European working conditions survey.* Luxembourg: Office for Official Publications of the European Communities.

Paterson, B. (2007). Millfields Charter: Drawing the wrong conclusions. *Learning Disability Practice,* **10**, 30–33.

Paterson, B., Bradely, P., Stark, C., Saddler, D., Leadbetter, D., & Allen, D. (2003). Deaths associated with restraint use in health and social care in the UK. *Journal of Psychiatric and Mental Health Nursing,* **10**, 3–15.

Paterson, B., & Duxbury, J. (2006). Developing a perspective on restraint and the least intrusive intervention. *British Journal of Nursing,* **15**, 22, 1235–1241.

Paterson, B., & Leadbetter, D. (2002). Standards for violence management training. In M. Gill, B. Fisher, & V. Bowie (Eds.), *Violence at work: Causes, patterns and prevention.* Cullompton, Devon: Willan Publishing, pp. 132–150.

Paterson, B., & Leadbetter, D. (2009). Towards restraint free care. In R. Hughes (Ed.), *Reducing restraints in health and social care: Practice and policy perspectives.* London: Quay Books, pp. 115–137.

Pitonyak, D. (2004). 10 things you can do to support a person with difficult behaviors. Available at www.dimagine.com.

Proulx, G. (1999). How to initiate evacuation movement in public buildings. *Facilities,* **17**, 331–335.

Popper, K. (1963). *Conjectures and refutations: The growth of scientific knowledge.* New York: Routledge and Kegan Paul.

Reason, J. T. (1990). *Human error.* Cambridge, UK: Cambridge University Press.

Reason, J. T., Carthey, J., & De Leval, M. R. (2001). Diagnosing 'vulnerable system syndrome': An essential prerequisite to effective risk management. *Quality in Healthcare,* **10**, 2, 21–25.

Richetin, J., & Richardson, D. S. (2008). Automatic processes and individual differences in aggressive behaviour. *Aggression and Violent Behavior,* **13**, 6, 423–430.

Rogers, P., Miller, G., Paterson, B., Bonnett, C., Turner, P., Brett, S., Flynn, K., & Noak, J. (2007). Is breakaway training effective? Examining the evidence and the reality. *Journal of Mental Health Training, Education and Practice,* **2**, 2, 5–12.

Schon, D. (1987). Educating the reflective practitioner. Paper presented at the *1987 Meeting of the American Educational Research Association,* Washington, DC.

Scott, C. L., & Resnick, C. J. (2006). Violence risk assessment in persons with mental Illness. *Aggressive Behavior,* **11**, 598–611.

Sequeira, H., & Halstead, S. (2001). Is it meant to hurt, is it? *Violence against Women,* **4**, 462–476.

Smallridge, P., & Williamson, A. (2008). *Independent review of restraint in juvenile secure settings.* London: Ministry of Justice, Department for Children, Schools and Families.

Stubbs, B., Leadbetter, D., Paterson, B., Yorston, G., Knight, C., & Davis, S. (2009) Physical intervention: A review of the literature on its use, staff and patient views, and the impact of training. *Journal of Psychiatric and Mental Health Nursing,* **16**, 1, 99–105.

Ulrich, R. E., & Azrin, N. H. (1962). Reflexive fighting in response to aversive stimulation. *Journal of Experimental Analysis of Behavior*, **5**, 511–520.

Van Den Pol, R. A., Reed, D. H., & Fuqua, R. W. (1983). Peer training of safety related skills to institutional staff: Benefits for trainers and trainees. *Journal of Applied Behavior Analysis*, **16**, 139–156.

Van Oorsouw, W. M. W. J., Israel, M. L., Von Heyn, R. E., & Duker, P. C. (2008). Side effects of contingent shock treatment. *Research in Developmental Disabilities*, **29**, 513–523.

Vincent, C., Taylor Adams, S., Chapman, J., Hewett, D., Prior, S., Strange, P., & Tizard, A. (2000). How to investigate and analyse clinical incidents: Clinical Risk Unit and Association of Litigation and Risk Management protocol. *British Medical Journal*, **320**, 777–781.

Watts, D., & Morgan, G. (1994). Malignant alienation: Dangers for patients who are hard to like. *The British Journal of Psychiatry*, **164**, 11–15.

Weiner, B. (1986). *An attributional theory of motivation and emotion*. Berlin: Springer-Verlag.

Weiss, E. M., Altimari, D., Blint, D. F., & Megan, K. (1998, October 11–15). Deadly restraint: A Hartford Courant investigative report. *Hartford Courant.*

Whittington, R., & Higgins, L. (2002). More than zero tolerance? Burnout and tolerance for patient aggression amongst mental health nurses in China and the UK. *Acta Psychiatrica Scandanavica*, **106**, 37–40.

Whittington, R., & Wykes, T. (1996a). Aversive stimulation by staff and violence by psychiatric patients. *British Journal of Clinical Psychology*, **35**, 11–20.

Wright, S., Gray, R., Parkes, J., & Gournay, K. (2002). *The recognition, prevention and therapeutic management of violence in acute in-patient psychiatry: A literature review and evidence based recommendations for good practice*. United Kingdom Central Council for Nursing, Midwifery and Health Visiting.

Yerkes, R. M., & Dodson, J. D. (1908). The relation of strength of stimulus to rapidity of habit-formation. *Journal of Comparative Neurology and Psychology*, **18**, 459–454.

Yorston, G., & Haw, G. (2009). Historical perspectives on restraint. In R. Hughes (Ed.), *Reducing restraints in health and social care: Practice and policy perspectives*. London: Quay Books, pp. 5–19.

Index